# A TODDLER'S LIFE

## Becoming a Person

MARILYN SHATZ

*University of Michigan*

New York    Oxford
OXFORD UNIVERSITY PRESS

Oxford University Press

Oxford   New York   Toronto
Delhi   Bombay   Calcutta   Madras   Karachi
Kuala Lumpur   Singapore   Hong Kong   Tokyo
Nairobi   Dar es Salaam   Cape Town
Melbourne   Auckland   Madrid

and associated companies in
Berlin   Ibadan

First published in 1994 by Oxford University Press, Inc.
200 Madison Avenue, New York, New York 10016

First issued as an Oxford University Press Paperback, 1995

Oxford is a registered trademark of Oxford University Press

Library of Congress Cataloging-in-Publication Data
Shatz, Marilyn.
A toddler's life : becoming a person / Marilyn Shatz.
p.   cm.  Includes bibliographical references and index.
ISBN 0-19-508417-9
ISBN 0-19-509923-0 (pbk.)
1. Child psychology—Longitudinal studies.
2. Cognition in children—Longitudinal studies.
3. Toddlers—Language—Longitudinal Studies.
4. Self-perception in children—Longitudinal studies.
5. Toddlers—Psychology.
I. Title.   BF721.S485   1994
155.42′3—dc20   93-29053

2 4 6 8 9 7 5 3 1

Printed in the United States of America
on acid-free paper

*In loving memory of my grandmother*
*Sarah Levinthal*

# PREFACE

This book is about early human development as revealed in the story of one little boy's passage through the toddler years from ages 1 to 3. The child, Ricky, is very special to me, in part because he is my grandson—my first. Determined to relive the wonderfully satisfying relations I had shared with my own grandmother, I quickly warmed to my new role when Ricky was born, and I happily gave much time and energy to developing an affectionate relationship with him. I like to think our closeness encouraged him to share with me many of the thoughts and feelings that make this book possible.

When I was midway through the writing of this book, I interrupted my work for a rare visit to Florida to visit my sister. As we sat in the family room catching up on news of our lives, the mother of four grown children extolled the skills of her pet cockatiel, "I swear, Wafoo is just like a 2 year old." So emphatic a claim from an experienced child-raiser—not unlike the claims of many animal researchers—caused me to consider again what I was trying to capture that was unique about the early development of human children.

There are indeed many similarities between Wafoo and a human toddler. They are both curious, sociable, and imitative creatures. They are sensitive to the emotional states of those around them, and their behavior can be controlled by auditory stimuli, including words. Toddlers, like birds, are emotional animals capable of associational learning. However, even at an early age, the human capacities for organized, self-reflective behavior begin to manifest themselves. By age 3, Ricky was a creative language user, and he had a concept of himself and an awareness of others as beings with intentions, desires, knowledge, and beliefs. My chronology of Ricky's toddler years is a way of exploring how human children acquire the knowledge needed to become persons, entities separable from yet comprehensible to those around them.

Ricky was the ideal informant for me in my search for the essence of toddlerhood. Just as adults differ greatly in their interests, talents, and energy levels, so do toddlers. Some are physical dynamos—too busy climbing from one challenge to another to allow anyone much access to the workings of their minds; others, despite their mental prowess, are shy and reticent, often difficult to read even by their parents. Ricky, however, was talkative and open, interested always in being with people, although a bit cautious and quiet with strangers. There was a transparency about him: he had an expressive face and voice and was very verbal. So, he was a rich and readily interpretable source of information about the way he understood the world and how he worked to learn from and about it.

Surely, some readers of this book will ask themselves whether the children they know are as verbal or as thoughtful as Ricky, or whether their developmental progress is more or less rapid. Such comparisons are only natural. As remarkable as some of Ricky's words and actions may seem, he was still very much a normal child. He reached developmental milestones for such accomplishments as walking, using single words, putting several words together, and showing concern for others well within the normal age ranges, that is, the age ranges during which most children reach them. Toddlers differ considerably on when they reach such milestones—the documented age ranges of normality are large; hence, some differences among children are to be expected. Ricky may more explicitly show us what this period of childhood is like than some children do, but all normal children in normal environments very likely make similar progress during the toddler years. I hope that when they read this book, adults who raise, teach, care for, or do research with children will not merely draw superficial comparisons, but will be helped to recognize and enjoy some of the progress the children they know personally are making during this most important and exciting time of life.

To give it more generality, I have set this case study in the context of other findings on toddler development. Often I rely on my own past observational and experimental research into the cognitive and linguistic development of toddlers. I also draw heavily on the important work of the last 15 years by researchers who have begun to map out the various competencies of toddlerhood—people like Jerome Kagan and Michael Lewis on the development of self-concept, Ellen Markman on early word learning, and Judy Dunn on the emergence of social skills within the family, Rochel Gelman and Susan Gelman on cognitive development, and Alan Leslie and Henry Wellman on the development of a theory of mind, to name just a few. What my work using the longitudinal case study method does, that research with more narrowly focused objectives cannot, is to provide a comprehensive picture of the whole child—and the rapidly developing competencies of toddlerhood and some of the interrelationships among them.

Many people deserve my appreciation for their helpfulness to me on this project. My daughter and son-in-law dutifully but agreeably arranged long visits both at my house and theirs so that I could see Ricky frequently. During my sabbatical, the staff and faculty at the Institute of Human Development at the University of California, Berkeley, provided a comfortable, supportive home away from home in which to write, as well as conversational partners who knew more about recent research in social development than I did when I began the book. Back at home, my students in language acquisition and child development classes at the University of Michigan heard (and read) endless examples and anecdotes, and argued about their significance. In particular, Tamara Halle gave me detailed comments on an earlier version of the manuscript, and Eric Loken asked challenging questions that inspired several of the expansions and qualifications found in the Notes. My colleagues, Susan Gelman, Jeffrey Parker, Brenda Volling, and Henry Wellman, offered references or suggestions based on their own specialties.

When I first began writing, Richard Feingold (Grandpa Richard) helped me find the appropriate voice for a text different from the typical academic one. My good friend Marjorie Horton took precious time to comment on the first draft of the manuscript from the perspective of her experience not only as a Ph.D. in developmental psychology but as a working mother of two young children. Agreeing to work on a tight time schedule, Susan Gelman and Susan Goldin-Meadow gave me detailed suggestions for improving the final draft. The high enthusiasm for the project shown by my editor, Joan Bossert, made it much less painful to spend countless hours at the computer. I owe all these people special thanks.

Foremost, of course, is my grandson Ricky, who made my research for this book truly a joyful labor. By now, the paradigmatic toddler, who endured my note-taking, my cameras, and my tape recorders, but occasionally insisted I put them down so that I would play undistracted with him, has been enveloped by but is still occasionally glimpsed in the kindergartner he has become. I hope someday Ricky will enjoy retrieving with this book a part of his childhood now past.

*March 1993*                                                    M. S.
*Ann Arbor, Mich.*

# CONTENTS

# CAST OF CHARACTERS

R     Ricky

M     Ricky's Mother, Alice

F     Ricky's Father, Robert

G     Ricky's maternal grandmother, the author

Gf     Ricky's "grandfather," Grandpa Richard

B     Ricky's maternal great-grandmother, Bubby Frieda

U     Ricky's uncle

# A Toddler's Life

# 1

## *Introduction*

At the age of 15 months, a human is still more infant than child. Having just learned to walk, most toddlers have acquired perhaps a handful of words and a few conventional social skills, such as waving goodbye. However, over the next 20 or so months, children undergo enormous change: they develop elaborate language and social skills, and they begin to use these skills to learn about the wider world in which they live, to govern their emotions and their social behavior, and even to reflect on their own knowledge and abilities. Toddlers are not just egocentric and stubborn; they can be caring, polite, and generous. They can comfort, cajole, persuade, joke, and argue. In short, by 3 years of age, a child has become very much a person—someone who knows about and participates in the social life surrounding him or her.

This book uses the case study method to investigate the essence of toddlerhood, the development of social-linguistic intelligence. Social-linguistic intelligence is what turns a human infant into a person. It is the capacity to understand and use accepted social means to interact successfully with others. There are many component skills a toddler must acquire in developing a social-linguistic intelligence, but its cornerstones are the abilities to use a language and to understand and explain social behavior as others in one's community do. At least in Western societies, and very possibly in all societies, social understanding requires one to think about the mental states of both the self and others and to recognize when and how people's mental states can differ. With such skills, individuals can express their intentions, justify their behavior to others, understand and predict others' behaviors, and negotiate with and adjust to others. At 3 years of age, children still have much to learn about when and how people differ and about the social rules governing their communities, but this case study reveals that by then a child's social behavior is well grounded in a basic social-linguistic intelligence.

## Situating a Study of Toddlerhood in Research on Human Development

Many decades ago, Jean Piaget (1952) observed his own children's behavior during their first 18 months of life and characterized what he saw as the development of sensorimotor intelligence, the capacity to acquire and apply knowledge of the world by using and interrelating information from their sensory perceptions and their actions on the world. Recent innovations in methods of studying infants have resulted in our revising upward our estimates of infant abilities. Very young infants have more capacity to organize their perceptual world and to understand the world of objects even earlier than Piaget (1954) believed (Baillargeon, 1986; Spelke, 1985). We also now know that infants are more socially aware than one might guess from Piaget's writings. For example, even preverbal infants look to their mothers for signals that guide their behavior in situations of uncertainty (Sorce, Emde, Campos, & Klinnert, 1985). Nonetheless, Piaget's detailed observations of the infant's interests and activities stand as testament to the importance of the development of sensorimotor intelligence as a critical achievement in infancy.

It was not until 6 to 8 years of age that, according to Piaget, children reached the next major stage of development, concrete operations. At this stage, he argued, children were still grounded in physical experience, but their thinking could now be described in terms of logical operations. Despite his voluminous output, Piaget never described the intervening time between 18 months and 6 or 7 years of age in ways that explicated the capacities or achievements of preschoolers. Although he took note of the onset of symbolic play and the acquisition of language (Piaget, 1962), he characterized preschool children more in terms of their deficits than their accomplishments. Young children supposedly lived in an egocentric world, unable to differentiate themselves well from others or to separate reality from nonreality. As with infancy, our view of preschoolers' capacities is much richer now than Piaget's, thanks to researchers' explorations of a broad range of cognitive abilities in the young child. For example, children aged 3 to 5 reason better about both the external world and the world of the mind than Piaget's theory had suggested (Gelman & Baillargeon, 1983; Wellman, 1990), although their abilities are sometimes fragile and can be masked or overwhelmed.

The accomplishments of the period between infancy and the preschool years have been less well documented, possibly because toddlers often defy researchers' efforts at experimental control. Also, because language learning is such a salient achievement and because research into it was stimulated by theoretical work in the field of linguistics, many researchers who chose to work with toddlers focused primarily on the learning of the grammar of a language. Nonetheless, as researchers have begun to examine other aspects of toddler behavior, it is becoming clear that a grammar is not the only important acquisition of the period. Toddlers develop self-awareness (Kagan, 1981), and they acquire social knowledge in the family (Dunn, 1988). But, it is still uncertain whether toddlers can give evidence outside the laboratory of many of the skills newly discovered in slightly older children through experimentation.

How independent are the skills a toddler is developing? As researchers seek to explore a domain in which young children's abilities are unknown, they necessarily focus narrowly on that area. Indeed, there is even reason to believe that domains have little formally to do with one another (Keil, 1981). The characteristics of the rules of grammar, for example, may have little or nothing to do with the character of the family's rules for how to behave with one's sibling; the organization of lexical knowledge may be very different from the organization of numerical knowledge. Differences among domains manifest themselves early to young learners (Gelman, 1990). Yet learning in one area can still influence learning in another. Language is an obvious example: It is both an object of and a tool for learning. Children can learn an enormous amount about the social and physical worlds by asking, and even a primitive grammar allows them to do that. Moreover, young children have strategies for learning that they can apply across areas, even when the rules of each are different. In addition to eliciting information, they can observe, imitate, analyze, practice, and organize, regardless of the domain to be learned. The toddler we study uses all these strategies to learn in a variety of domains, including language.

In the rest of this chapter, I describe more fully what it means to be a person, and I provide some background on the two foundational aspects of social-linguistic intelligence—coming to talk as others do and coming to account for behavior as others do. The two achievements of language acquisition and the development of a folk psychology are not wholly independent. We will see how Ricky uses what understanding he has of language to increase his knowledge about others, and how his developing social knowledge enhances his learning of language. These two accomplishments provide him with the means to operate in the social world with a set of communicative tools comprehensible to his community; they make him recognizable as a person. Finally, this chapter includes a short discussion of the methods I used to collect and interpret the data on Ricky's progress toward becoming a person.

## Personhood and Social Identity

What does it mean to be a person? First, persons must be human beings. People often attribute person-like characteristics to their pets (witness my sister and her bird), but they say their pet is "like" a person, not that it *is* a person. Being a human being is necessary for true personhood, but it is not sufficient. To be a human being is to have a biological status: It entails certain physical characteristics and capacities. Human infants are human beings, but they are not yet fully persons.[1] They have the potential to become persons, but attaining full personhood requires a gradual process of development founded on interaction with others. To be a person is to have a social status: It requires a certain relationship between an individual and the social group to which the individual belongs. Persons are individuals who show through their behavior that they have a recognizable mental life and that they recognize others' mental lives. To be a person means to act and communicate as a rational member of a society—one who understands and uses social means to interact with others in mutually comprehensible ways.

Social philosophers have observed that, despite their particular expectations of how persons should behave, all societies essentially adhere to this definition of personhood. The evidence for this is that human beings who do not behave accordingly are typically considered mad—or "out of their minds"—and, as Jonathan Miller has noted, they lose their right to be considered persons. Thus, personhood is intimately connected with behaving in ways understandable and explainable by others.

How do children learn to act like persons? Children need a human social environment in which to flourish. Without caretakers who attend to them, talk to them, and interact with them, infants do not realize their potential to become persons. Often children lacking the attention of other persons do not even survive; when they do, we recognize them as unfortunate human beings, but we rarely grant them the status of persons. The woeful tales of "wild" children raised beyond the bounds of human communities attest to this.

Being a person requires knowledge of a culture's many rules and conventions for behavior, knowing when to use those rules, knowing when they can be broken or modified, and taking responsibility for doing so. Obviously, the learning of it all goes beyond toddlerhood. Every social group must decide when to grant children the status of personhood. Some of the privileges of personhood are not granted until adulthood; children cannot vote, marry without parental consent, or buy alcoholic beverages. But, long before adulthood, the recognition of personhood begins. In the United States, at least, even preschoolers are encouraged to select the clothes they wear, the foods they eat, and the friends they play with. Freedom to choose in such instances assumes that the child is an intentional being and recognizes his or her potential for rational thought and reciprocal communication.

Some cultures recognize the capacity for personhood earlier than others. Researchers report that middle-class mothers in the United States talk to their children from infancy as if they are beings with desires and intentions, whereas in other cultures (e.g., the Samoan), parents prefer not to make such assumptions about their infants (Schieffelin & Ochs, 1986). Apparently, in some cultures, children must first produce some evidence that they have the potential to grow into persons. Indeed, language itself can be an important benchmark of an individual's status. History is full of examples of limited status being accorded to those who do not use the language common to a culture's dominant social group. The very word *infant* traces its roots to the Latin words meaning "incapable of speech."

How do children make progress toward personhood? In all cultures, children's early language is their most important tool for learning how to be a person. Learning a language involves more than just learning vocabulary and the rules of grammar. Children must learn rules of discourse: when and how to speak so that they seem to be recognizing the same implicit beliefs that organize the social and mental lives of others in their society. In learning to use a language, a child learns what justifications and explanations of behavior are comprehensible and acceptable, and how important it is to communicate unobservable mental states. Being a person means one can be trusted to behave rationally, as "rational" behavior is defined by the community. Through one's use of language, a person conveys his or her acceptance of that covenant.

## Becoming a Native Speaker

Native speakers of a language, those who acquire it as their first language when they are very young, seem to have considerable advantages over those who learn it as a second language even a few years later. Native speakers talk with no accent discernible by others in that community, and they seem to know all the grammatical subtleties of the dialect even better than second-language speakers who have lived in the community longer (Newport, 1990). They know the nuances of expression and the idioms and patterns of everyday speech that so often trouble non-native speakers. They also know how to use their language to talk like persons, to justify and explain behavior in terms understandable to others in their communities.

It is remarkable that so much of this prodigious knowledge is acquired by young children with little or no apparent direct teaching, yet older children and adults have difficulty learning the same material, no matter what the teaching method. Chomsky (1975) argued that children have an innate capacity to acquire a first language and that they need only be exposed to a language to analyze and acquire its grammar spontaneously and comparatively effortlessly. Years later, his position is still controversial, although few would argue that there are no innate constraints at all on acquiring language. The controversial questions are how those constraints are to be characterized and whether they are specific to language or are responsible for more general cognitive and social capacities that make language acquisition possible.[2]

Whatever detailed answers to the questions about innate constraints are ultimately found, it seems clear that human infants come prepared to learn to communicate as others around them do. Over the course of several years, they develop a linguistic system based on what they are exposed to. Undoubtedly, what they acquire — and how — is constrained by the evolution over thousands of years of human capacities for communication. Yet, this does not mean there is no room for learning. Children do not acquire a native language effortlessly or unconsciously; they work at language learning. They think about what they are learning, and they have strategies for learning more. They seek information and confirmation from helpful adults, they practice, and they listen to and revise their own productions (Shatz, 1987; Shatz & Ebeling, 1991). Indeed, many of Ricky's grammatical errors seemed to follow from too much mental effort—too many incorrect but reasonable analogies and attempts to regularize inconsistencies.

Moreover, close observation of Ricky's everyday life revealed that he spent an enormous amount of time in language activities—he was almost always either talking or listening to others, talking to himself, engaging in verbal pretend play, or just singing. At times, he could be seen working on word meanings, relations among words, or word categories; at other times, he worked on how to use language for social purposes. In the fullest sense of learning how to use it appropriately, acquiring language occupied much of his attention. In consequence, a considerable portion of this book is devoted to discussions of Ricky's progress in acquiring language and how it relates to current issues in the study of early language and cognitive development.

Undoubtedly, learning to speak like those around them starts very early for children. Language acquisition may even have its beginnings in the womb, as fetuses hear the speech rhythms of their mothers. Certainly newborns are attentive to the sounds in their environment, and even if they are not addressed directly, all but the most deprived will hear a great deal of speech and thus come in contact with the patterns of the language spoken in their community. Two month olds delight in vocalizing back when spoken to, and they can engage in "conversational" rounds of vocalizing.

By 1 year of age, most children have assimilated many of the sound patterns of the language; by then they have begun to babble in sounds common to the language, and they string those sounds together in ways that imitate the rhythms and intonation patterns of the language. Indeed, many parents report that their children sound as if they are speaking full sentences, but there are few if any identifiable words! By 15 months, many (but not all) children have begun to produce some identifiable words and to use them at least occasionally in appropriate circumstances. Language-like behaviors, then, are found in children younger than Ricky was at the start of this book.

Why does this book begin only when Ricky is 15 months of age? It was about that time I noticed what were concerted—one might even say conscious—efforts to use language *to learn more*—more about language and more about people. Before that age, Ricky was certainly a social creature; he played the kinds of games initiated by adults that most infants play—peek-a-boo, bye-bye, pat-a-cake, and so on. He also directed vocalizations to adults when he wanted attention from them. But, when Ricky was 15 months old, during my first visit with him after a three-week separation, I noticed something new. Ricky was now using his primitive language and play skills to engage others in well-known games or variations on those games. In short, Ricky was doing all sorts of things with language to engage others amusingly and to keep them engaged, not because he had some obvious material or emotional need, but because, apparently, it was fun, and it provided him with information—about language, about people, and about the way people behave.

So, those very early language skills, those months of practicing sounds and learning to associate words with objects and contexts began to pay off. Ricky could use them to learn more. He now had an extremely powerful tool at his disposal, one that was compellingly engaging to those around him. It was at this point that I decided to study Ricky's development throughout the toddler period.

## Developing a Theory of Mind

To be a person, one has to be able to give culturally acceptable explanations for why people behave the way they do and to make accurate predictions about how others will respond in various situations. At least in Western societies, such explanations are based on the belief that unobservable internal states can be the causes of an individual's behavior.[3] Persons in such societies must be able to make reasonable inferences about the internal states of others. In current terminology, persons have theories of mind. Theories of mind can be simple, based primarily on a *desire* psychology. For example, we can explain why someone is looking for cookies by saying he or she wants one. Or, our theories can be somewhat more sophisticated, recruiting ideas about others' access to information about reality. For example, we can explain why someone looks in the pantry for the cookies by saying that the searcher saw them put there or knows that they are usually kept there. This would be a *knowledge* psychology.

Desire and knowledge theories of mind work well in some situations, but not all. A still more sophisticated psychology allows for the complication that what people represent in their minds may be based not on knowledge of reality but only on their *beliefs* about reality—and those beliefs may be true or false.[4] Suppose someone looks for the cookies in their usual location in the pantry even though the cookies actually have been put in the refrigerator on this occasion. In such an instance, the searcher has a *false* belief about the location of the cookies. With a belief theory of mind, we can explain the searcher's erroneous behavior because we know that people can act only on their *beliefs* about reality, which can be different from reality itself. In some circumstances, preschoolers have the ability to draw on a belief psychology to explain others' actions (Wellman, 1990), but it has been hard to find evidence that toddlers have this level of sophistication about minds.

As with language, the development of a theory of mind undoubtedly begins long before 15 months of age. Infants recognize the differences between animate and inanimate objects very early (Gelman & Spelke, 1981), and by a year of age, they attribute independent agency to animate beings (Poulin-Dubois & Shultz, 1988). It is with the onset of language, however, that children acquire powerful means to learn about the causes of animate behavior.

During the time I studied Ricky, he gradually acquired many of the skills necessary for developing a mature theory of mind. For example, he began to take account of others' perceptual needs and knowledge levels, even when they differed from his own. By 3, he had reached at least the beginning level of a belief-based theory of mind, if not a full-blown one. Intense, long-term observation allowed for the discovery of the path he took toward a belief psychology as he thought and talked about mind and reality.

## The Methods of the Study

Ricky is the first child of a stay-at-home mother with slightly more than a high school education and a father who worked and went to college part time. Ricky is a true product of the American melting pot: his mother's family had East-European origins, and his father came from a mixed background of Mexican and Irish origins. During the time of the study, Ricky lived with his parents in Dearborn Heights, a small city in the suburbs of Detroit, in an apartment complex where he had a few playmates. Toward the end of the study, he began attending a half-day program several days a week at a local university-run nursery school.

From the time Ricky was 16 months until his third birthday, I took extensive notes whenever I spent any time with him. Most often I wrote down exact utterances on a nearby pad during our visits and then elaborated on these by writing contextual notes on the computer immediately after we parted. Sometimes I was able to audiorecord parts of our visits, and occasionally I took videotapes as well. Recordings became less useful as Ricky grew older, as he quickly grew impatient either with being restrained to a location near the recording equipment or with not having my full attention when I was videotaping. Importantly, though, the electronically recorded data confirm with precision my account of his progress in language, supplementing and supporting the handwritten records. I myself transcribed the electronically recorded data, and I reviewed all the videotapes again in the course of writing the book.

Ricky lived about 40 minutes away from me by car, and we saw each other often, about every 10 days on average during this period. The three longest periods without a visit were of three weeks' duration each, when I was traveling. Most visits were relatively long, lasting 3 hours or more. One of the richest periods of observation was when Ricky was 22 months old, and we spent a week together on vacation. Around that time, Ricky started to visit for overnights without his parents, and these too were especially rich times for data collection. However, there were also opportunities to observe him with his parents, more distant family members, and friends. These periods gave me added perspective both on Ricky's social knowledge and on his strategies for learning. In all, I collected data on more than 60 different occasions, constituting hundreds of pages of transcripts and computer printouts of notes.

A study that concentrates on a single child has both advantages and disadvantages. Obviously the size of the data set just described is rare even in naturalistic research. A researcher usually does not have the time with or access to even a single child that I had with Ricky. Longitudinal observations by a trained observer familiar to the child can make multiple contributions to our understanding of child development; among them are better descriptions of both the subskills involved in increasingly sophisticated behavior and the interrelations among different behavioral developments, as well as descriptions of the kinds of effort over time the individual child makes to learn.

Excepting clinical case studies and the many insightful studies done by parents and students (usually linguists) of children's language development, research on child development has relied more often on experimental or survey methods than on case studies. Such methods give us good ideas about ranges of behavior at varying ages, and experimental studies can also test specific hypotheses about causes of change. However, because toddlers typically do not test well in experimental settings and because their newfound knowledge is fragile, they often do not display it in experimental settings. Even though experimentation with toddlers has grown increasingly sophisticated and revealing in recent years, it is likely that we still underestimate their abilities when we limit our research to experimental techniques. The intensive case study method provides an opportunity to capture emerging abilities too elusive to find readily with other methods.

Nevertheless, in writing about a toddler's everyday life, one has to interpret what one observes. Toddlers are different from older children and adults. At the very least, they have less experience of and knowledge about almost everything. Nonetheless, they can often talk and behave in remarkably sophisticated ways, producing adult-like behavior in appropriate situations. Such behaviors are often ephemeral, appearing only sporadically, or they break down under probing or more demanding situations. What should one conclude from inconsistent performance? Are examples of maturity mere imitations with no import for understanding the nature of toddler thinking and no consequences for development?

It requires some detective work to figure out specifically what a single toddler's behaviors tell us about development. Sometimes I use converging evidence to confirm an emerging higher level of thinking; sometimes I conclude that, no matter how tantalizing the instance, a more conservative estimate or interpretation of it is warranted. The data from other children studied in laboratory or natural settings are helpful, and I use such data where available to reason about the meaning of Ricky's behaviors. My cautious interpretations, however, should not obscure the importance of the increasingly sophisticated but still fragile social-linguistic intelligence I saw Ricky display. Its development provided him a solid framework on which he could scaffold more mature social and conceptual knowledge in the future.

A study like this one can provide us with insights about child development that are unlikely to be obtained solely with other methods. Still, Ricky's story is best taken as only indicative of what children at this age can be like. We can relate his development to what we know of other children, but we cannot blithely generalize to all children on the basis of his particular experience. We can use Ricky's story to generate ideas about what develops and how, but however plausible those ideas are, one child's example does not prove them.

This book is organized as a chronology. Each chapter describes incidents covering approximately two-month intervals in Ricky's life. The narratives illustrate Ricky's developmental progress by reporting behaviors characteristic of him during the period. However, initial instances of some behaviors may have occurred earlier than first observed, and many continued to occur after the period in which they are reported. Thus, the two-month segmentations are practical, not theoretical ones. The time span of a chapter is large enough to give us a sense from chapter to chapter of how Ricky was changing over time and small enough to detail some of his concurrent behaviors. Sometimes the descriptions of everyday life may seem rather ordinary, but we should keep in mind that they illustrate how fully a very young child participated in that life. When we consider how quickly the knowledge behind that participation is being acquired, we cannot fail to be impressed.

I have included in the book a wealth of research findings spanning a broad range of topics and ages. In each chapter I discuss what Ricky's behaviors mean for understanding a toddler's growing mental, social, and language skills; and I relate Ricky's progress to the general knowledge we have about children's growth at each age. Thus, topics of development that rarely meet in highly specialized disciplinary journals get discussed together. Moreover, because toddlers emerge from infants and grow into preschoolers, I often refer, when relevant, to the literature on either younger or older children, to add a sense of continuity as well as generality to Ricky's life story.

Now, to begin, meet Ricky at 15 months of age, using single-word utterances as he plays with a toy dog in his living room.

> R: Mouth. (R points to the mouth of the dog.)
> Mouth. (R points to his own mouth.)

When we leave him well on his way to becoming an American person less than two years later at the age of 3 years, Ricky will be telling us about his plans for his future.

> R: When I grow up and I'm a baseball player, I'll have a baseball hat, and I'll put it on, and I'll play baseball.

## Notes

1. Rights of personhood are not the same as human rights. Societies can and often do grant human rights (such as the right to life) to any member of the biological category human while reserving the rights and responsibilities of personhood (such as the "right" to be held accountable in a court of law for one's actions) for only a subset of humans.

2. Tomasello, 1992, is one who takes a strong anti-language-specific position. See Shatz, 1992, for a critique of his views, and Pinker and Bloom (1990) for a position that advocates language-specific constraints but with a learning component as well.

3. It is unclear whether reasoning about the causes of behavior universally recruits notions of internal state. Recent research (Avis & Harris, 1991) shows that such reasoning is not limited to Western societies. What may differ across cultures may not be whether internal states are recruited at all, but how much reliance is placed on them as opposed to other explanations, such as supernatural ones, that may be warranted as well.

4. One could argue that even a desire psychology implies at least an implicit understanding of belief states. For example, if one explains John's looking in the cookie jar by saying he wants a cookie, one must implicitly attribute to John two beliefs: (1) looking for the object of desire is a reasonable prelude to satisfying the desire and (2) cookies are to be found in the cookie jar. However, for individuals with a desire psychology, (1) and (2) may be more like background conditions or customary presuppositions than belief states that can be true or false and that are attributable to John.

# 2

## *15–16 Months*
## Doing a Lot with a Little

It was mid-October. An August vacation and a busy first month of the new school year had limited the time I had spent with Ricky the previous two months. Even so, I had noticed in recent short visits an increase in vocabulary from the occasional few words he had been using over the previous two or three months. Ricky was easier to understand and was beginning to use language more. Nonetheless, his behavior that October day was a bit of a surprise.

I had come for a visit and dinner. I had just entered the living room and greeted the family when a giggling Ricky scampered out of the room, down the hall, and into the bathroom. He then repeatedly called out, "Where? Where?" with a sing-song intonation. Alice (Ricky's mother) informed me that Ricky had begun this game during the week; his calling "where" was my cue to respond, "Where's Ricky?" in a loud voice, at which point he would reappear. When I did as I was told, he indeed came running out, right into my arms. He repeated this sequence about 10 times with great glee before finally tiring of it.

A week later, at my house, Ricky produced a new variation of the "where" game. He had discovered he could hide his face behind a dishtowel that hung on the handle of the oven. As he draped the towel over his face, he called, "Where?" Once again, an adult took up his invitation by calling, "Where's Ricky?" Thereupon, he whipped off

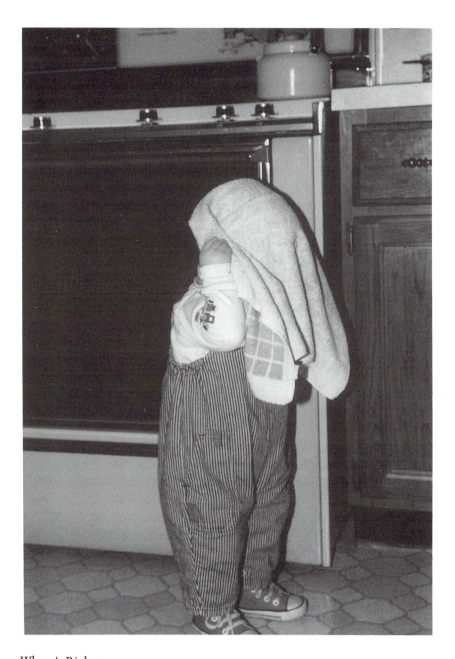

Where's Ricky

the towel to reveal his smiling face. As before, this sequence was repeated over and over.

Probably Ricky's game was adapted from the hide-and-seek games adults often play with infants, and that his parents had played with him. Especially striking was his use of "where?" to signal to others that he wanted to play the game. Other children about this age also engage in repeated coordinated actions with others (Eckerman & Didow, 1989). Less well documented is the use of language to initiate and maintain play interactions. Irrespective of children's use of language, the coordinated play behavior maintained over several cycles suggests that by early in their second year, children are able to engage in complementary, multi-turn interactions with others. This gives them the chance to practice behaviors, get feedback on them, and make modifications over time, all of which are important as they learn from others. If, by using language, they can engage others and sustain their participation as well, they increase their opportunities for all this.

## Paralinguistic and Linguistic Expressions of Meaning

The day I had first seen Ricky play the "where" game, I heard him respond to his mother with the same word, *where*, but with a different intonation pattern. Now the word was lower pitched, with less of a rising, then falling contour.

> M: Where is your book?
> R: Where.

In this instance, he was asking his mother to identify the book's location. I realized Ricky had a word and intonational variations on it that gave his interactive abilities a new status: He could respond in somewhat appropriate ways even when he did not know how to answer the question being asked ·of him. Indeed, his strategy of using the word *where* with a flat intonation in reply to questions had the effect of getting his mother to supply the substantive answer for him and, before long, he was also using *what* in a similar way in response to "What is that?" questions. These responses made his linguistic interactions with others longer and more informative. His use of the same words to initiate naming or finding games also made for more frequent interactions involving language. Ricky's progress on verbal initiations may have been more gradual than it seemed to me, but Alice reported that she too had noticed a marked improvement in his verbal interactions in the previous week or so.

Varying the intonation of a limited set of sounds or words to accomplish different communicative purposes is a strategy other toddlers have been reported to use (Halliday, 1975). Even before he began to use intonation in this way, Ricky showed that he had some knowledge of the role of paralinguistic devices like intonation and intensity in communication. He used an exaggerated soft tone and slightly raised pitch when he sang, thereby showing that he recognized singing as a different way of using language from speaking. And he increased the intensity of his vocalizations when he was calling to someone in another room. Possibly he had already learned something about how sound is dampened by barriers, or perhaps he was imitating what he'd observed others doing when conversing from different rooms. In either case, he seemed to have an inkling that both intentions and physical conditions influence one's vocal behavior.

Bates (1976) has described how toddlers use early language to make demands and draw attention to things. Ricky was using language to accomplish both these ends by 15 months. He used words like *more, up, down, juice,* and *water* to ask for actions or objects he wanted. He labeled objects and people in the environment, often pointing at them at the same time. But, at 15 months, he had only about a dozen nouns to use in this way. He also had a few verbs (*rock, walk, push, pull*) which he would use to label his own ongoing actions. In addition, he had a small set of greeting words and a large set of animal noises that he delighted in using whenever he saw an appropriate animal or picture thereof or when he could engage an adult to play the "What does a (dog, duck, etc.) say?" game. Like many children of this age (e.g., Steffenson, 1978), he recognized yes/no questions as calling for a verbal answer, and he regularly said "no," even when he showed by nonverbal behavior that he meant *yes*.

So, Ricky did a lot with relatively little. At the start of this period, he had no more than 30 recognizable words, including his repertoire of animal sounds. Yet, with only this much language he could greet others, make requests, seek attention, initiate play, and respond to questions, if not always with the correct word.

Ricky used both conventional and creative gestures to supplement his arsenal of verbal devices for engaging others in interaction and getting his needs and desires met. He would wave hello and goodbye, and point to objects he wanted. He developed an idiosyncratic gesture of opening and closing the fingers of both hands when he wanted something done. He loved to play the piano at my house.

One day he stood at the bench, holding up his hands for us to see, and opening and closing his fingers until he was lifted onto the bench. Then he looked at me, pointed to the bench, and again moved his fingers in the same fashion until I sat down next to him. However, this gesture was not restricted to the context of piano playing. Ricky used the same motion for many desired actions, such as to indicate that he wanted to be taken out of his high-chair or his car seat. Other children use this sort of gesture; it is claimed to be very common in the repertoires of prelinguistic children (Petitto, 1988). Children just starting to use language typically alternate between gestures and words and even combine the two into the same communicative act (Morford & Goldin-Meadow, 1992).

## Help in Comprehending Language

Like most children his age (Benedict, 1979), Ricky understood more than his limited productive vocabulary indicated. He could respond appropriately in various ways to others' requests that he act (or stop acting). ("Get me a diaper." "You are not supposed to stand on the sofa. You'll fall.") When asked to identify objects, Ricky could point to many things he did not spontaneously name. He also played games that involved pointing or touching responses rather than verbal ones (e.g., "Where's your nose? Where's Mommy's nose?")

Undoubtedly, Ricky's ability to respond appropriately to language of this sort was supported by several factors. For one, his mother used intonational cues and exaggerated facial expressions to convey her intent. Without raising her voice, she made it clear when she disapproved of or supported his actions, and she used her eyebrows and mouth to express surprise, consternation, dismay, and pleasure. Also, her language usually mapped closely to the context. She asked Ricky to get a diaper when he needed a change and to climb into his chair when a meal was ready. Still, he typically did not do those things unless or until she asked, suggesting he had at least made the temporal connection between the specific verbal request and the appropriate action response.

Ricky's mother directed an enormous amount of language to him—naming, questioning, and explaining almost constantly as she went about her caretaking tasks. She was an enthusiastic respondent to his verbal initiations for interaction and readily engaged in his repetitive games. She regularly repeated more clearly or expanded on his attempts at language, taking his utterances and setting them in fuller sentence contexts. She often spoke simply to him and encouraged him to respond or imitate. On these occasions, she used exaggerated intonation. On many other occasions, she spoke to him in full and sometimes complicated sentences with more normal intonation. She was not a believer in talking down to children; indeed, she once expressed dismay at a relative who copied her own child's mistaken labels for objects when talking to the child. Nevertheless, she disavowed any interest in actively or directly teaching Ricky language, and she did not overtly correct his errors. Her clarifications and expansions of Ricky's speech seemed to be motivated more by the need to be sure she had understood him and to keep the conversation on shared ground than by attempts to teach language. Although I did not systematically observe her gesturing, I had studied gesturing behavior in other mothers (e.g., Shatz, 1982; Schnur & Shatz, 1983), and it seemed to me that Alice's gestures were not particularly abundant.

Ricky's father, Rob, had less time with Ricky, but was an attentive parent too, spending some part of every day talking to and playing with him. Consequently, Ricky had considerable support from those around him for language learning. Rob used his hands when he spoke more than Alice did, and I had noticed Ricky trying on occasion to imitate Rob's gestures; but it did not seem as though Ricky was using the gestures to discern what was being said.

How much was Ricky's language development dependent on the way his parents spoke to him? The fact that he and Alice were very frequently engaged in conversation very likely facilitated his vocabulary growth. The amount of language mothers direct to their children does seem to affect their rate of word learning (Huttenlocher, Haight, Bryk, Seltzer, & Lyons, 1991). Also, expansions of the child's own speech have been found to facilitate the acquisition of particular grammatical forms (e.g., Hoff-Ginsberg, 1985; see Hoff-Ginsberg & Shatz, 1982, for a review). However, the idea that there are well-described parental styles that can generally account for children's progress at language acquisition receives little support (Pine, 1991; Shatz, Grimm, Wilcox, & Niemeier-Wind, 1989). The fact of a supportive environment, then, is no reason to discount Ricky's own efforts to learn language.

## Working at Language Learning

Ricky was relentless in his desire for social interaction. He was happiest when he was in the company of other people, and he was attentive to others' talk. Little more than a year old, he was already finding ways to gain and maintain the verbal attention of others. With adults willing to nourish and encourage his overtures, he was well on his way to using what little language he had to learn more.

Ricky made rapid progress over the next few months in language learning, yet the road was not always a smooth one. Many of the constructions of English were not transparent to him, and omissions and errors took a considerable time to change. For example, toward the end of this period, Ricky began to use plurals, saying words like *cars*, *birds*, and *bugs*. However, he didn't seem to know what the -s on such words stood for. For example, he referred interchangeably to a single car as "car" or "cars." One day, we tried to correct his labeling of a toy tricycle with the word "cars" by repeatedly responding "trike" or "car"; he persisted throughout the interaction with "cars." Even when Ricky had heard many corrections, he could not modify his own productions. In the child language literature, there are similar anecdotes involving other toddlers unable to accommodate to direct language instruction. Such incidents are evidence that, although children must be sensitive to the language they hear, they often follow their own path in acquiring the language of their community, no matter how instructive and facilitative the speech of their parents.

By the end of this period, I had counted more than 50 words in Ricky's productive lexicon. About three-quarters of them were labels for objects, including words for animals, food, items of clothing, and a few less common but salient objects (e.g., snowball). The list of action words Ricky produced was growing too, but more slowly. The predominance of object labels in Ricky's vocabulary is similar to that reported for other children about this age with vocabularies this size (Nelson, 1973).

Gentner (1982) has argued that nouns predominate over verbs in early lexicons because most early nouns are labels for objects that are readily discernible, whereas verbs require an understanding of how words can express relations between objects as well as label them. Therefore, it should be cognitively easier for young learners to assign meanings to nouns than to verbs. However, the composition of a child's lexicon may be subject to external influences as well. A recent study suggests that the tendency for nouns to dominate early lexicons may be enhanced or diminished depending on whether parents emphasize objects or feelings and social relations in their talk to infants. American mothers were more likely to emphasize objects than were Japanese mothers, who focused more on feelings or the mother-child relationship; and parental checklists of children's vocabulary revealed that the American children produced more nouns than did their Japanese counterparts (Fernald & Morikawa, 1993).

Alice talked a great deal to Ricky about objects, but she also talked about feelings and actions. The ease with which Ricky imitated and then spontaneously used new labels for objects lends credence to the notion that the object labels are somewhat more accessible for toddlers than verbs, regardless of emphases in the input. Nonetheless, it is likely that Alice's responsiveness to Ricky's interest in and attempts to talk about objects enhanced his tendency to acquire nouns easily.

Ricky was just beginning to use multiword phrases at 15 months. He regularly imitated phrases longer than a single word.

> G: Are you going to take a shower? (R was playing in the shower stall.)
> R: Take a shower.

He said, "light on," as he turned on a light, and "slide down" as he climbed up the stairs of a slide. Utterances like these may have been rotely learned phrases or parts of phrases acquired as unanalyzed wholes. He did have a few phrases, such as "where my ___?" and "more whee" (said as a request to be pulled down a hill on a sled) that seemed to be more creative constructions. Also, he sometimes embedded his conventional words in longer strings of jargon that carried a recognizable sentence intonation. Thus, he seemed to know that utterances longer than a word were the norm in conversation.

One may ask why Ricky could not produce more multiword utterances if he knew that more than one word per utterance was common in conversation, and he could produce a string of sounds with an English-like intonation. One possibility is that he simply could not easily or quickly enough retrieve from memory the words he stored there. An anecdote about an 18 month old supports this possibility. When first using two words in an utterance, she would substitute *this* or *that* for object labels that she nonetheless used regularly in single-word utterances, saying, for example, "eat this" instead of "eat apple" (C. Kalish, personal communication, November 15, 1992). Apparently, retrieving the general-purpose lexical item was easier for her than retrieving a specific one when it was to be combined with yet another word.

Alternatively, using the vocal tract to produce the extended strings of precise articulatory movements that are required for multiword speech may be hard for a 15 month old (see Branigan,

1979). At first blush, research on the acquisition of American Sign Language (ASL) seems to support the possibility that vocal articulation is the cause of the difficulty. Children learning ASL as a first language tend to produce single manual signs somewhat earlier than children learning a spoken language produce single words (Abrahamsen, Cavallo, & McCluer, 1985; Orlansky & Bonvillian, 1985). For 1 year olds just embarking on lexical development, then, the hands may be a bit more agile than the mouth.

If young signers are advantaged relative to speakers only because of the speakers' vocal articulatory limitations, then one would expect the signers' advantage to continue into the multiword stage. However, the productive advantage early signers enjoy does not appear to continue once children have to start combining symbols systematically (Meier & Newport, 1990; Shatz, 1985). It is necessary to search for another possible limitation on putting symbols together. One that speakers and signers share is grammar: Neither words nor signs are strung together in arbitrary fashion; instead, they are constrained with regard to their placement relative to other symbols. Whether children are acquiring a spoken or a manual language, they have to learn *how* to put the symbols together in order regularly to produce well-formed multisymbol utterances. The fact that signers, despite their earlier advantage at the one-word stage, have not yet been shown to maintain their advantage over speakers when acquiring their respective grammars suggests that the articulatory difficulty is not the main problem for one-word speakers. Instead, learning grammar requires a level of linguistic and cognitive maturity that seems independent of the age when words or signs first appear, how many words have been acquired, or the modality in which the words are learned.

In addition, there appear to be individual differences among children. Some children produce words early and stay in the one- or two-word stage for a relatively long time, whereas others begin to produce words somewhat later but then move on to learning grammar fairly soon thereafter. Undoubtedly, several factors influence the nature and rate of a child's progress at language acquisition, including brain maturation, individual differences in attention and interests, and opportunities for and encouragement of language learning in the environment. Some aspects of the process seem more easily influenced by environmental factors than others. When children first produce "words" depends in part on which modality they are encouraged to use; and which words or signs children first learn are undoubtedly influenced by the objects around them, the activities they engage in, and the topics their caretakers initiate. As to when they begin to construct a grammar based on what they are exposed to, that seems to be more an internal matter, waiting on their ability to attend to, segment, store, and analyze what is in their input language.[1]

During this period, it was fairly clear that Ricky's attention was largely focused on single-word learning, in particular practicing and playing with the pronunciation of words. For example, as he stood in the shower stall, he said "wash" to himself several times, then "water" repeatedly, and finally some amalgam of the two, "warsh," which he said over and over. He also tried to improve his articulation of words in response to feedback.

R: Urs. (Playing with toy cars.)
G: Hurts? What hurts?
R: (Emphatically) Urs. (Holding out a car to G.)
G: Oh, is that for me?
   Oh—"yours." (Realizing I had misunderstood and repeating and clarifying R's word.)
R: Yurs. (Confirming what I had said and improving the pronunciation.)

## What Do Early Clarifications Mean?

Initially, the "urs" example suggests that Ricky recognized when he was being misunderstood, that he persisted in trying to get his listener to understand, and that he seemed to recognize that his own inadequate articulations needed improvement. However, that may be too generous a characterization of the communicative competence of a 1 year old. On many other occasions, Ricky regularly imitated his interlocutor's last words. Sometimes he seemed to be using imitation to signal assent ("Do you want juice?" "Juice.") or just to maintain verbal contact ("Daddy's at work." "Work."). Often his intent was unclear, and the imitations were almost like automatic recapitulations of the last word heard, as when he would be asked, "Do you want milk or juice?" and he would respond "juice," but then refuse to drink it. In the "yurs" example, he had an imminent model of the pronunciation of "yours" to emulate, and he did a better job of enunciating the word than when producing it spontaneously from memory. Therefore, his improved pronunciation may not indicate a sophisticated awareness that his inadequate articulation caused his listener's misunderstanding and that he needed to practice matching the conventional model with better precision.

Alternatively, it may have been a more automatic imitation of my prior utterance.

Nonetheless, when I first phrased his message incorrectly, although he could not enunciate his word any better, he did add emphasis to the repetition of his earlier pronunciation, suggesting he at least knew my production had not matched what he had intended. Of course, I had not acted in the way he intended either; I had not taken the car he had designated for me. One year olds can be quite persistent about getting others to act in the way they want. Whether this means they know that others have minds that can understand and misunderstand has been a matter of some controversy (e.g., Golinkoff, 1993; Shatz & O'Reilly, 1990).

Even if it is not a very sophisticated strategy, imitation can be a good learning device, since it maintains interaction and results in the practice of more adequate articulations. Not all children imitate as much as Ricky did in these early months, and not all children who imitate use their imitations to hold up their end of conversations as much as Ricky did (Bloom, Hood, & Lightbown, 1974). For a sociable but as yet linguistically unskilled child like Ricky, however, imitation was an effective means to stay in verbal contact with others. As with verbal signaling, he was indeed doing a lot with a little.

## Note

1. Apparently the internal capacity for grammar is so strong that toddlers can even develop more systematicity in their communicative systems than they are exposed to, for example, when their grammatical input is nonexistent, as in the case of deaf children whose hearing parents do not sign (Feldman, Goldin-Meadow, & Gleitman, 1978), or when it is comparatively meager, as in the case of deaf children whose parents learned sign as adults and are not fully as adept as native signers (Singleton & Newport, 1987). Paradoxically, this grammatical capacity shows itself only in the context of viable social interaction. As far as we know, children isolated from human society do not develop idiosyncratic grammars just for the sake of talking to themselves.

# 3

## 17–18 Months
## Just One of the Family

Language is an incredibly powerful tool for learning. At 17 months, Ricky had much more still to learn about language itself, about people, and about how people use language in the world of social interaction. Yet, even with his limited linguistic skill and all his naiveté about people, he increasingly used his language to interact with others in ways that provided opportunities to learn—about himself and other people and about the way his language encoded the world.

### What Was Ricky Listening To?

From their earliest days, children have at least two kinds of experiences with language: They hear people talking directly to them and they overhear people talking to others. Apparently, at a very early age, children can tell the difference between infant- and adult-directed speech due to the acoustic characteristics of the speech stream. Speech directed to young children typically tends to be slower, higher in pitch, and with more exaggerated pitch and stress contours (Garnica, 1977). These characteristics have the effect of making the speech more attention-getting; even 4-month-old infants prefer to listen to speech with such pitch characteristics (Fernald & Kuhl, 1987). Speech of this sort probably aids learning: It is very likely easier for children to segment the speech stream, to recognize sounds they have heard before, and to follow the patterns of phrases in speech that has been slowed and exaggerated.

By the time they are toddlers, of course, children have had many months' experience attending and responding to linguistic stimuli. Language, especially when spoken forcefully, not only captures their attention but can have an effect like physical force on their actions. This was well illustrated one day when Ricky, his mother, and I went for a walk. We came upon a large dog penned in a yard, who barked incessantly at us. Despite the fence, Ricky was afraid to walk past the dog. His eyes never strayed from the animal as his mother tried to control the dog by saying, "Sit! Sit down!" The dog was immovable but Ricky promptly plopped down on the sidewalk as if physically pushed.

Although young children are highly attentive to simple, high-pitched speech, they do not simply ignore more complex language addressed to adults and older children. After all, they can learn much about the way people relate to each other by observing how they talk and what they say. Such useful social information may be worth the effort of dealing with language that may be hard to understand. Indeed, recent research shows that 2 year olds monitor the conversations between their mothers and older siblings (Dunn & Shatz, 1989). The evidence is based on the frequency and kind of intrusions toddlers make into mother-sibling conversations. That toddlers can be intrusive is unlikely to surprise anyone who has spent much time with them. Of more interest is the fact that their intrusions can often be appropriate to the topic at hand. The children seemed to want more than just to divert their mothers' attention—they wanted to be included in the ongoing interaction as a member of the family group.

Because we question their ability to understand much and we often modify our speech when talking to young children, we tend to treat them at times as though they are not part of the larger group. When they insist on inclusion and participation, it can be amusing as well as surprising, especially with a 1 year old. During one holiday meal, Ricky informed us that he considered himself a full member of the family group. Ricky was the only child at a dining table of seven adults. He was sitting next to me, in his high-chair. I had made a noodle dish that he loved, and in response to my attentively asking him whether he wanted more, he had said "more" or "more noonles" and been rewarded with several servings. At the end of the meal, as I prepared to clear the table, I asked the adults, "Does anyone want more noodles?" From my elbow came a little voice—

"More noonles"

"Yesh." Believing that the question had been addressed only to the grown-ups, all seven adults began to laugh. Ricky at first looked puzzled, then decided it was worth laughing as well. Recovering, I said to him, "Well, give me your plate then." Ricky looked down at his plate for a moment, then picked it up in two hands and held it out to me.

Ricky's response suggests that he saw himself as just another part of the group, not as a unique entity requiring special attention. His joining unselfconsciously in the laughter suggests he was still quite naive about himself as an individual with different skills and social roles from others around him. As an older child, when adults laughed at his childish comments or interpretations, Ricky would sometimes get a bit defensive and try to explain his behavior. As a young toddler, his view of himself was less complicated: he saw himself as like everyone else and did not really understand why others found that perception amusing.

It seems, then, that children regularly listen to and try to engage in the conversations around them. If they sometimes ignore what they hear, it is probably because they cannot understand quite enough of the conversation to find a way to participate in it. In any case, their apparent lack of attention should not be attributed to a belief that the speech directed to others is of no interest or import to them.

## Starting to Take Account of What Others Can See

Part of what makes it so hard in most circumstances for 1 year olds to understand the speech of adults or older children is that such speech is constrained by knowledge about listener perspective. When we talk, we constantly adjust our speech to take into account what our listener knows, given the conditions of our conversation. For example, it would be bizarre to say to a listener on the telephone, "How do you like the color of the dress I'm wearing?" Similarly, it would be odd to ask an educated adult who had just commented on the brightness of Jupiter in the night sky, "Did you know Jupiter is a planet and not a star?" With the exception of speech directed to pets and infants, the conversations that children typically overhear involve speakers and listeners with both more communicative knowledge and more sophisticated understandings about the world than they have.

Taking account of what we can reasonably expect others to

know in various circumstances requires a wide range of abilities, from an understanding of perceptual capacities to a recognition that different people can have different memories and experiences. Such knowledge takes years to accumulate. In its absence, misunderstandings can be frequent. One way to minimize misunderstandings is to limit conversation to topics to which both speaker and listener have equal access. Conversations between parents and young children avoid much misunderstanding because they regularly focus on objects both participants see and/or manipulate. By the beginning of their second year, children monitor others to see where they are looking, and they can both direct (with gestures) and follow another's line of regard (Leung & Rheingold, 1981; Scaife & Bruner, 1975).

More sophistication is involved, however, as soon as listener and speaker do not or cannot share a perspective. For example, a child looking at a picture must turn it toward a listener facing opposite her if the listener is to see it. Appropriate behavior in these cases requires the child to take account of the listener's line of sight, even when doing so results in the obstruction of her own view of the object. Ricky had not yet acquired this ability, but a series of communicative misses suggested that he was at least thinking about how to share information with a listener. One day he was sitting on the hall stairs looking at a book. Seeing a picture of a butterfly, he ran toward where I was sitting in the living room, shouting "Butterfly, butterfly." He stopped near me, pointing at the butterfly, but he did not turn the book so that I could see the picture. He seemed to have taken proximity but not my line of sight into account. On another occasion, I asked him to show me a duck in a book he was reading with his father. He pointed to it, but again made no effort to turn the book so that I could see it. His father turned the book, saying, "Turn it this way so Grandma can see."

It is possible that in these instances, Ricky's interest was so captured by the pictures in the books that he did not think to look up at me and see whether the book was indeed in my line of sight. However, an incident during a phone conversation suggests that this interpretation of his failure to consider others' visual perspectives is probably too generous. One day on the phone with me, Ricky said "house," trying to tell me he was playing with his toy schoolhouse. I misinterpreted him, and started to talk about a visit of his to my house. Ricky dropped the phone, went to the schoolhouse, and dragged it over to the telephone, apparently in the hope that its proximity to my voice would somehow give me access to his intended referent. Thus, even though he could direct and follow lines of sight in simple communicative situations, where pointing or following points would result in *shared* perspectives, his solution in more demanding situations that required taking a perspective different from his own was to rely on proximity, but not line of sight.

Nonetheless, during this period, Ricky's play showed that he was at times thinking about and trying to take account of others' lines of sight. When he played with toy people, he meticulously aligned them so that their eyes were facing in the appropriate direction for the activities in which they were to be engaged. For example, he turned toy drivers of cars so that their eyes faced forward, and he set toy children down in a waiting line, all facing in the same direction toward a toy slide. Not surprisingly, about four weeks later I observed Ricky's first spontaneous turn of a book to show his grandfather seated across from him a picture he had been looking at.

After Ricky had returned the book to its original orientation, I explored the robustness of this emerging skill a bit by saying, "Show the bear to Grandpa." Ricky pointed at the bear and lowered the book so that the bear was visible to his grandfather but was upside down. Apparently, Ricky thought the appropriate response to "show" was to point, and the task of pointing as well made it too difficult to turn the book all the way around. Also, with the book just lowered, Ricky could see the bear too. Likewise, in response to "Show the apples to Daddy," Ricky first pointed, then got up and walked over to his father, holding the book so that they could both see the objects.

By 19 months of age, Ricky seemed to be taking another's line of sight and not just proximity into account, but he still found it difficult to orient an object for another, especially if it meant changing his own view of it or coordinating it with a second behavior such as pointing. Watching a toddler struggle with behaviors adults perform so effortlessly makes one realize how much learning and development goes into a seemingly simple communicative skill. Orienting an object so that another can see it requires knowing that others' vision depends on unobstructed paths of viewing, computing what that path is, and maneuvering the object to be seen so that it intersects with that path—all this while trying to attend to the object oneself. In the laboratory, 3 year olds can readily do tasks requiring this level of competence (Flavell, Shipstead, & Croft, 1978; Yaniv & Shatz, 1988), but observations of other toddlers confirm how difficult visual perspective-taking is for children under age 2 (Lempers, Flavell, & Flavell, 1977).

## Language Development

### *Uncoupling Language from the Here and Now*

In most cases, Ricky tried to tie language to the immediate context in any way he could, possibly because it was his way of assuring some mutual focus in the absence of full understanding. I said to him on the phone one day, "It's a beautiful day out. You and mommy should take a walk to the park." Ricky dropped the phone, ran to the door, and said, "Door. Outside." It took some convincing by his mother that the activity did not have to be immediate.

However, *where* was clearly a term that he understood referred to something absent rather than present or immediate. Not only did he continue to play the "where's Ricky" game, but new versions of hiding games were created, such as asking his father "where" and then pulling up his shirt to reveal his navel. He also spontaneously and appropriately used the word when seriously searching for something.

G: Go get your jacket in the kitchen.
   (R runs into the kitchen but doesn't see his jacket which is hidden under his mother's coat.)
R: (Calling to me) Where, where?

The *where* sequences may have played some role in Ricky's beginning to understand that absence or separation can be temporary and need not be frightening. Although over the last year, Ricky had stayed alone with me on several occasions, he had usually experienced dismay at his mother's absence. His unhappiness was often relatively shortlived, but it nonetheless required some effort on my part to comfort and distract him. Now, however, Ricky began to accept verbal explanations for his mother's absences with equanimity. One day at his home, in the midst of play with me, he realized that Alice (who had been gone about an hour) was not in the apartment.

R: Where mama?
G: Mommy went to get Daddy; she'll be home soon.

Ricky immediately returned happily to playing, without showing any further concern. Language now was a mediator of immediate experience and hence could have some impact on Ricky's emotions.

Language was able to mediate desired actions as well. Ricky was sitting in a chair at the table, eating lunch. He stuffed some food in his mouth, and then swung his legs to the side, preparing to leave the table.

R: Down.
G: Wait until you finish what's in your mouth. You can't walk around with food in your mouth.

Ricky turned back toward the table and finished his mouthful, then motioned to be taken down.

Conversational engagements were also sources of information about how to organize the world with language. Traditionally, researchers studying how children develop semantic categories assumed a kind of "bottom-up" approach. A child might notice an object, learn a label for it, and then notice another object that is either perceptually or functionally similar. The child might then use the same label for the second object, and in that way build a category of objects that fall under the same label (Clark, 1973; Nelson, 1974). In such cases, the referent-word ties, or world-word ties, underlie the semantic categories developed.

Linguistic discourse itself, however, can be a source of information about semantic categories for children, even before they discover just how certain words relate to the world. This is especially true for categories that may not have as obvious referents as object categories do. For example, just as children apparently learn that *yes* and *no* are answers to certain sorts of questions before they fully understand the meaning of the words, so, too, do they seem able to learn that certain words form good answers to questions like, "What color?" or "How many?" In essence, experience in conversation demonstrates for the children that there are sets of words relating to something called "color" or counting even before they understand what individual terms in those classes like *red* or *two* might refer to.

Even at this early age, Ricky seemed already to have learned that the appropriate answer to a "what color" question was a term like *red* or *blue*. The term he favored was blue ("boo"), which he used in most instances. Very occasionally, he was correct, as when we were reading a book about colors and he said "boo" and pointed to the page of blue objects, but he used the same term in too many other instances when it was incorrect to grant him knowledge of what it referred to. He also answered "two" in response to "how many" questions, regardless of the number of objects to be counted. However, he did not say "two" when there was only one object referred to; so it seems he used the term to refer generally to plurality, and not duality.

In these months, Ricky began to use other color names (orange, green, yellow) that alternated with blue as a (usually incorrect) response to the color question. The most recently acquired word would be privileged for a few days as the response to a color question. By the end of the period, Ricky had a set, or category, of color terms but no knowledge of what any one of them specifically referred to. What conversational experience had given Ricky was a word-words tie—a set or category—of terms that related to "color." Assigning specific referents to those terms would come a bit later.

Recent studies examining over 100 toddlers about Ricky's age revealed similar behavior with color terms (Backscheider & Shatz, 1993; Shatz & Backscheider, 1991).[1] About half of the 20 month olds studied produced a color term in response to "What color is it?" questions from their mothers, but they were almost always incorrect in their choice of term and in a color comprehension task as well. Interestingly, only a few children answered such questions with something other than a color term, for example, an object label or a number term. Therefore, the children at least knew that terms like *red* or *blue* were the right sorts of answers to questions about color.

## Talking to Self and to Others

One incident demonstrated especially well that language served nonsocial cognitive functions as well as social ones for Ricky. One day he was playing by himself. He tried but failed to put a large ball into a small boxcar. Giving up, he set the ball on the floor, saying softly to himself, "Big."

Ricky was talking quietly to himself more frequently. Several instances suggested he was practicing how language encoded some conceptual relations that were new to him. For example, toward the end of this period, he became fascinated with the notion of duality (or, possibly, plurality) and he took every opportunity he could to use the word *two*. When he noticed two towels hanging on a rack, he said to himself, "Two," whereas earlier he might have labeled them with the word *towel*. As he was playing with a toy car he was pushing along a track, he suddenly said, "Two," and went to get another car so that he had one in each hand. About the same time, he stopped using the plural forms of nouns for single objects, as he seemed to have achieved the understanding that -s was a marking for multiple objects. For example, he called his toy Jeep and Porsche by their individual names, but labeled them together "Cars."

He often spoke softly to himself about names and relations, as when he took a pair of his trousers from the laundry basket, held them against himself, and said, "Mine." And, one day, sitting at the breakfast table, he quietly named the other members of the family as they came into the room and sat down.

One new social use of language sometimes resulted fortuitously in information about basic conceptual category distinctions. Ricky recognized that adults could be called on when he needed assistance of some sort. He had learned the word *help* and used it appropriately and effectively to solicit adult assistance. Sometimes, adults responded in ways that illustrated differences among objects in the world that he might not have noticed or that were not obvious. For example, on a walk one day, he picked up a pine cone and tried to open it with an unscrewing motion. Frustrated after a few minutes, he handed it to me, saying, "Help." After I had broken it open by snapping it, Ricky tried several times to put it back together. The incident may have allowed him to discover that some kinds of things found outside on walks in the woods usually don't work the way that things in the house do.

Ricky's mistaken actions with the pine cone were grounded in ignorance about one of the basic distinctions that adults have come to take for granted between natural objects, entities with natural origins, and artifacts, objects made by humans. Preschoolers are still working out those distinctions (Carey, 1985). For example, 4 year olds understand better than 3 year olds that living things, both animals and plants, have some power to regenerate their parts whereas artifacts do not (Backscheider, Shatz, & Gelman, 1993). How something opens, and whether it can be reclosed, is another kind of knowledge about the natural object-artifact distinction that might depend on early trial-and-error action, observation of more knowledgeable others, or both.

In the realm of social behavior, Ricky's ignorance about conventional practices in his society sometimes led him to use his newfound language skills in violation of expected social practice. One day as we were leaving a restaurant, he stopped at each booth on the way out, smiled, waved, and said, "Bye-bye." Although greeting the other patrons may be conventional practice in some parts of the world, it is not in the United States. Ricky could not have observed such behavior by others in restaurants, yet it must have seemed to him to be an appropriate extension of leave-taking behavior within the family. Needless to say, there was considerable mirth in the restaurant by the time he reached the door.

Even though Ricky's inappropriate actions in the pine cone and restaurant incidents resulted from the lack of knowledge in two very different domains, his naive behaviors reveal a general tendency in children to use whatever knowledge they do have, however incomplete, to engage both the physical and social worlds. Without added knowledge further constraining his understanding of objects or of leave-taking behaviors, Ricky overgeneralized his actions to inappropriate contexts. In doing so, however, he was practicing his skills and seeing how far his knowledge would take him.

## Progress with Vocabulary and Multiword Phrases

There are reports in the child language literature of vocabulary spurts in children, cases where children go from having a few dozen words to close to a hundred in a matter of weeks. A recent study of two dozen children found that slightly more than half of them exhibited a relatively rapid spurt in word learning, with more than 60% of their vocabulary as they approached the 100-word mark being nouns. The other children seemed to progress in a more linear fashion, and a slightly smaller proportion (about half) of their words were nouns (Goldfield & Reznick, 1990). I had not kept weekly records of Ricky's early vocabulary growth, but his pattern of word acquisition suggests that he may have been somewhat like the word spurt children. From 15 to 16 months, he went from 30 to over 50 words (see Chapter 2), and by 18 months he had over 100 words, about 60% of which were concrete nouns.

Ricky had also begun to use two- and three-word phrases with some regularity. His mother reported being so surprised by his first full sentence that she couldn't remember what it was. I heard him say two spontaneous three-word sentences on a single day for the first time about the middle of the period. The first was when we were seated in a restaurant, waiting for food. Ricky grabbed a wad of dollars that his father was holding.

R: Doyyars. (Starts to put them in his mouth.)
G: Oh, no, Ricky. Don't eat that. It's dirty. (Ricky's father retrieves the money.)
R: (To me) No eat doyyars.

Later the same day, after his father had gone out to the car, Ricky said, "Daddy go outside."

Not all multiword utterances were so well formed. Subjects and predicates occasionally were reversed from their normal order, as in

"go wa-chine" (washing machine is going). Many times Ricky produced strings of jargon in which only one word was intelligible. One
day after arriving at my house, he traipsed upstairs as he often did
just to look around. I followed him up to find him climbing on the
couch in the den. Settling himself, he pointed to the television set
and said, "bo-ball," his word for football. Apparently, he remembered
having watched football with his father and uncle on New Year's
Day six weeks earlier. I turned on the set and twirled the dials, but,
alas, football season was over. Disappointed, Ricky went downstairs, earnestly greeting his grandfather at the foot of the stairs
with a long string of jargon (the only discernible word of which was
"bo-ball") while at the same time pointing upstairs. Ricky clearly
had more to say about his attempt to recreate a pleasant afternoon
than he could yet put into words.

In sum, Ricky's behavior was a charming panache of mis-
matches between levels of cognitive, social, and linguistic knowledge. At times, his language use seemed more advanced than his
cognitive understandings (as with color terms) or his knowledge of
social conventions (as with his multiple farewells in the restaurant).
At other times, his attempts to express his thoughts were clearly
thwarted by his immature language skills. His naiveté undoubtedly
was something of a virtue. It allowed him unselfconsciously to keep
entering the social fray and to keep trying out his nascent skills—
regularly getting feedback from the delighted adults around him
about his social, physical, and linguistic environment.

## Note

1. Bartlett (1978) and Rice (1980) report similar phenomena in slightly
older children.

# 4

## 19-20 Months
## Emerging Skills

### Learning in a Literate World

When we think about language skills, it seems reasonable to assume that oral language must be highly developed before a learner's attention focuses on reading or writing. In a literate Western society, apparently that is not so. Young children are exposed to print media just about everywhere they look. From newspaper kiosks to billboards and television ads, print is ubiquitous. For children whose parents read to them or even just read the newspaper and write letters or checks, literacy events are everyday happenings. Researchers are discovering that even preschoolers—and not just ones from advantaged homes—know a considerable amount about the conventions of printed language. (See Teale & Sulzby, 1986; van Kleeck, 1990.) Still, it was surprising to find how much, at a year and a half, Ricky was already attuned to the literate world.

### Experience with Pictures and Print

When Ricky was just a few days old, his mother had propped a book with simple colored figures in his cradle so that he would have something interesting to look at when he opened his eyes. From that time, books were a part of Ricky's life. At first they were more fun to chew and to throw than to peruse, but by 1 year, Ricky was intensely interested in examining the contents of books either alone or with others. By 18 months of age, he had an extensive book collection that he treated with pride. Whenever I came for a visit, his first act was to guide me to his room to show me his latest acquisition. He was especially fond of books about animals and vehicles, and he learned a great many new words such as *parrot*, *monkey*, *alligator*, and *tractor* from them.

Young children learn vocabulary at an amazingly rapid rate during this period, and so Ricky's acquisition of new words from books is not surprising, especially since researchers who have studied parent-child behavior with books have noted that parents of young children spend considerable time conversing with their children about the labels and attributes of depicted objects in books (Ninio & Bruner, 1978). Early interactions with books have long-lasting benefits: School-aged children who had such preschool experiences are more advanced in vocabulary than children who did not (Whitehurst, et al., 1988).

More surprising than his vocabulary growth was the fact that Ricky had already picked up some knowledge about the process of reading. He understood that the squiggles on the page were related to what was said in reading. As he was looking at a picture book one day, he turned to the frontispiece (where, unlike on the other pages, there was writing), held the book close to his face, and began to jabber in a "reading" intonation. He then pointed to the letter *I* and said, "I."

Ricky was also attentive to letters in other contexts. We were playing a video game, and when letters began to pop up on the screen, he became excited and began to shout out letter names, albeit incorrect ones. He had a set of blocks with letters on them, and liked to play with them and have adults label the letters so that he could repeat them.

Reading activities in nonbook contexts had also caught his attention. One day, we celebrated my birthday with a feast of Chinese food. When we got to dessert, Ricky passed out a fortune cookie to each of us. He bit into his, saying, "paper." He needed another bite before he finally got to the fortune. He pulled it out, held it up before his eyes, babbled softly, and then threw back his head and laughed. Despite all that goes on at mealtimes and the relatively rare occasions on which he had seen fortune cookies, he had nonetheless noted carefully the details of the social ritual of reading cookie fortunes. His desire to participate like everyone else in the happy ritual may have outdistanced his literacy skills, but he had associated "reading" with a pleasant social event.

Ricky was also fascinated with the music books for children that I kept on my piano. I had told him earlier that the markings on the musical staffs were "notes" that I had to "read" in order to play the music, and when he pretended to play a song, he insisted on opening a music book and having the pages turned for him. He quickly learned to recognize the locations of particular songs in the book by their accompanying pictures and would sing a song only when the book was turned to the appropriate page, as if he were reading the words from it. Thus, he associated the act of reading with some interaction between the eyes and the printed page. Although he did not really understand what "reading" was, it was already related in his mind to interesting and pleasurable adult activities having to do with books and music—activities he was very attentive to and tried to emulate. Ricky also expected pictures as well as words or notes to appear in books. When he came across an adult music book with no pictures, he showed some consternation, bringing it to me and saying in a concerned tone, "Dis no pictures."

Ricky's interest in printed materials undoubtedly was stimulated by the adults in his milieu. However, it was not just occasions of book reading between adult and child that caught his attention. The fortune cookie incident illustrates that he took note of literacy activities in all sorts of situations; reading behavior was woven into the fabric of the everyday life of the adults he observed. As he closely watched and tried to understand how adults managed the world around them, Ricky was discovering the centrality of activities involving printed material in that world, and he tried hard to be included in them in some way. Even the arrival of the daily mail became an opportunity to engage his mother in such activities. He began to listen expectantly for the mail drop each day, and on hearing it, excitedly to urge Alice to take him to the box to see what had arrived. At only 20 months of age, Ricky was already embedded in a literate society.

## Developing Number Concepts

There has been much research on the development of number concepts in young children. (See Frye, Braisby, Lowe, Maroudas, & Nicholls, 1989, for a review and discussion of findings.) Like an interest in reading and print, an interest in concepts of quantity may get a boost from caretakers who engage their young children in activities involving quantity like counting. Many children under 2 have a routine for responding to their mothers' "how many" questions. They answer by pointing one at a time to an array of objects, and some respond with a number term as well (Shatz & Backscheider, 1991). Many 2 year olds learn a sequence of numbers that they recite as they "count," although the sequence is not always correct.

Ricky's interest in numbers increased during this period. Early in it, we overheard him spontaneously practice counting to five to himself. When asked to count with me, he pointed to objects in sequence without any repetition, but he refused to produce the numbers himself until I said "four," which he then repeated several times. Later on during the period, he became less reticent about counting publicly. One day, when I was wearing a set of beads, he reached up, touched several in turn, saying "One, two, three." Although he still answered "how many" questions with the verbal response "two," he could clearly count beyond that. As he collected Easter eggs we had spread around the lawn, he stopped regularly to take his eggs out of his basket, counting them one by one and then returning them to the basket the same way. He occasionally was stymied by a number in the sequence, but managed to get up to 10 several times with relatively few mistakes.

It may seem surprising that Ricky maintained his earlier-learned conversational response of "two" to "how many" questions even as his counting skills grew. However, children acquire an understanding of ordinality, the sequential relations between numbers, before the notion of cardinality, the idea that a number stands for a particular quantity (Fuson, Pergament, Lyons, & Hall, 1985). Thus, Ricky's verbal response to "how many" questions may have been rote; he didn't seem to relate it to the process of "counting," the sequential pointing to an array of objects that often accompanied his response. Yet he did seem to know that *two* stood for a particular quantity; he used it appropriately as a cardinal number to describe various duplicates of objects, such as "two buses." Although he spent much time playing with number words, not only reciting a sequence of numbers, but often picking a single word like *eight* and saying it over and over to himself, he did not extend his knowledge of any other number words beyond the counting context. He seemed to have three situation-dependent concepts of number that he kept somewhat separate: a rote response to "how many" questions, cardinal duality, and ordinal counting. At first, *two* was the only number term that was linked to all three.

An incident about a month later showed that Ricky's terms for answering "how many" questions were expanding, but he still had not integrated his concepts of number, even through the word *two*. At my house, Ricky expressed an interest in going outside, and I had told him he had to put his shoes on first. After playing around for a few minutes with a key he was holding, he ran to get one of his shoes, which he brought to me. As he turned to get the other one, he said, "Two," repeating the word twice more as he ran back to me with it. At my request, Ricky sat down at the foot of the stairs so that I could put his shoes on.

M: Why are you putting your shoes on, Ricky?
R: Shoes bye-bye.
M: You going bye-bye?
G: Yes.
M: (To G) Are you sending us home?
G: No, he has this idea he wants to go outside.
M: (to R) Oh, you want to go for a walk?
R: No walk.
G: I have a feeling that's not what he wants to do.
M: How many shoes do you have, Ricky?
R: Four.
G: You don't have four shoes [overlap].
M: [Overlap] You have four shoes?
M: How many feet do you have?
R: Four.
G: You don't have four feet [overlap].
M: [Overlap] You'd better check.
   Count them.
   Let's see.
R: Check. (Ricky gets off the stairs, moves toward the door, and stops.)
   Check. (R bends down and points a finger at one shoe.)
M: One—
R: (R moves his pointing finger to the other shoe.)
   Two.
G: Two [overlap]!
M: [Overlap] Two feet [overlap].
R: [Overlap] Two. (R. goes to the door.)
M: So, how many feet do you have?
R: Four.

Four had replaced two as his favorite response to "how many" questions and continued to do so for several weeks. On the putting green at our vacation house (see Chapter 5), Ricky ran toward me with a golf ball in each hand.

M: Tell Grandma how many balls you have.
R: (R looks down at his hands.) Four.

## Working on Words

Number words were not the only ones Ricky practiced. His pattern of picking a word and working on it for a day or more became increasingly frequent. In this period, he developed an interest in adverbial modifiers that was to last for several months. The first such word he picked up was *now*. He imitated it after I had used it in a sentence, said it a few times then, and continued to repeat it throughout the day in different contexts.

Word practice was not limited to single words. One day I heard him reciting to himself a series of antonyms—"in-out, up-down, hi-bye." His mother reported she had heard something similar, although she herself had not introduced the exercise to Ricky. Apparently, his language practice involved organizing his lexicon in rather abstract and complex ways. Organizing a set of spatial terms into opposites would have been impressive, but because he had coupled *hi-bye* with such words, he seemed to be thinking on an even more abstract level—more generally about words that were polar opposites.

For 70 years, language researchers have noted that young children practice or play with language, repeating and varying bits of speech for themselves without any communicative purpose (Cazden, 1976; Garvey, 1977; Jesperson, 1922; Kuczaj, 1983; Weir, 1962). Most often, children have been observed practicing a single word in different sentential contexts, as Ricky did with *now*, or substituting different words in a single context, for example, "Give Mommy drink, give Daddy drink, give Baby drink." Possibly the sort of practice that focuses on sentence construction is much more common than practice that organizes words into grammatical or conceptual classes, as did the antonym instance. It is also possible, however, that researchers interested in grammar development have been more attentive to the former than the latter. Although Ricky's practice with classes was not abundant, the antonym example was not unique for him.

Another new behavior for Ricky was overextension, a phenomenon regularly reported in children about this age (Clark, 1973; Rescorla, 1980). An overextension occurs when a child uses a label to designate an object not covered by the adult usage for that term, thereby taking the label beyond its usual reference set. There are often perceptual or functional similarities between the usual referent and the referent to which the term is overextended. For example, a child might call a cow "horse" (Clark, 1973). There has been some controversy over the meaning of overextensions—whether children overextend because they believe, say, that cows and horses are the same kind of thing and belong in the same group or category, or because their vocabularies are limited and they have to stretch the words they do know to cover circumstances for which they lack the correct word. There may be times when children draw their categories too broadly, but there is considerable evidence in favor of the vocabulary stretching view as well: Children reportedly produce overextensions in order to call attention to similarities they have noticed (Nelson, Benedict, Gruendel, & Rescorla, 1977; Foster, 1979), and children who overextend their productions can often make the appropriate differentiations in comprehension tasks that ask them to "show me the cow" (Fremgen & Fay, 1980).

It seemed that Ricky used overextensions to call our attention to similarities. As we were spreading a tablecloth on the table, he said "sheet." On another occasion, we were playing with blocks, several of which were cylindrical.

R: Ball? (Holding up a cylindrical block.)
G: Cylinder. See, this part is like a ball—or a circle. (Pointing to the end of the cylinder.) But the whole thing is called a cylinder.
R: Cy-a-der.

In this case, Ricky's questioning intonation suggested he knew his use of "ball" was incorrect, but its production got me to provide the correct term for him.

Interestingly, overextensions tend to become more frequent at about the same time that children apparently prefer to have only one label per object. Markman (1987) has proposed that learning new words is easier for children if they abide by a principle of mutual exclusivity: They assume when they hear a new word that it labels something other than an object for which they already have a word. At first it seems somewhat paradoxical that children would extend words beyond the conceptual categories to which they have heard them applied at the same time that they make the assumption that objects have only one label. (It seems more reasonable for children to assume that if one kind of thing has only one label, then a different kind of thing should have a different label.) But suppose children use overextensions to tell listeners that they see similarities as well as differences across situations. For example, when he said "sheet," Ricky may have been trying to say, "This looks like a sheet" or "Spreading something on a table reminds me of spreading a sheet on a bed." As in the "ball" case, he may have been wondering whether another word covered this similar but different instance. If children use overextensions to communicate about similar but different instances, then the paradox is resolved. Both children's overextensions and their tendency to treat words as mutually exclusive labels for different referents would be indications of the same process of trying to sort out the culture's semantic categories and their labels in the language being learned.

Although Ricky earlier had seemed to accept more than one label for an object (e.g., he used both *Porsche* and *car* for a single object), he now showed that, at least sometimes, he adhered to a principle of mutual exclusivity. One day, when he was looking at a book with his grandfather, they engaged in a rather argumentative dialogue about the label for a baby bird.

> Gf: Chick (Pointing to the small, yellow, furry object.)
> R:  Bird.
> Gf: Chick.
> R:  (Insistently) Bird!

They repeated the cycle several more times, with Ricky getting more agitated each time his grandfather persisted in using a term different from his. Other children have been observed engaging in similar arguments (Macnamara, 1982).

Still, children learn new words very readily, and sometimes this must occur after they hear adults use different words for objects they have already labeled another way. Thus, some of the time when they reassign labels, they undoubtedly have to redraw the boundaries of the category to which their original label applied. (If "horse" originally did include instances of horses and cows, learning the word *cow* would allow for the restructuring of the conceptual category "horse.") Researchers have begun to study when children make assumptions of mutual exclusivity to do such restructuring and when they make other inferences about the relations between new words and old ones. For example, they might consider the new word as labeling a subcategory of the old, as in the example of *Porsche* and *car*.

Several factors seem to affect whether toddlers will accept a new label for an object that already has one and how that new label will be integrated into the lexicon. Such things as how much information the child is given about the differences between the referents of the new label and the referents of the old (Banigan &

Mervis, 1988), the perceptual similarities between the referents (Waxman & Senghas, 1992), and the language accompanying the new label (e.g., whether the adult says, "That's not a horse; it's a cow"). Possibly, if Ricky's grandfather had said explicitly, "A chick is a baby bird," Ricky would have been more willing to accept the new label. It would then have been useful to know whether he would have accepted both *bird* and *chick* as labels for the object, in which case he might have entered the new word into a hierarchical relation with the old, or whether he would have insisted on only the new label, in which case he would have created a mutually exclusive relation. Children need to be able to do both if they are to achieve an organization to their lexicons that they hold in common with other speakers of their language (Shatz, 1993). We will see that sorting out the referents of words and the relations among words was a task that occupied Ricky for many months.

As for putting words together and acquiring grammar, this period was largely a time of consolidation for Ricky. He continued to use many two-word utterances, but in the first month, three-word utterances were rare, as were two-word utterances that included verbs. Instead, there were many comment-topic combinations that made some statement about an object. For example, Ricky said "more ball" when he found another ball next to the one that had just been tossed toward him. He said "out porch" when he wanted to go outside and "off horse" after he tumbled from his rocking horse. Therefore, although his multiword utterances did not usually violate what would be the conventional word order of more mature expansions of them into full English sentences (e.g., I want to go out on the porch; I fell off the horse), they seemed to require only a simple ordering rule—and not much knowledge of English grammar—to generate them.

By the time Ricky was 20 months old, the range of relations expressed by two-word utterances had expanded considerably. Common now were phrases with verbs like "eat it" or "make it," adjective-noun combinations like "blue balloon" and "big car," prepositional phrases like "in here," and determiner-noun phrases like "a school" and "a pig." Three-word utterances with verbs reappeared ("I want juice"). However, many of these had the character of frames with open slots into which different words could be dropped (e.g., I want ____; here ____ is). Thus, during this period, grammar acquisition seemed to progress with the addition of bits and snatches of adult forms rather than via the learning of obligatory rules. For example, I could find no systematic patterns of occurrence either for determiners or sentence subjects. Sometimes Ricky would correctly include an "a" or an "I" in his utterances, and sometimes he would drop them. Such a pattern of variable use in new acquisitions of form is not well understood, but it is one that has been frequently observed for children learning language, and we will see it repeatedly.

## A New Social Skill: Teasing

Ricky had been waiting for us on the stairs in the lobby of his apartment house. When we arrived, he greeted us, then turned and walked up to the landing between two stairways, only one of which led to his home. Ricky went to the stairway opposite that one and made as if to descend that flight, thus moving *away* from his own apartment. He looked back at me with a coy little smile. Was he making a joke? Was he teasing? His attitude certainly suggested he was teasing, but I couldn't be sure. I said cheerfully, "Oops. Wrong way. I'm going this way," as I headed for the correct stairway. Ricky laughed and followed me.

At the end of the afternoon, when I put on my coat to leave, Ricky went to get his coat, saying, "out porch." He knew I was planning to leave, but instead demanded to be taken onto the porch to forestall my departure. A few days later, when I was again visiting, there was a similar incident. As I was preparing to leave, Ricky grabbed my purse from a chair near the door and ran laughing into his bedroom. He knew I would not leave without the purse. After considerable rough-and-tumble play and much laughter, I retrieved the purse.

All these incidents indicated that Ricky was developing an awareness of how he could influence others' behavior. He seemed to know that others had expectations about events that he could violate with his own ends in mind. Such knowledge is relatively subtle, and I had not observed behavior based on it before in Ricky. Interestingly, his first attempts at spontaneous teasing and manipulation of others (as opposed to ritualized games) were essentially nonlinguistic. Regardless of how verbal interactions had helped him build a representation of others' expectations, his own linguistic skills did not yet support conversational jokes, although, as we will see, that would soon change.

Teasing behavior has been reported in children even younger than Ricky. Younger siblings by 16 months of age will know what sorts of things upset their older brothers or sisters and will engage in behaviors such as grabbing a favored toy that will engender an emotional response from the sibling (Dunn, 1988). Ricky's behavior seemed designed less to annoy than to violate expectations: the emotional response appropriate to his teasing was surprise rather than dismay. Both kinds of teasing rely on knowledge about how other people usually behave, but the knowledge needed for younger children's teasing may be accessible earlier. Dunn has suggested that young children show so much insight into their siblings' emotional states because they have the opportunity to observe what upsets or comforts them in very salient, highly emotional situations—for example, when they are in conflict with their parents. Violating expectations may be a later form of teasing because it relies on knowledge of how others behave in less emotionally volatile circumstances.

## Emerging Organizations

### *Creating Domains of Knowledge*

This chapter began with the suggestion that toddlers' acquisition of knowledge might diverge from the order that commonsense logic predicts. In particular, learning about writing begins long before oral language learning is very advanced. Similarly, there is evidence that commonsense sequences for learning are violated elsewhere as well. It seems reasonable to learn what red is before learning that red and blue are color words, or to come to recognize the letter A before being able to distinguish letters from numbers more generally. Yet Ricky was acquiring, as have other children observed in my laboratory and elsewhere, some of the more general distinctions before the more specific ones. Although he rarely labeled a color, letter, or number correctly, he never confused the sets of labels, always selecting a letter from the alphabet when labeling a letter block and a number from 1 to 10 for a number block. Strangely enough, it was easier for him to learn that two was a number and not a letter than to recognize even R, which was pointed out to him frequently because it was his initial.[1]

Ricky was, then, creating domains, or areas of information, even on the basis of very little knowledge about the entities in those domains. Such areas of information may be the foundations on which children construct understandings about the world. Clearly, children have to be able to differentiate a great many things in the world if they are eventually to understand them. Numbers indeed behave differently from letters, and we acquire different kinds of knowledge about them. Similarly, children need to acquire different understandings about people and about inanimate objects. Consequently, a crucial aspect of acquiring knowledge is creating domains or areas in which entities that are constrained by the same rules of logic or laws of nature are grouped. When adults have knowledge about the ways in which groups of entities commonly operate (and what causes them to operate in those ways), they are said to have domain-specific theories.

Researchers are working to discover what sorts of understandings preschoolers have about these different groups of entities in the world, whether their understandings are coherent, and whether they provide the children with ways to explain their experiences. If their understandings prove to be coherent and explanatory, we can say that children have theories about the various domains that comprise world knowledge, even though those theories may be different from the ones held by adults. As their experience and knowledge grow, they have to revise their theories and possibly even restructure their domains.

Toddlers probably do not yet have specific, coherent theories, but it is clear from our observations of Ricky that even before age 2, toddlers are busy creating pretheoretic domains, separate areas of information on which to build their knowledge of the world.[2] How can young children begin to create domains without having a theoretical basis for doing so? One possibility is that they have some bases for grouping things together that either look alike or behave similarly. Mandler (1988, 1992) has suggested that an innate ability to do perceptual analysis provides the foundation for early conceptual differentiations as early as infancy.

An additional possibility is that the language toddlers are learning gives them clues. Parents ask different sorts of questions about color and number ("what color," "how many?") and different labels apply to sets of letters and numbers. If children are prepared to assume that things that are labeled or talked about differently are different kinds of things, then language would be a powerful tool for organizing domains of knowledge even at a very early stage of language development. Language should be especially useful for conceptual domains that are not characterized by easily detectable perceptual characteristics and for children without normal access to perceptual information, for example, blind children (Landau & Gleitman, 1985).

## The Nature of Toddler Learning

The creation of knowledge domains is one piece of evidence that Ricky was organizing his knowledge even as he was acquiring it. His practice of opposites is another. His attention to words and their appropriate range of referents is another (e.g., the bird-chick and ball-cylinder incidents). Moreover, the organization can be somewhat abstract in nature. Entities are not necessarily organized together just because they all look alike. Rather, for example, opposites of varying sorts are practiced together because they all have the same within-pair relations. And words like *red* and *blue* are organized together because they are all called "color." This latter example also shows that learning can be "top down," or general to specific, instead of always "bottom up," or specific to more general.

Yet there is chaos as well as organization in toddlers' behavior. Certainly, language behavior is very variable: Sometimes toddlers produce grammatical phrases, but just as frequently, required elements are missing. Much of their language seems better characterized as based on utterance frames than productive grammatical rules. Ricky's language behavior typified these patterns. Still, like those of other children, his errors were mostly ones of omission. For example, although he often omitted the determiners *a* and *the*, he never used them with pronouns or verbs. And, he only occasionally violated the word orders of English. The chaos is not complete, then, but rather constrained by partial knowledge.

In sum, toddler knowledge is piecemeal, but it is not totally unorganized, and it is neither completely simple nor concrete. Even with minimal knowledge, toddlers can operate on various levels of abstractness and complexity. What they lack is the intricate web of integrated knowledge that allows for context-appropriate, mature behavior.

### Notes

1. How readily children differentiate numbers and letters depends on the nature of their early experience with the symbols. Still confusing numbers and letters at age 4 was one child whose very early experience with them was of their common placement on a computer keyboard (S. Goldin-Meadow, personal communication, January 1993).

2. See Wellman and Gelman (1992) for a review of the evidence that young children are building foundational theories.

# 5

## 21–22 Months
## Self-Concept and
## Object Concepts

Because children acquire knowledge in a variety of domains during toddlerhood, we can often observe rapid progress in several areas of development within a very short time span. The period between 21 and 23 months of age was one such period for Ricky. He was developing his sense of self as well as learning more about how to use language to interact with others in playful ways. Indeed, progress in these two areas was very likely related. Mead (1934) argued that only through language can one discover fully how to see the self as others do, and that this perspective-taking is essential to the development of an adequate self-concept.

Mead's general proposal to interrelate the developments of self-concept, language, and an understanding of mind was seminal. In the intervening years, much research on each of the three areas revealed more complexity in their development, and in their relations to one another, than Mead's original theory can comfortably account for. For example, children begin to differentiate self from other very early in development even without the benefit of language (Butterworth, 1990; Sroufe, 1990). Moreover, independent considerations of linguistic form influence the timing of children's acquisition of self-other language and hence may mask early knowledge about self and other (Bates, 1990). Nonetheless, the basic insight that the three areas promote and sustain each other is still viable and is an essential aspect of this book's framework.

Ricky's language was generally becoming more sophisticated; he added more verbs and modifiers to his vocabulary, as well as labels for general object categories like *animals* and *clothes*. He was producing more complex utterances, with some grammatical markers such as plurals, but at times what he wanted to say still seemed to exceed his ability to express it grammatically; consequently, he occasionally produced long strings of jargon and words combined.

## Developing a Self-Concept

If children are to develop mature theories of mind, they must understand that they themselves are individuals, separate from other people, with unique physical and mental existences. Children's self-concepts develop over time as they recognize that they have feelings, intentions, and thoughts, and that these can differ from those of other people. One of the most important issues for students of human development is the question of when and how self-concepts develop. In creating appropriate mental representations of the world they experience and their place in it, children must discover both how they look and how their experiences differ from others'. This is what defines them as individuals and what they elaborate on to construct their sense of self.

Sometime after their first birthdays, children begin to recognize themselves in mirrors (Lewis & Brooks-Gunn, 1979). Ricky by 15 months would smile shyly when he caught sight of himself in a mirror, and he liked to mug in front of mirrors when he thought no one was watching. Still, his view of himself was far from complete or solid. Even six months later, he was elaborating his visual image of himself, comparing himself to others, and sorting out his relations to the rest of the world. A trip to the zoo was the occasion of some revealing examples of this, in addition to providing opportunities to practice other emerging skills.

### A Tale of No Tails

Ricky, accompanied by his parents and grandparents, was having a busy day at the Toledo Zoo, a place where he could discover how the creatures of the world, including himself, differed from one another. He was fascinated by blindfish housed in a dark fishtank lit only by infrared light; he could not seem to accept that some creatures would prefer a habitat without light.

R: Why inna dark?

G: The fish like the dark. The red light is on so that we can see them.

R: Why in here dark; why inna dark in here?

Even his visual image of himself was tested at the zoo. In the carnivore house we watched a magnificent Siberian tiger cleaning its paws with a huge pink tongue. Ricky stuck out his own tongue and handled it. Then he wanted to see my tongue and his mother's tongue in turn, as if to compare their sizes to his own and the tiger's. The tiger began to swing his tail slowly back and forth. Pointing to it, Ricky's mother said, "Look at the tiger's long tail." Ricky watched attentively, then turned to look over his shoulder and felt his bottom to see the status of his tailedness. It would, of course, be a long time before he understood why people and tigers both have tongues (albeit of very different sizes) but only tigers have those majestic tails.

After visiting all the animals, we stopped at the carousel, and Ricky and I mounted a horse for a spirited ride. Amid squeals and giggles, Ricky began to call out to the smiling audience of grandfather and parents each time we whirled past. "Hi, Ricky," he shouted, and occasionally, "Hi, bapa!" (Grandpa), not quite able in his excitement to sort out his appropriate role in the greeting process.

A week later, Ricky happily examined the photographs from the trip to the zoo. He enjoyed labeling all the animals, and repeatedly named his parents and grandparents in the pictures. However, he only reluctantly named himself a few times. He was clearly uncomfortable labeling his own image, and he was more reluctant to point to his image when asked, "Where's Ricky," than he was to point to others in response to the appropriate questions. His behavior was reminiscent of his reticence before his image in the mirror months earlier.

What accounted for Ricky's discomfort in such situations? Was it the simultaneous recognition of the self as an observer and as an object of observation? Sometimes adults report that they produce their most fluid behaviors when they do not monitor their own performances too closely. Perhaps children, who need to be focused so completely on the outside world to take in as much information as they do, would be too distracted by conscious monitoring to learn as fast as they do. Their reluctance to consider themselves objectively in social situations may be an attentional device to help them concentrate their energies on others. Or is the appropriate explanation an emotional rather than a cognitive one? Is it just too threatening to see oneself "captured" in a mirror or in a photograph?

At the zoo

We certainly do not fully understand this sort of behavior in toddlers, but one thing is clear. Ricky treated his own pictorial image differently from those of others, even his mother's, suggesting that he knew very well he had a separate identity.

## We Are What We Are Called

Dealing objectively with his physical image in a social context may have been problematic for Ricky, but he had no trouble using descriptive labels to construct his self-concept. About a month after the trip to the zoo, Ricky showed that he thought the labels applied to him were important to his self-identity in some way. He would indignantly correct anyone who he believed had mislabeled him.

> Gf: (As he, Ricky, and his mother were driving to a resort for a week's vacation with me and my mother.)
> You're a very lucky boy to be going on this nice vacation.
> R: No, my man. (His father often referred to him as "my man.") I a MAN.

Yet he was not above referring to himself as a boy or even a baby when he thought it would achieve his ends. When put to bed before the grown-ups at the vacation house, he would importune us from the loft with a variety of demands and entreaties. Among the most charming was this attempt to touch our sympathies. His grandparents, great-grandmother, and mother were seated in the living room below him, and he called out to each of us in turn.

> R: Mommy, come up a-tairs.
> M: Ricky, it's time to go to sleep.
> R: Grandma, up a-tairs.
> (No response from G, on M's instructions.)
> R: Ba-pa, ba-pa.
> (No response from Gf.)
> R: Hi, Bubby. Bubby, come up a-tairs.
> (No response.)
> R: (Dolefully) Mommy, baby boy.

Clearly, by this time, Ricky had little trouble considering himself objectively in talk about himself. Indeed, he could even joke about his identity, sometimes playfully insisting he was "Rob" (the nickname for his father) and not Ricky.

Ricky also showed considerable interest in the fact that other people could be referred to by more than one name or label. To minimize confusion with me, we had told him his great-grandmother's name was Bubby, but he heard his mother calling her "Grandma" instead of "Bubby," while I called her "Mom." He then began to play around with the names, occasionally calling me "Mom" and his mother "Alice," and trying a variety of terms for my mother. Whenever he did this, he would emphasize the names as though he was encouraging us to respond to his usage. We often did, repeatedly telling him in the simplest terms we could find how the familial relation between speaker and addressee determined the particular label. These discussions would often end with a little game about who was whose mother.

> G: So, who is Mommy's mommy?
> R: Grandma!
> G: And who is Grandma's mommy?
> R: Bubby!
> G: And who is your mommy?
> G: Alice!

Again, Ricky had found a way to engage us to help him understand the relationships of the people around him and the ways those relationships were encoded by language.[1]

Within a few weeks of all this talk about names, Ricky seemed to reach a new level of understanding about reference, image, and reality. Two incidents illustrate that perhaps he had accepted that an image of a person and an actual person could be labeled identically without modifying the identity (or existence) of the person. First, Ricky began to refer blithely to images of himself.

> (Ricky was making faces in front of a highly reflective ceramic lamp.)
> G: Who is that funny face in there?
> R: Ricky.

He also made an overt joke about identical reference as he was sorting through some photographs.

> R: (Pointing to an image of me in a photograph he is holding up to his father as he talks to him.) That's Grandma. (Laughing and pointing at me.) THAT'S Grandma.

### We Are What We Have

In American society at least, possessions play an important role in the development of self-identity. Children learn early about belongings: they are told not to touch Daddy's stereo or to lose Mommy's car keys, to ask before touching their sibling's possessions, and to share their toys with their friends. What we own, or have the access rights to, then, becomes part of our representations of self in the context of the larger social world. Yet the English language gives the young child relatively little help in sorting out different kinds of access rights. For example, English uses the same grammatical devices (possessive markers on nouns and possessive pronouns) for expressing temporary (as with shared, borrowed, or commonly used objects) or permanent access rights (as with ownership or exclusively used objects).[2] By interaction with others, a child learns which social rules for access apply to which objects.

In many incidents, Ricky showed he was experimenting with limits on his rights to access. He may also have been trying to make distinctions in speech that the standard language did not. He seemed to be trying to figure out the appropriate referents and functions for possessive pronouns. Sometimes he seemed to be using *my* to establish his temporary rights to an object. For example, he walked into the den where my exercise bicycle stood and asked about it.

> R: My bike?
>    My bike?
> G: Do you want to ride it?
> R: (Nods yes.)

Another day he saw his grandfather's jacket hanging on a chair.

> R: My coat.
> G: Whose coat is that?
> R: Bapa coat.

A week later, he referred to a possession of mine the same way.

At the same time, he regularly used names to indicate permanent possession, even when someone other than the owner had temporary control of the object. For example, when I drove Richard's car in Richard's absence, Ricky commented, "Grandma drive bapa car." Thus, he may have been exploring whether personal pronouns were a way of explicitly differentiating more temporary circumstances of possession from reference to permanent ownership.

Ricky's use of personal pronouns chiefly to refer to temporary possession was not limited to *my*. Within the month, he was regularly using other possessive pronouns appropriately the same way. (He had begun to use *yours* occasionally months earlier, as in the example in Chapter 2.)

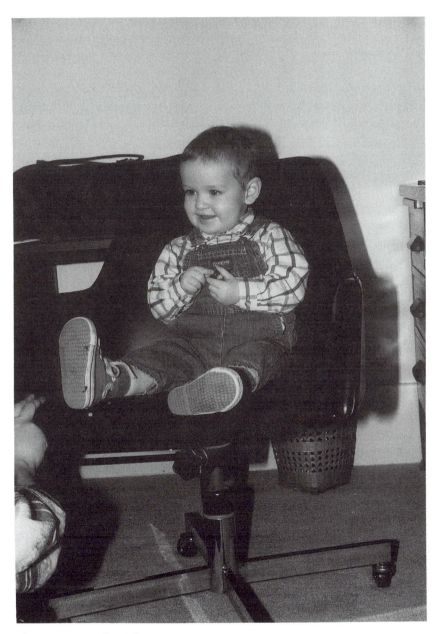

Playing at Grandma's house

(Ricky and I were playing with some toy dishes. He handed me a cup.)

R: Here's yours.

Possibly even a very temporary turn with an object allowed the use of *my*. Thus, when he wanted a ride on the bike, he called the bike his—he would be in possession of it at least for the time he was riding it. In the case of the coat, he may have been testing what response he would get if he declared the coat to be his. This may have been a way of helping to define himself and his posssession rights vis-à-vis others.

As further confirmation of his interest in possession, other incidents during this period show how much Ricky enjoyed being engaged in sequences of play or teasing about possessions. He had been playing with a small pot cover that had a knob in the center, putting the cover in his mouth and sucking on the knob as a pacifier. When he set the cover down, his grandfather picked it up and made as if to put it in his mouth.

Gf: This is my barse. (Ricky's word for pacifier.)
(R looks knowingly at Richard and laughs. Gf puts the cover back on the table.)
R: Now MY barse. (R picks up the cover and puts it in his own mouth; everyone laughs.)

Ricky also enjoyed play about giving or trading objects that belonged to him, but he was clever about not giving away anything he valued. One of his prized possessions was a golf ball Richard had given him and that he was allowed to hold when riding in the car. To amuse him one day, I pretended to be a golf ball monster, croaking for his ball and wiggling my fingers toward him. Ricky laughed, shaking his head no. I kept up my demands. Finally, he put his toy tractor in my hands. I refused it. He tried his pacifier, but again I refused it. Then he tried a diaper and the pacifier again. This time I accepted the pacifier.

G: Okay, I'll keep this for a while.
Maybe we should trade. I'll give you the pacifier. You give me the golf ball.
R: (R nodded yes, laughing.)

We made the trade, and I suggested we trade again, ball for pacifier. This time, Ricky took the ball, but he gave me the tractor instead of the pacifier. He laughed gleefully, as he now had both his prized possessions back.

## Humor and Objectivity About the Self

In an insightful paper, Jerome Bruner (1972) pointed out that play is a child's way of working at understanding the world. Some of the incidents described thus far illustrate that play as a way of learning was not limited to the world of action and objects for Ricky. Playfulness in linguistic exchanges had become a way for Ricky to explore who he was and what his relations to others were. He showed that he reflected on the nature of these exchanges, and was beginning to use playful language to place his own behavior in social perspective.

On the first day of vacationing together, Ricky had joined his grandparents and mother in the resort's swimming pool, but he had been conflicted over his experience in the water, alternately delighting in playing with the adults and asking anxiously to be taken out of the water, saying "No more, out now." The next morning, Ricky sat on his grandfather's bed, looking at some books. Richard, who regularly used language in playful ways with Ricky, started to tease about the pool incident.

> Gf: (Putting his face close to Ricky's and murmuring quickly.) No more, no more, no more.
> Out now, out now, out now.

Ricky at first looked nonplussed, then took Richard's face gently between his hands and smiled lovingly.

> G: Grandpa is teasing you again.

About an hour later, I overhead Ricky talking to himself.

> R: No more, no more. Tease me.

On another occasion, Ricky and Richard were reading a book about Curious George, one of Ricky's favorite characters. Knowing that Ricky pronounced *George* and *doors* similarly ("dorch"), Richard pointed first to the image of George and then to a door in the book.

> Gf: What's this?
> R: Dorch.
> Gf: What's this?
> R: Dorch.

They repeated this sequence three or four times, picking up speed with each repetition. Finally, Ricky looked up at Richard and started to laugh, possibly realizing that his replies were indistinguishable. Later, when Richard recounted the incident to other family members, I added "he got the joke." Ricky, who had been listening intently, said "doke," and laughed heartily once again.

About the same time, Ricky began to play his own jokes using language, by denying circumstances that both he and his listener knew to be true. When his misrepresentations were acknowledged, Ricky would laugh gleefully. Ricky and Richard were telling me about a walk they had taken.

Gf:  Did we see leaves on our walk?
R:  No, no leaves.
Gf:  We did so see leaves.
R:  (Laughs.)

Later the same day, we were walking to the car we had left in the parking lot.

G:  Where is Grandpa's car?
R:  I don't know.
G:  You don't know? Sure you do.
R:  (Laughs.)

In Chapter 4, Ricky teased others nonverbally by defying their expectations for his behavior. Now he could tease others by defying their expectations that his language would map to reality. In the realm of action, an even more intriguing instance of misrepresenting reality occurred. Ricky was in the car with the family, asked his mother for his pacifier, reached into her pocket to get it, and pulled it out.

Gf:  May I have the barse?
    (Ricky ignores him, and puts the pacifier in his own mouth.)
Gf:  May I have the pacifier?
    (Ricky gives it to him.)

A bit later, after Ricky had retrieved the pacifier, Richard asked for it once more. This time, Ricky kept the pacifier but pretended to put it back in his mother's pocket. When Richard looked in the pocket, Ricky laughed gleefully.

## Theory of Mind and the Development of Self-Concept

Ricky clearly made much progress during this period in creating an image of himself as an individual. Many different kinds of knowledge contributed to that effort. He had discovered that pictures and mirrors were self-reflective objects in which he could take some pleasure, and he learned how language expressed various relations between himself and others in his milieu. He began to talk about himself as an intentional being, announcing his intentions before he did an act, not just saying, "I want . . . "

R: (Climbing into the driver's seat of a car) I go drive.

This more sophisticated sense of self seemed to free him from being bound to an ongoing reality. Ricky showed some understanding of jokes about language use, and even began to make some himself. And, in his play with others, he showed that he could engage in pretense and enjoy it. Nonetheless, we must be cautious about the kind and amount of knowledge about others' minds that we grant Ricky. Leslie (1987) proposed that the cognitive structure supporting the ability to engage in pretense is the same as that supporting an understanding of false belief. However, most researchers would agree that skill at pretense is not sufficient for a belief psychology, and not all would even agree that it is necessary (Hobson, 1990, Lillard, 1993b). What pretend play indicates about the child's understanding of his own and others' mental representations has proven to be a difficult question to answer. (See Lillard, 1993a, for an interesting discussion of this issue.)

When Ricky pretended to hide the pacifier in his mother's pocket, did he think that he was engendering a false belief about the pacifier's location in his grandfather's mind? And was his glee at Richard's looking in the pocket pleasure at achieving a successful ruse? It may be granting Ricky too much to give him an understanding of false belief (cf. Fodor, 1992). Rather, without actually thinking about misleading his grandfather as to the pacifier's whereabouts, Ricky may simply have been delighted by Richard's actions because he had successfully engaged him in joint pretend play. That is, he may have been "acting-as-if" the pacifier was in one location when it was in another, and Richard's action confirmed joint participation in the "as-if" game.

In this scenario, Ricky believes both he and Richard jointly recognize that reality (the actual location of the pacifier) is one thing, but they act as if it is another. We do not have to grant Ricky the ability to represent Richard's *beliefs* about reality as different from his own. There is knowledge about the real location, and they both have it, but they both *pretend* it is elsewhere. If, for young children, pretense is "acting-as-if" (Harris, 1991), then it need not involve sophisticated notions of false mental representations.

Both the joint pretense and false belief accounts of the pacifier incident require the child to think simultaneously about a real and a nonreal entity or event, as well as to recognize that the other person also is representing the situation. However, in joint pretense, the other's thought is basically the same as the self's. The same location is tagged as the real one. An understanding of false belief requires the recognition that someone can have a different—an incorrect—representation of what reality is; the representations of self and other are not alike. For Ricky to think Richard's looking in the pocket means Richard thinks that is where the pacifier *really* is, Ricky would have to represent Richard's reality as different from his own, as well as represent to himself the two different locations correctly. This is why the representation of false belief is a more complex mental act than shared pretense. (See Flavell, 1988, for more discussion of the representations of beliefs.)

Only more studies of toddlers will tell whether a conservative interpretation of incidents like the one involving the location of the pacifier is justified. In any case, it is good science to be skeptical in the face of ambiguous incidents, especially when it has been difficult—at least experimentally—to show understandings of false beliefs even in 3 year olds (Lillard, 1993a; Ruffman, Olson, Ash, & Keenan, 1993). Still, even the conservative interpretation presents a very positive picture of the toddler's developing theory of mind. The ability to reflect on the real and the nonreal is itself a kind of dual representation, or perspective. Having that ability and attributing it to others as well may be two precursors to the more complex mental operations involved in an understanding of false belief.

To date, researchers who study developing theories of mind have not identified all the kinds of abilities that allow individuals to reason about their own or others' minds, nor do they agree on a list of stages leading up to a belief psychology. Wellman and Woolley (1990) proposed that during the preschool years children move from accounting for people's behavior on the basis of their desires (desire psychology) to explaining people's behavior on the basis of their beliefs (belief psychology). This movement presumably takes place as children recognize that what governs people's actions is their mental representations about reality, not reality itself.

One of the identifiable intermediate stages during the development from a desire theory of mind to one based on belief is one in which children realize that they and others can represent both real and nonreal states, and can act on the basis of both as well. A genuine belief psychology awaits the further understanding that those internal states can be correctly or incorrectly tagged with regard to their status as real or true. Ricky will show us he has such an understanding, but only months in the future, after he has thought much about states of knowledge and their relation to reality.

Where do children get the idea that others have mental representations? Toward the end of the second year of life, children internalize caretaker standards of performance or behavior, and then, with their recently developed senses of self, begin to relate their own conduct to them (Kagan, 1981). So, children have an "ideal" or nonreal state and the reality of their own behavior to compare. Possibly these internal metrics help children see that they are simultaneously representing actual and possible states of affairs, and perhaps, because their internal standards are based on caretaker behavior or teaching, children are also encouraged to attribute similar awareness of the real and nonreal to others.

## Knowing What Others Know

At about this time, Ricky started talking about past events. If such talk depends on an ability to retrieve some mental representation of a past event as well as to recognize that the listener can also represent the event, then it is not surprising that talk about the past begins during this period. Ricky enjoyed recalling events both he and his listener had participated in, but he rarely distinguished his talk about such events from those in which his listeners had not participated. Conversations about past events often came up at mealtimes, such as at dinner the day after we had gone together to the airport to pick up Ricky's great-grandmother.

> R: Bye-bye Daddy. (His father had stayed at home.)
>   Go airport.
> G: Yes, we left Daddy at home and went to the airport.
>   What did we do there?
> R: Airplane Bubby — — Bubby.

Later, during the same meal, Ricky initiated talk about his trip with his mother to my house that very day.

> R: Bye-bye Daddy. (Again, his father had stayed at home.)
>   Drive car go Ba-pa's house.

Bruner (1983) has said that children are naive realists: they assume everyone has the same access to reality as they do. Recognizing that the self's knowledge of an event may be different from the knowledge of another person who did not witness the event is another kind of perspective-taking that is necessary for yet another stage in the progress toward a belief psychology: a knowledge-based theory of mind. With such a theory, an individual would assess whether the self and others both had the same knowledge or whether one was ignorant of some fact or event. Whether Ricky talked about shared and nonshared experiences in the same ways because his language was limited or because he didn't take into account that my knowledge of the two trips was not equivalent or the same as his, we cannot know for sure.

One incident during this period suggests that at least on some occasions Ricky did consider that someone might not possess the same knowledge that he himself had. I had come for a visit several days after another visiting relative had brought Ricky two animal puzzles that were laid out in his room. As soon as I entered the apartment, he drew me into his room.

R: See? (Pointing to the new puzzles.)
G: Oh, you have new puzzles.
   What are they?
R: Hippopotamus.
   Baby whale back mommy. (Showing me the baby that fits underneath the pieces that make up the mother whale.)

Ricky's actions suggest that he thought (correctly) I had had no prior knowledge of the puzzles. A few months earlier (Chapter 4), Ricky had exhibited similar behavior with new books he had received between my visits. Thus, in circumstances where the child witnessed an event but the other person was not present, even children under 2 may be able to recognize they have knowledge the other does not. In the coming months, Ricky provided more evidence that he was developing a knowledge psychology as a precursor to a more sophisticated belief psychology.

## Summary

In multiple ways, Ricky showed he was both developing his sense of himself as an individual and situating himself in a group of like members. He recognized that he, as well as others, could be represented in pictures. He could express possession rights for himself and others through language, and was beginning to see that people were identified in part by their relations to others (e.g., who was whose mother). Importantly, he seemed to attribute the skills he had for disengaging from reality in play and language to other people as well; this may not be surprising since others had initially engaged him in teasing and pretense. At the same time, he at least occasionally saw, as he had with visual perceptions months earlier, that although others had the same internal capacities he did, they did not necessarily have the same access to substantive knowledge. For example, he could recognize that he had to tell me about the new toys or books that arrived in my absence; I was not privy to them otherwise. Thus, Ricky was discovering what people (and he himself) were like while at the same time recognizing how they could be different.

## Language Development

Learning about similarities and differences among people is one explicit instance of more general learning that children must do as they learn to divide the world into conceptual categories. As children learn a language, they must discover how the words of that language divide up the world and how they relate to the concepts the child has acquired nonlinguistically.

### *Organizing the Lexicon*

As discussed in Chapter 3, early in the language acquisition process, children begin to learn words at a much accelerated pace compared to the rate at which their vocabulary previously was growing. This increased vocabulary often is accounted for by the rapid acquisition of a large number of nouns. Researchers and parents alike have noted that some children are voracious in seeking out labels for objects once they realize there are names for things.

Nouns learned early on are typically words that characterize sets of objects at a level of generality researchers call the *basic* level. *Cat, dog, car,* and *plane* are examples of words that label basic level categories, where *animal* and *vehicle* are examples at a more general (superordinate) level and *schnauzer* and *sedan* are examples at a less general (subordinate) level. At the basic level, the within-category items are easily seen to be much alike compared to the items outside the category. For example, two within-category instances of *car*, say, sedans and coupes, seem much alike and quite different from outside-the-category instances of *airplane*; whereas at the subordinate level, two within-category kinds of *sedan* are very much alike but not that different from outside-the-category instances of *coupe*, and at the superordinate level, within-category instances like cars and airplanes are not much alike although they are both instances of *vehicle*.

Words for different level categories provide a way of organizing a lexicon. The relation the different level categories bear to one another is one of hierarchical inclusion. A sedan is also a car and a car is also a vehicle. Thus, the same object can be labeled with more than one word, depending on the level of categorization.

As noted in Chapter 4, Markman (1987) has proposed that young children assume objects have only one label. Such an assumption would help them learn new word-referent relations, because each time they heard a new word, they could assume it referred to an object for which they did not yet have a label. However, learning superordinate terms should be difficult for children if they already have basic level terms for the objects that can also be classified at the higher level. Also, superordinates might be difficult to learn because labeling at this level requires the ability to abstract a general property or relation from a range of often fairly dissimilar instances. Indeed, laboratory studies suggest that superordinates are hard to learn (Horton & Markman, 1980; Mervis & Crisafi, 1982).

Ricky's use of words during this time both supports and challenges this view of lexical development. His vocabulary of common, basic-level nouns was indeed growing rapidly. In one afternoon of tracking his output, I counted 64 different nouns, mostly basic-level words found in the home environment, such as kitchen and bedroom furnishings (*pillow, brush, spoon*), toys (*puzzle, blocks, cards*), and insects (*bug, ant, bee*). He certainly knew many more nouns than these, since few of his words for people, animals, or food happened to come up during that time, and on only one day of my tracking food terms, he had produced 14 different words, including *guacamole* (a favorite), *potatoes*, and *waffle*.

What is more interesting from a developmental point of view, however, is that these object labels were already being organized into categories, and the categories themselves given labels. One day Ricky was "helping" me put laundry away. Removing items I'd just put into his drawer, he labeled them each in turn, "socks, sweater." Then he took them down the stairs to where his great-grandmother was sitting, showed them to her and said, "clothes."

Soon after, we took a trip to a pet store where we saw birds, fish, mice, hamsters, and guinea pigs, all of which were labeled either by or for Ricky, but the word *animal* was not used. On the way home I asked, "so what did we see in the pet store?" Ricky replied, "animals." This incident confirmed what I had observed two months earlier when Ricky had said "more animals" when asking to see more photographs of zoo animals we had been naming individually as we looked at the pictures we had taken of them earlier. On both occasions Ricky was able to use the appropriate superordinate term to cover the disparate class of individuals he had in mind.

Ricky's use of terms like *animals* and *clothes* raises an interesting question. Did Ricky know that a single entity, say a dog, can also be called by a more general term? Or was Ricky using the more general terms as labels only for a *collection* of disparate items that formed a group but individually could be labeled only with their own terms? The question is an important one because the ability to use both a basic level and a more general term for a single entity would imply a hierarchical organization to the lexicon, and that sort of organization is the basis for scientific classification and certain kinds of logical reasoning about classes. Piaget and other students of young children's thinking have typically not been willing to grant them the ability to create true hierarchical classes. Markman (1981b) has proposed that children first understand words like *toys* or *animals* as labels for collections and not as superordinate terms that can be applied in the singular to individual instances (e.g., a rattle or a dog) as well. There are no studies with children under age 2 addressing this claim. However, one experiment with 2 and 3 year olds showed that they had considerable ability to use language hierarchies appropriately, although their occasional errors suggested to the authors that a collection organization might nonetheless have been the prior one (Callanan & Markman, 1982).

One evening Ricky did use the singular form of *animal*, but in circumstances that did not make clear whether one or more referents were being labeled. We were sitting in a restaurant, and on the wall was a painting of several grazing sheep. Ricky pointed to the picture and said, "Animal beep" (sheep). This might be glossed as, "That animal is a sheep," thereby implying a hierarchical classification. But because there were more than one sheep in the picture, we can't be sure Ricky was referring to a single sheep, even though he used the singular form of *animal*. He may have seen them as a collection of animals that were sheep. However, as we will see later in the chapter, Ricky had not mastered irregular plural forms by this time, and it seems that if he had been referring to more than one sheep, he would have said something like "animals sheeps."

Even if Ricky had only been organizing his lexicon according to collections and not hierarchical classes, that too would have been an accomplishment, since it suggests the ability to discover rather abstract relations among diverse instances. After all, socks, shirts, and shoes do not look much alike, and grouping them together under the single label *clothes* requires the ability to see a relation in the face of physical difference. Thus, toddlers' apparent difficulty in learning superordinates does not appear to be due to the inability to abstract nonobvious relations. If that were the case, they would have trouble recognizing collections as well.

More research is needed to discover whether children under age 2 use superordinate terms like *toys* or *animals* in the singular to refer to only one referent for which they also have a basic label. If they do not, that would be evidence that the difficulty in learning superordinates is due to the assumption that each type of object can have only one label. It may be that while the assumption helps children learn new words quickly, there is a cost in the development of hierarchical classifications.

## The Bases of Object Labeling

Visual characteristics are important criteria for categorizing and labeling objects. Things that look alike often have the same name. But toddlers must quickly learn that physical features are usually insufficient for categorizing objects. Young children are often said to be bound by perceptual phenomena. They seem to overcome that tendency to create collections. Can they overcome it as well in creating basic-level lexical categories?

Ricky regularly pointed out similarities of shape between objects of very different sorts. For example, as he took a walk with his grandfather one day, he pointed to a telephone pole with a cross-bar at its top and said, "hammer." Food play provided Ricky many opportunities to extend his vocabulary to unusual referents. One day he ate all the white off a hard-boiled egg, made throwing motions with the remaining yolk, and said, "ball." Another day he made a piece of cheese he'd been eating "walk" on his high-chair.

R: Oink-oink.
G: What do you think that is?
R: Pig. (R turned the cheese toward me so that I could see it was indeed in the shape of a pig's head.)

Was Ricky creating overly general categories based on shape or just using his simple language to draw attention to similarities of shape? His use of language in other circumstances supports the inference that Ricky's utterances should be glossed as "that looks like a hammer," "that looks like a ball," and "that looks like a pig" rather than "that is a hammer, a pig, a ball." When Ricky wanted cheese, he always asked for it by name, never with "pig." And he had a large vocabulary of *ball* words, including *football*, that he always used appropriately, suggesting that he knew that spherical shape was not a necessary feature of *ball*. He also used the word *hammer* (although as a verb) in appropriate circumstances. Ricky was in his room, and having watched his mother put something up on the wall, he took his toy hammer and banged on the wall. I came in from the living room.

> R: Hear noise, Grandma?
> I hammer wall.

Also, although Ricky used appearance as an important clue to category membership, he was able to go beyond physical similarities in making inferences about animal behavior. At the zoo, when Ricky saw a panther, he started to make noise.

> R: Meow, meow.
> M: That's a panther.
> It's more like a tiger than a cat.
> R: Grrrrr.

Thus, Ricky was able to make use of Alice's words to infer that, even though an animal may look like one thing, if it *is like* another thing, it will behave like the other thing. Researchers have shown that older children make inferences based on their notions of internal essences (Gelman & Markman, 1986; Gelman, Coley, & Gottfried, 1994). Ricky's example suggests that, although appearance is an important clue about how to categorize the world, even before age 2, children discover more subtle organizations than those based on appearance alone. Names for things are important clues to categorization.

Ricky's language use, then, reflected rather abstract principles of lexical organization. He grouped together things that can be labeled with a single word but that can be quite different in appearance (e.g., clothes), he recognized that things that have the same shape are not necessarily the same kind of thing (cheese that looks like a pig), although he seemed to think it was appropriate to draw analogies between different kinds of things based on shape, and he knew that things that look alike don't necessarily behave similarly but that things that are said to be alike do (panthers and tigers).

## Using Language to Learn

Talking about similarities between objects was one way in which Ricky showed he was working at organizing the world through language. It was easy to see Ricky using language to foster his own growth in other ways as well. Sometimes, he would try to sort through his experiences on his own, as when he talked to himself about teasing, or when on car trips, he would sit in the back in his car seat and talk softly to himself, practicing language and reciting bits of remembered conversations.

At other times, he would engage adults in interactions that either were informative about language or helped him reflect on past events. The day we went to the zoo, he discovered an exception to standard plural markings as we stood at the deer pen.

> G: Look at the deer running.
> R: More deers? (As several more come toward us.)
> G: Yes, there are three deer.
> R: More deers?
> G: Three DEER.

We repeated this last interchange about 10 times, as Ricky apparently tried to figure out why I said "deer" and not *deers*. Perhaps I should have explained that *deer* was a "funny" word, but I did not realize that his repeated questions were very likely attempts to get me to reiterate my presumably unexpected construction. Only retrospectively did I see that he regularly used the tactic of getting his interlocutor to repeat unfamiliar or unexpected constructions by reinitiating the conversational sequence in which he noticed them, either with a self-repetition, a "what?" or (much later) a "say it again." In the absence of a more explicit way of asking about exceptions to linguistic regularities, his strategy at least allowed him to check on whether he had heard right and whether the surprise construction had been intended by the speaker (was not an error) and would be used consistently.

He was able to ask direct questions more easily about events, as happened when we picnicked at a rest area where a tractor had just finished mowing the lawn.

> R: Tractor go?
> G: The tractor's gone.
> R: Why?

G: I guess he had to go away and cut grass somewhere else.
R: Tractor goed away.
G: Yes, the tractor went away.

It was clear from the knowledge he acquired about variable names for family members that Ricky listened attentively to language that was not directed to him. He even tried to be included in some conversations directed to others. When I recounted, in his presence, the incident about "animal beep" to his grandfather, he began to bleet, "ba-ba-ba."

In these months, Ricky seemed to be a more adept conversationalist than a linguist. He had various little phrases for carrying on smooth verbal interactions such as *oh my, oh boy, okay, let's go, ready, right back,* and *now,* all of which he used appropriately, at the same time that he only variably produced appropriate grammatical markings such as auxiliaries, articles, and verb inflections. He enjoyed carrying on conversations, despite sometimes struggling to find the words he needed. He even occasionally fell back on topic-comment utterances like "gas buy," instead of following conventional word order. Six months earlier (see Chapter 2), he had embedded a conventional word or two in strings of jargon. Now, especially when he was talking about past events, he would produce relatively long strings of words, but still they would sometimes be jumbled with jargon; as with his attempt to tell about his search for a football game on TV in Chapter 3, he had more to say than he could produce in meaningful words.

It seemed that the act of engaging others in conversations was itself so important to Ricky that even the difficulty of doing it grammatically was insufficient restraint for talk. Indeed, he would often work to make himself understood, as he did the day we were on the deck of our newly rented vacation cottage and he noticed the striated, tilted bannister.

R: 'tar. (Making a strumming motion.)
G: Car?
R: TAR. (Continuing to make the strumming motion.)
G: Oh, a guitar.
   Are you playing a guitar?
R: Yes.
G: That's called strumming.
   You strum a guitar.
R: Strum a 'tar.

Possibly Ricky was persistent when he was misunderstood because the adults in his family were attentive to his talk and often expanded his utterances to include new words and information, as I had on the deck. Thus, they were an important source of information as well as social pleasure.

## Summary

During this period, Ricky demonstrated behaviors that suggested progress in the development of his self-concept and his understanding of the relation of himself to others. He used personal pronouns, became comfortable with self-reference, began to make jokes with others, to talk about the past, and even (more rarely) to take account of another's knowledge state. Typically, researchers have searched for and documented only one or another of these behaviors in samples of children about the same age. Documenting their co-occurrence in a single child highlights possible interconnections among the behaviors and suggests that the development of self-concept and early theory of mind go hand in hand. Given the independent documentation of individual behaviors like Ricky's in many samples of other children, it is likely that Ricky's progress exemplifies a kind of complementary insight into self and others that is attained by most children around this age.

Similarly, many of the phenomena observed in Ricky's language have been noted in other toddlers approaching age 2: the long, jargony sentences, the variable use of grammatical devices, and the rapid vocabulary increase. Yet children seem to have different styles of language use at this age. Some, like Ricky, are voluble; they talk a great deal even though they have not mastered grammar. Others seem more restrained, waiting perhaps until they are more certain of how to say something before they attempt to say it. Such children may eschew Ricky's style of frequently eliciting conversational interaction as a way of learning about the world for a more observational one. Even with family, they may hang back, watch more, and talk less, as Ricky did when he was with strangers. It is likely that children use both strategies, but to different degree.

Differences in how children distribute their efforts among the strategies for learning from those around them are to be expected. However, we know little about why children differ—whether, for example, interactional patterns between parent and child set down early in infancy influence them, or whether temperament is an important factor. Nonetheless, the developmental time line looks robust: on the eve of their second birthdays, toddlers will have taken major steps toward becoming persons.

## Notes

1. It is likely that Ricky did not fully understand that one person can fill both the roles of, say, mother and grandmother simultaneously. Even 6 year olds are still struggling with the notion of intersecting roles (Watson, 1990).

2. A third device, prepositional phrases with *of,* is largely reserved for cases of permanent possession bordering on the object being essential to its host or owner, as in "the blood of Christ." More formal, this device is likely to be rare in parental and child speech.

# 6

## 23–24 Months
## Consequences of
## Self-Awareness

Two year olds have bad reputations. Generations of parents have bemoaned the transformations around 2 years of age that seem to turn sweet, compliant babies into aggressive, recalcitrant "enfants terribles." Child development experts often assure parents that their children are just going through a stage, experimenting with their newly developed sense of self. Surely 2 year olds' behavior can be exasperating, but the same effort at self-development has a positive, almost poignant, aspect to it as well. At this age, toddlers often begin enthusiastically to try out new roles and activities, only to end up vacillating between bravado and dismay when they find themselves in situations that are unfamiliar or uncertain. Kagan (1981) has shown that around this time toddlers also begin to think about their own behavior and skills relative to others. Ultimately, their self-evaluations and comparisons will result in better social understanding of themselves and others and form a basis for more mature social interactions. However, at first the character of their social behavior alternates between brashness and bashfulness, as they work at managing a wider range of interactions with less parental intervention. One has to feel some sympathy for toddlers as they try to meet the challenges of independent action in an uncertain world.

## The Struggle for Independence

Given Ricky's progress in developing a self-concept in the past several months, it is not surprising to see him producing some new self-assertive behaviors in this period. At times, he seemed to be intentionally naughty, and his increased teasing of others was occasionally aggressive. At other times, his desire to create an independent self led him bravely to attempt new activities and new kinds of interactions with others.

Ricky took a big step toward independence when he accepted my invitation to sleep over at my house without his parents. He was very excited about the prospect, talking about it with his mother for days in advance. Indeed, when Richard and I arrived to pick him up, he became upset when his parents started to walk out to the car with us, because he believed they would accompany us after all. Only after I explained that they were just coming downstairs to the car to help carry his "gear," did he stop trying to prohibit them from leaving the apartment.

For the 40-minute ride in the car, Ricky was generally happy and playful, although after only a few minutes he had calmly asked, "Where Mommy go?" I explained that she would pick him up the next day, and he asked about her just once more during the ride, the rest of the time commenting about trees, flags, and trucks he saw along the road and practicing counting.

R: One, two, three, four.
G: What comes after four?
R: Five.
G: What comes after five?
R: Six.

Once in Ann Arbor, we went to an informal outdoor concert, where we enjoyed ice cream and the warm summer night. Ricky indicated he was having a good time by saying, "Nice park." Going to bed would not be quite so pleasant. When we arrived home, Ricky was at first reluctant to go upstairs, saying, "No sleep." But, after a few minutes of play, he was clearly tired, offered to go upstairs, and ran up to his room.

R: This Ricky's room.
This Ricky's bed. (Jumping on the bed.)

We had a pleasant enough time getting him ready for bed and reading stories. At the last page of the last story, however, Ricky again asked, "Where Momma go?" Once more, I explained where

Counting pine cones

she was and that she would be coming for him the next day, but after we finished the story and it was time to turn off the light, Ricky cried, "No light off!" He got weepy, asked for his mother and father, gathered up his stuffed animals and said, "Mommy home." I reassured him once again and got him back into bed, but Ricky's courage had failed him, and he begged me to stay with him.

R:  Grandma, lay down. (Patting the bed next to him.)

I gave in. I turned off the light, lay down on the foot of his bed, and rubbed his stomach for 2 minutes, by which time he was asleep, and I tiptoed out.

The rest of the night was uneventful. Ricky awoke in the morning happy and content as could be. All through breakfast, he didn't mention his parents or going home; still, he clearly wanted me nearby. While I showered, he asked his grandfather where I was, even as they were playing happily together. And, when I was busy with kitchen chores as he played in the living room, he called to me to join him. When his parents arrived that afternoon for a trip to the circus, he was resting, but as soon as he heard them, he jumped up to greet them excitedly with a big smile, hugs, and kisses.

Overall, Ricky's first night away from home was a success, but I had been an important source of comfort and support during this experiment in independence. He had wanted to try being away from his parents, but when he experienced the reality of separation, he needed to be assured that I, a trusted parental surrogate, would stay close to him. Thereafter, Ricky made many happy overnight visits; he still liked having me nearby when he was visiting, but we didn't need to be in sight of one another constantly. He continued to want me to stay in his room until he fell asleep for most of the next year, but there were no further displays of dismay over separation from his parents. Many months later, when Ricky could express himself much more completely, he told me that he liked me to be in the room with him when he went to sleep because (unlike his one-floor apartment) there were two floors in my house, and the bedrooms were far from the living room and kitchen. Ricky felt he would be too far from me if I went downstairs. When I assured him that I would stay on the same floor as he, but in one of the other rooms, his need to have me in his room as he fell asleep disappeared. Apparently, Ricky measured his tolerance level of independence very specifically by physical proximity to a trusted caretaker.

The struggle for independence is often a struggle with the self for the confidence to face new situations without the parents or primary caretakers. For young children, it may be helpful to have some support like a trusted other nearby who can provide a secure backup in situations where the child first attempts independence from the parents. It may be that children who experience "assisted independence" in toddlerhood have an easier time with later situations requiring self-confidence and independence, such as entering school.

Ricky experimented with independence in other "safe" contexts. He was often naughty at times when he could test the resolve of his caretakers without putting himself in real jeopardy. For example, one day we attended an outdoor children's show on a large lawn bounded by a busy street toward which Ricky headed when he got bored. I urgently cautioned him to stay on the lawn. He decided to make a game of challenging me, repeatedly running toward the street, but abruptly turning back to the grass and laughing just before I caught up to him. It was as though he was playing at willful independence, recognizing that running into the street was not a good thing to do, but teasing me nonetheless about my authority over his behavior by refusing to adhere strictly to my admonition.

One day at home, he intentionally turned his cup over and blithely watched the juice spill onto the rug. He was unsurprised by his mother's negative reaction and willingly helped to clean it up. Only when she insisted that he also take a short time-out in his room did he protest. Apparently, this was more punishment than he had anticipated. After complaining a bit, he acceded, saying "Oday [okay], time-out."

That night we went to a restaurant where Ricky recounted the incident to me as he sat next to me in his high-chair.

> R: Juice on a floor.
> G: Yes, you spilled some juice today, didn't you?
> Juice doesn't go on the floor.
> It stays on the table.
> R: Yes, juice on a floor. (Laughing, R pretended to turn an imaginary cup's contents onto the floor.)
> Juice on a floor.

We repeated this scenario several times, with Ricky taking great pleasure in his pretended naughtiness.

Incidents like these suggest that toddlers know the rules of the household very well, and that their misbehavior is often intentional—a way to assert themselves and affect their caretakers' emotions and actions. If 2 year olds were not aware of the voluntary nature of their own behavior, or did not have an awareness of family standards, it is hard to imagine that they could take such delight in their minor violations of others' expectations of them. (See Dunn, 1988, for a related discussion.)

On many other occasions, Ricky strove to establish his new-found sense of self. He would often stubbornly refuse help, saying "Ricky do it." One day he was trying to walk to the car with a cup of juice (this time *not* wanting to spill it).

> G: Why don't you give me the juice while you get into the car?
> R: (Emphatically) Ricky hold it.

He would insist on having his way about play activities as well. He had been playing upstairs with a favorite set of coasters I kept in the TV room, and he refused my repeated requests to come down-stairs with me until I agreed to let him bring the coasters with him. He loved pretending to feed adults imaginary food from the coasters, which he pretended were plates. When his grandfather called a halt to Ricky's "feeding" him from the coasters by saying, "no more," Ricky insistently responded, "yes more."

With peers, he was willing to share his toys, but only after he had made explicit that they were indeed his. On his second birthday, one of his closest friends visited. Whatever Jonathan began to play with, Ricky would touch or grab and then announce was his ("Ricky's dumptruck"). Having established his rights, he would readily return the toys to Jonathan, with no need for parental intervention.

As bold as he was in asserting himself with familiar others, he was tentative and shy with strangers. On a walk to the park one day, we came across several children playing on the sidewalk. One of their toys was an appealing tractor with a Mickey Mouse doll sitting on it. Ricky stopped and watched the children longingly.

> R: (Turning to me.) I play a tractor?
> G: You have to ask the children.
>    I think they will let you play with it.

Ricky turned back to the children, watched them silently, and then moved on. At a younger age, he probably would have headed for whatever toy attracted him. Now he knew enough about self and other to recognize that he needed a permission warrant to play with other children's toys, and he turned to me to get it. It would be several more months before he had enough social knowledge and self-confidence to make his own overtures to unfamiliar children.

Ricky's reluctance to approach unfamiliar children was confirmed at the park where we came across a small boy tossing stones through the openings of a concrete play structure. Ricky scrambled onto another piece of play equipment and watched the child from there. When the boy moved away, Ricky asked, "Boy gone now?" When I said, "Yes," Ricky headed for the structure and promptly imitated the other boy's actions of throwing stones. It is clear he was intrigued by the other child, but did not feel comfortable approaching him.

Ricky's behavior with familiar children was very different. At his birthday party, there were about a dozen children aged 1 to 10, a few of whom Ricky knew only slightly. Nonetheless, he enthusiastically engaged in all the planned activities and games with them. Indeed, he was concerned that all the children participate, and he urged the few who hung back to join in. He even encouraged me to join an impromptu band by bringing me one of the musical instruments his mother was handing out and saying, "Play music, Grandma."

Such instances show that Ricky was not restrained in all circumstances. Rather, his behavior was distinctly different in situations with familiar and unfamiliar others. On the one hand, he was happy and comfortable interacting with a broad group of familiar others, even testing his limits without fear of unanticipated consequences. On the other hand, unfamiliar others, especially away from home, invoked caution, watchfulness, and silence. It was as if he was unwilling to chance interactions in situations where he had no information on which to base an expectation of the response his behavior might invoke.[1]

Ricky showed similar patterns of caution in other circumstances. When confronted with a novel physical challenge, such as a new piece of play equipment to climb, he was tentative and careful. So, his caution in unfamiliar social situations may have been a manifestation of a more generally cautious temperament. Children with different tendencies to cautiousness might test their senses of an independent self somewhat differently. Less cautious children might be more self-assertive and aggressive in a broader range of circumstances, and children more inclined to shyness might be less intent on overt experimentation than was Ricky, in all circumstances.[2]

A pensive moment at the birthday party

## Awareness of Internal States

### *Knowing One's Own Mind*

Self-awareness has consequences beyond the realm of actions. Ricky began to use language in ways that indicated more awareness of his internal states. Whether he had such awareness earlier but could not or would not express it through language, we cannot know for sure. Now, at least, there was some linguistic evidence to suggest that Ricky was able to turn his attention to the workings of his own mind. For example, Ricky understood that the word *remember* signaled that he had to do some mental work to recover information. He had played in the morning with little purple cylindrical blocks that he had called "hot dogs" and had pretended to cook in a small pot that he liked to play with whenever he came to my house. Late in the afternoon, he rediscovered the blocks and wanted to cook them again, but he apparently had forgotten that he had taken the pot into the bath and that he had played a new game of hiding a golf ball in it.

> R: Pot?
> G: You want the pot?
> R: Yes.
> G: We left the pot upstairs because you took it into the bathtub.
>    Do you remember what's in the pot?
> R: (Laughs.) Golf ball.

During this period, Ricky began to comment on things that were pleasing to him. These were not just statements about satisfied desires like "nice hug" or "good cookie." Instead, they were statements of aesthetic feeling—comments about things that gave him pleasure. When Ricky said "Nice park" at the outdoor concert, he seemed to be commenting on the nature of the experience of being outdoors listening to music on a lovely early summer evening. The "park" itself was really just a rooftop with some potted trees. He said, "Nice pictures up here," as he sat on my bed and carefully inspected the objects on the bedroom walls. This was not a polite phrase he was imitating. He went on to describe rather creatively a woodcut that particularly delighted him.

> R: Two birds (Pointing to two birds in a tree.)
>    Mommy bird, baby bird. (The birds are the same size.) Leaves blowing in the wind. (There is no overt depiction of wind in the woodcut.)

On another day, Ricky and his mother were engaged in a scenario of pretend play in which Ricky repeatedly took the hat from a wooden doll and refused to give it back despite the "man's" entreaties (produced by Ricky's mother in a falsetto voice). Ricky, looking intently at the doll, grabbed the hat.

M: You have my hat!
That's NOT funny.
R: (Now looking up at his mother seriously yet mischievously.) IS funny!

Not quite understanding the idiom Alice had used in talking for the doll, Ricky nonetheless thought that the scenario he and his mother were creating was indeed amusing, and he wanted to be sure she agreed with him.

Ricky also showed he was monitoring his own language. He pointed to flowers, saying, "Faiyers." Without waiting for a response, he repeated the word, improving on the pronounciation, "Fowers." He began to distinguish his word for sheep ("beep") from the noise he made for car horns ("beep") by saying "beep-maa" for sheep. The addition of the bleeting sound made the two previously undifferentiated words very distinguishable. At some point Ricky must have realized that his pronunciations for the two words were the same, although he meant two different things by them. Students of early child language have reported that children will sometimes mark meaning distinctions creatively when the adult language does not do so. For example, French children find ways to distinguish the meaning *one* from *a* even though the French word *un* encodes both (Karmiloff-Smith, 1979). What is interesting about Ricky's behavior is that he created a way to distinguish his own pronunciations, which he had to be monitoring, rather than to mark a difference in meaning that his input language neglected to mark.

Was Ricky spontaneously clarifying his speech to make it more understandable for his listeners? It is more likely that he was doing it for himself. Although toddlers will clarify their speech for others when listeners make requests for clarification (Gallagher, 1981), the monitoring and spontaneous revision of their own speech seems to be more a matter of their testing and evaluating their output against some internal standards separate from the goal of listener understanding (Shatz & Ebeling, 1991). The contexts in which Ricky uttered his "beep" utterances were so different that his listeners did not misinterpret them. Consequently, Ricky's attempt to distinguish them seemed to be motivated more from a need to represent overtly a meaning difference he recognized than from a desire to correct any misunderstandings indicated by or expected in his listeners. Although Ricky may have been motivated to learn language in part because it is such a central means of interacting with others, it was nonetheless, to use Karmiloff-Smith's (1983) words, a "problem space" in its own right.

## Inklings About Others' Minds

The ability to adjust one's speech for a listener implies that the speaker recognizes the listener as having capacities or knowledge different from one's own. Obviously, this skill rests on a developing theory of mind. By looking for speech adjustments in young children, researchers have discovered that, in some circumstances, 3 and 4 year olds can recognize differences in mental states among listeners and take account of them in their speech. The inference can then be made that preschoolers have achieved a theory of mind at least sophisticated enough to support some spontaneous speech adjustments. For example, 4 year olds are more explicit with blindfolded than sighted listeners (Maratsos, 1973) and they hedge their assertions not with 2 year olds but with adults who have the knowledge to question their correctness (e.g., "I think these are lambs"; Shatz & Gelman, 1977).

There are several possibilities for why toddlers may not make as many speech adjustments for others as 3 year olds do. Toddlers may not yet have enough of an understanding of others' minds even to entertain the possibility of adjustments. Alternatively, they may have developed enough understanding of mind, but simply apply it less for various reasons. If toddlers are busy evaluating their own linguistic output against internal models, they may not attend as much to their listeners and may not notice some cues to possible misunderstandings. Not needing to monitor their own speech as much, preschoolers are able to turn more attention to listener cues to misunderstanding. Secondly, the language experiences of toddlers with attentive families like Ricky's are largely with listeners who do much of the communicative work, making every effort to understand and respond appropriately even to the children's most primitive speech. Hence, toddlers may be less aware of the need for speech adjustments than preschoolers, who have had more opportunity to interact with less familiar and accommodating listeners. Also, with less experience generally than preschoolers, toddlers should be less able to assess what specifically their listeners need;

nor do they have as much linguistic skill in adjusting their messages to take account of their assessments. That is, they may not have the knowledge needed to make appropriate adjustments even when they sense that adjustments are necessary.

There was no opportunity to see whether Ricky would adjust his speech with a younger child. However, there were other incidents, including several in which Ricky tried to justify his behavior to others, that suggest Ricky had some ability to think about others' feelings and mental states. One day we were at a swimming pool, and with a mischievous glint in his eye, he began to pour cold water on my feet.

M: Does Grandma want water splashed on her?
R: (Laughing) No!

He began to justify his refusals to fulfill requests, instead of simply saying "no" or ignoring them as he had in the past when he didn't want to do as asked. One day just after Ricky and his parents had arrived for a visit, Alice invited him to go with her to see a new porch swing. As Ricky began to follow her to the porch, Richard appeared and demanded a hug for a greeting. Ricky refused, and continuing to run down the driveway, said, "Grandma got a new swing." On another occasion, playing his pretend "feeding" game with his father, he refused a request from Rob for more "food" by announcing his intention.

F: Give me more.
R: Ricky put away. (R then took the coasters he was using as plates and put them back in their box.)

Statements like these show that Ricky believed (1) others (adults at least) had the ability to understand through language the reasons why he behaved the way he did, and (2) he needed to tell them these reasons for them to know them. That is, he did not seem to think adults had access to the same knowledge about his intentions as he himself did. Therefore, he did seem to have the rudiments of a theory of others' minds—that they too, as he did, could learn and understand through language, but that they and he could have different mental access to information.

Of course, the inferences that Ricky made about what others knew and did not know were often wrong or inappropriate. A more experienced speaker, in justifying the refusal of a hug, would have realized that Grandpa must have known about the purchase of the new swing, and that the more appropriate justification was not just the news of its existence, but some declaration of need, desire, or intent to see it, such as "I'm going to see Grandma's new swing." So, Ricky recognized the need to explain his refusal, yet his specific justification was not explicitly adjusted for his grandfather's perspective but rather came from his own.

Partial success at taking account of others occurred with regard to perceptual ability too. To amuse Ricky in a restaurant, I had given him a small dish with a cover, and he began to hide small objects in the dish. I covered my eyes with my hands as he was about to hide the object, then uncovered them, asking, "Where did it go?" Delighted, he lifted the cover to reveal the object. Very quickly he realized that he might be able to surprise me if on some occasions he put the object somewhere other than the dish. What he apparently didn't realize was that the object had to be out of my sight—and not just out of the dish—if I was to be fooled. For example, I responded to his calling, "Open now, Grandma" by uncovering my eyes to find him holding the object in plain view with one hand while making ready to lift the cover with the other. It seems Ricky did not anticipate that I would *see* more than what he wanted me to *look at*—namely, the empty dish.

In sum, at 2, Ricky had developed a theory of mind that included an understanding of himself as a separate individual with desires, feelings, and intentions different from others. He knew that language could be used to make some of his internal states explicit to others. Moreover, he recognized that others had, at least, the ability to understand what he said and that they had a range of perceptual and emotional capabilities not unlike his own, but that at any given moment, they could be in a different state from him. However, working out and taking account of the specifics of what others knew or perceived often seemed to be beyond him. Nonetheless, the rudiments of personhood—the beginnings of recognizing a mental life in the self and in others—were already in place.

## Ways of Conversing

Ricky seemed to be a good conversationalist. Although he occasionally ignored verbal overtures, he usually made some sort of verbal response and had a variety of ways to extend conversations. At times he answered others' initiations with topic-relevant comments of his own. We walked out of a restaurant one evening into a glorious sunset.

G: (Pointing to the most vivid part of the sky.) Look, Ricky, see all the
beautiful colors in the sky?

R: (Waving his hand across the horizon.) More sky all over.

Ricky was thoughtful as well as sociable, and these characteristics came together most clearly when he tried hard to answer novel questions that had been posed for him. On these occasions, one could see him thinking hard about what had been said to him before responding to it. Two months earlier, he had been pretending to make oatmeal in a little pot.

R: I cook more oatmeal.

G: You need to stir the oatmeal.
What do you need to stir it with?

Ricky looked away from me and pensively stared out the window for several seconds. I had just about given up hope that he would respond when suddenly he brightened and turned back toward me.

R: Poon![3]

With typical 2-year-old curiosity, Ricky regularly asked, "Wot dat, Gramma," listening carefully to the responses and often repeating snatches of them to himself. He usually imitated a label when told what an object was called, but occasionally showed some reluctance to give up his old word for the new one. We had been playing with a little garage, driving trucks and cars up a ramp. Ricky vacillated between saying "up a hill" and "up-a-tairs" as he drove his vehicles up.

G: (Touching the ramp.) This is called a ramp.

R: Truck go up-a-tairs a ramp.

About this time, Ricky began to use imitation to convey information from other adults. When talking with one adult, he would receive information from a second person (often his mother) and he would then pass it on to the listener as if he or she had not also heard it from the other speaker.

G: What are you drinking, Ricky?
(R looked toward his mother.)

M: Same stuff Mommy is.

G: What is that?

R: Apple juice. (A rote response.)

G: Apple juice?

M: Pineapple-banana.

R: (To G) Pineapple-nana.

That same day, I noticed he was attending to the sound of the wind chimes on the porch.

G: What's making that noise, Ricky?
R: Ding-dong.
G: What's making the ding-dong?
R: Bells.
M: (To G) He knows they go off when the wind blows.
R: (To G) Wind blows.

Imitations of these sorts were clearly different from those following an adult response to Ricky's "what's that" questions. In the "what's that" instances, his soft voice and thoughtful expression suggested his imitations were largely for himself, a way of entering the new word offered by the adult into memory. In contrast, eye gaze and body orientation indicated that these conversational imitations were not just for himself but were listener-directed. He did not seem to note—or care—that his listener would already have heard his mother's comments as well. What seemed to matter was that he convey the information relevant to the dyadic interaction that had been in progress before his mother's interventions.

As the months went by, Ricky began actively recruiting information from his mother to pass on to the person with whom he had been conversing. For example, if he was asked, "What did you do at the park," he would turn to his mother and ask, "What?" Mother-directed referrals were so common that family members joked about how Alice was Ricky's encyclopedia, dictionary, and external memory bank all rolled into one. Such instances show us that Ricky had great faith in Alice as a knowledge store; he expected her to know and remember more than he himself did—or at least to be able to verbalize better than he.

The fact that Ricky himself went on to direct some version of Alice's responses to his listener suggests that his referrals to her were not simply due to a desire to get out of talking. On the contrary, Ricky maintained and extended conversations by using his mother's comments to take his conversational turn, answering questions that had been directed to him or offering "new" information he had obtained from her. His behavior suggests that his model of conversation included requirements for active participation once engaged; in asking for (and getting) help, his goal was to fulfill his conversational role, not relinquish it.

The philosopher Grice (1975) has proposed a set of conversational maxims governing adult conversations. Primary among them is the notion that conversational participants must be coooperative. Cooperation can be operationalized as speaking when spoken to, not talking at the same time as one's partner, and so on. Additionally, speakers are expected to be relevant and concise, saying mainly what their listeners don't already know. Ricky's behavior suggests that being cooperative by responding when spoken to may have overridden any notion he may have had of following the maxims of relevance and conciseness. More likely, while focusing on what the answer was to be, he may have neglected to take account of the fact that his listener would already have heard it from his mother at the same time he did. Once again, a seemingly simple task, in this case, the ability to participate appropriately in a three-way conversation, turns out to be quite complicated when analyzed according to the cognitive and social knowledge that must be brought to bear in the situation.

Routine and repetition generally played an important role in Ricky's interactions involving language. Just as when he was younger, he delighted in playing the games he created with others over and over, sometimes reinitiating the same games for a period of several weeks until they took on the status of little interaction routines or rituals. Occasionally, bits of repeated games became rote responses that had to be unlearned later. Ricky had been fascinated four months earlier by pretend play that I had initiated one day about going to Bubby's house. At his insistence, we had played it over and over with toy people and cars throughout a 5-hour period. Thereafter, we had played it a few more times before Bubby's visit; after she arrived, he showed little interest in playing the game again. Nonetheless, even long after she had returned home to Florida, whenever he was asked where he was—or we were—going, he would almost always reply quickly and seriously, "a Bubby's house."

After several months of such behavior, he recognized, when his grandfather teased him about it, the humor in his routinized response. On the way to my house for Ricky's first sleepover, when his destination was very salient, Richard wanted to see whether he would still give his rote response.

Gf: Where are we going, Ricky?
    Are we going to Bubby's house?
R: (Laughing) No Bubby's house.
    Gamma's house.

A few weeks later, as we were driving to a picnic at a lake, his grandfather again brought up the question.

Gf:  Are we going to Bubby's house?
R:   No, a yake.
Gf:  Where is Bubby now?
R:   In Forida.
Gf:  How did Bubby get to Florida?
R:   Pane. [Plane.]

Even with this awareness of its inappropriateness, the old response continued to appear occasionally almost automatically.

Despite his often thoughtful and creative conversation, routinized or rote responses were an important part of Ricky's linguistic repertoire. Possibly, like imitations of his mother, they made it easier for him to sustain conversations. Caretakers frequently engage children just learning to talk in little conversational rituals such as "What does the [animal] say?" (Allen & Shatz, 1983). These kinds of interactions give children the opportunity to practice language in situations where the child's roles are complementary to the interlocutor's but nonethelss clearly specified, and not just imitative, as they are when parents label objects for children and then request them to repeat the words. In contrast, carrying on a fully spontaneous and complementary conversation requires that a speaker must monitor what his or her interlocutor has said and then find novel appropriate expressions that both take account of the interlocutor's language and convey what is on the speaker's mind. Apparently, this is a difficult task for toddlers. Although even 19 month olds know that they should answer when spoken to, only gradually does toddlers' speech become contingent on what's been said to them without being imitative (Bloom, Rocissano, & Hood, 1976).

Ricky's creation of idiosyncratic, routinized responses and his recruitment of his mother's help were both ways of easing the burden of carrying on conversations without giving up his central role as respondent. It is not hard to see how Ricky developed these devices. Family members had frequently engaged him in complementary language routines like the animal sounds game early in his second year of life, and his mother had been a ready and willing third-party informant in early conversations others had initiated with him.

Conventional rituals were important to Ricky, too. He was intent on following the appropriate script for his second birthday party. He had joined in the singing when "Happy Birthday" was sung, only to stop after a few words. He looked a bit embarrassed, apparently remembering that the birthday person was not supposed to sing at his own party and he was that person! He also was adamant that other children not usurp the right to unwrap any of his presents, admonishing anyone who made as if to do so: "Ricky do it."

Ricky may have been generally devoted to routine and ritual because they helped give him a sense of predictability and control over his interactions. Routines and rituals make no surprising demands on children; they allow children to attend closely to how others behave in usual situations without having to work too hard to come up with appropriate behavior themselves. Indeed, sometimes 2 year olds become recalcitrant precisely when their routines for doing things are violated by parents who do not recognize the role such routines may play for the children.

Paradoxically, 2 year olds sometimes exercise their newfound independence in just those same situations, because in them they can be sure of what is a violation and that it is likely to be noticed by others who also are accustomed to the routine. It is likely no accident that Ricky's early attempts at naughtiness, teasing, and jokes involved violations of others' expectations of behavior in usual circumstances. Relying on routines while nonetheless occasionally violating them is a way for a newly self-aware toddler to engage a world both predictable and controllable.

## Notes

1. In general, having to interact with unfamiliar others induces more stress than interacting with familiars. Videotaped observations of preschoolers suggest this is true for children slightly older than Ricky; they are more subdued in play with unfamiliar peers than familiar children, even in the same physical context. See Doyle, 1982, for a review.

2. Longitudinal research on children deemed extremely inhibited or uninhibited suggests that the tendency to cautiousness is maintained throughout early childhood (Reznick, et al., 1986).

3. In American culture, answering questions quickly is often taken to be a sign of competence. Apparently in some Asian cultures, answers that are slow in coming are seen as evidence of an answerer's thoughtful stance, and hence are considered in a more positive light (H. Stevenson, personal communication, February 1, 1993). Ricky's example suggests the appropriateness of that view.

# 7

## 25–26 Months
## Two-Year-Old Talk

While Ricky had been making progress in developing an awareness of self in the prior months, his language skill had been growing too. On his second birthday, I heard a five-word sentence for the first time, when he said of his friend's action, "Jonathan knock over more tower." In the months following his birthday, he displayed new ways of using language to express his recently acquired social and cognitive knowledge. His vocabulary continued its rapid expansion, and there was more evidence that he was busy organizing his lexicon. In comparison, grammatical development seemed more fitful; at times he showed some sophistication with the forms of the language, and at other times his grammar seemed to be remarkably primitive.

### New Ways with Words

#### Talk to the Animals

Ricky's increased sense of self seemed to be the basis for several new uses of language. Previously, he had sometimes talked for toys in pretend play or even talked to them when another human was pretending to talk for them. Now, I observed him talking directly to toys and animals with a tone that ranged from bossy to authoritative to affectionate. The character of his speech on these occasions suggested he was trying out social roles and speech registers (ways of talking). Watson (1990) has suggested that this sort of behavioral role-taking in toddlers precedes the interactive role play observed in children aged 4 to 7, who take on the roles of, say, "mother" or "doctor" (Andersen, 1990).

Practicing with toys or animals the kinds of language that functions to order, instruct, protect, or comfort may be especially useful for children who have little opportunity to use those functions with others in daily social life. As an only child with no regular day care or playgroup experience with younger children, Ricky was almost always the youngest and most immature speaker in conversational interactions, and he regularly received rather than sent messages with such functions. Still, in play at least, he apparently saw himself as capable of being the more competent or authoritative speech partner, and he appropriately chose less "competent" toys and animals as recipients of his authoritative language.

Ricky and his parents had come to meet me at the airport on my return from a trip. As he and I entered a public restroom, a woman thrust two stuffed gorillas at Ricky and asked him to watch her souvenirs while she used the facilities. Ricky was at first a bit nonplussed by the request, but when I explained what he had been asked to do, he began to take his duties very seriously. He solicitously set the two animals next to one another on a sofa. Then, picking up the baby gorilla, he leaned it over an ashtray.

R: (In a high-pitched, soft voice to the toy) See?
See? Moke. [Smoke.]

When we got home, we went out to the yard where the apple tree had dropped its annual plethora of wormy apples. A neighbor's cat appeared and began to follow us around the garden.

R: (Picking up an apple.) Eat this apple?
G: No. These apples aren't good to eat.
   (R collects a few apples, lines them up in a row, scoops up the cat, and sets him down in front of the apples.)
R: (Sternly) Eat apples, cat.
   (The cat sniffs the apples and runs away.)

A few weeks later, he met the cat with an affectionate, high-pitched "Hi, cat," and on another occasion, he greeted a picture of cats in a book, with a high-pitched "Hi, catties." A child with a younger sibling might have used the sibling to exercise these linguistic ways of expressing status and authority roles. Without that possibility, Ricky found an alternative audience in toys and animals.

## *Telephone Talk*

Ricky also became much more interested in telephone talk during this time. Although previously he had been willing to talk to me on the phone when I called his home, only now did he want to initiate calls on his own. The day I had returned from my trip, he had wanted to stay overnight with me, saying to his father, "Go home daddy. Ricky stay Grandma." I had to work the next day, and so could not accommodate him. The next morning I received a phone call from him because he wanted to tell me he was playing with the toys I had given him the day before.

> R: I play bird.
>    Babar car. (This was a little car driven by Babar the elephant.)

A few weeks later I arrived home to find a message from him on my answering machine; he had found the car that he had misplaced a few days earlier and that he had told me was "lost."

> R: Hi, Gramma.
>    Found Babar back stroller.

At 17 months, Ricky had dragged the schoolhouse to the telephone when I had not understood him; now, he knew how to talk on the phone so that his unseeing listener could understand, and he realized he could convey information his listener did not have. His mother confirmed that it was his idea to call me to tell me the toy had been found. He became so comfortable talking on the telephone that he even agreed to talk to more distant family members like my mother, who were not as good as I at understanding him over a phone line. He also enjoyed pretend play with the telephone. Ricky and I had just finished a conversation on a toy telephone when his mother picked up the phone and pretended to make several calls to various family members. When she got to Ricky's 4-year-old cousin Nadine, she asked him whether he wanted to talk.

> R: Yes. (M hands R the phone.)
>    Hi, Nadine.
>    Sitting here Mommy Grandma in Grandma's house.

Despite the lack of a few function words (with, and), Ricky had very nicely described his situation for his imagined, unseeing listener.

Telephone talk

## *Beyond Labels*

Ricky began to use his language to describe and narrate. His interest in books continued to grow, along with his library, but now instead of simply labeling objects as he looked at books, he often described the pictures and actions in more detail.

> R: Fox drive a schoolbus.
> Wolves in a truck.

On occasion, he even spontaneously related short sequential narratives.

> R: Shovel pick up dirt.
> Dump it.
> Dump it 'nother truck.

He was also able to sustain a conversation long enough to give a reasonably complete report about a past event to others, although his listeners supported his efforts with pointed questions. Ricky had gone to a berry farm and taken a ride with his father on a wagon pulled by a tractor. He began to relate the event to his mother and me.

> R: Ride.
> Tractor.
> Man driving.
> M: What color was the tractor?
> R: Green
> M: Was it a big tractor?
> R: No, small.
> M: Were there other people taking a ride, or just you and Daddy?
> R: Other people ride.

Ricky seemed to have more confidence about his use of language; he often became adamant about his word choices and was insistent about getting his listener to understand or acknowledge what he had said. He had been playing with me in the living room and went into the kitchen to show his mother something. She told him she was almost finished with her cooking. Ricky returned to the living room.

> R: Mommy's almost finished.
> G: Oh, you're all finished.
> R: No, MOMMY ALMOST finished.

One day he came into the kitchen where his mother and I were talking. He imitated a greeting he had heard at his paternal grandparents' home, "What's doing, babes?" Later that day, when he again entered a room I was in, I asked, "What's doing, fella?" Ricky was quick to correct me, but nonetheless willing to accept some instruction.

R: No, "babes."
G: Well, I'm a babe — YOU'RE a fella.
R: Grandma and Mommy are babes.

At other times, possibly when he felt more sure of himself, he was less amenable to alternatives. Ricky knew both the word *alligator* and the word *crocodile*. One day he and his mother were looking through a book of animal pictures and came across a reptile.

R: Alligator.
M: Maybe it's a crocodile.
R: Not a crocodile.
   (Emphatically) A alligator!
A: Are you sure?
R: Yes!

It was unlikely Ricky could distinguish alligators from crocodiles (nor was it clear what the reptile actually was), but it seems that Ricky at that moment had enough self-confidence to take up his mother's challenge and even to declare his certainty. Possibly he did not fully understand what "Are you sure?" meant, but he had used the word *sure* in another context as a very strong assent, so he must have had some idea that it indicated at least a strong commitment to his claim, if not a strong sense of certainty about its veridicality.

## Development of the Lexicon

### *A Mushrooming Vocabulary*

Although Ricky's increasingly rich and varied uses of language depended in part on his advances in social understanding, they also drew on an expanding vocabulary. By 26 months of age, Ricky had acquired hundreds of nouns, including multisyllabic words like *hopscotch*, *chuckwagon*, *raspberries*, *watermelon*, and *cantaloupe*. He also used compound nouns like *flatbed truck* and *water fountain*.

As impressive as the growth in numbers of nouns, however, was verb development. During this period, I heard Ricky appropriately use more than 80 different action verbs, a dozen verbs encoding different states, and half a dozen verbs of perception. (See Table 7.1.) Of special interest are occurrences of mental-state verbs like *think* and *know* and the meanings they express because, for some of their uses, they specifically indicate that the child is thinking of internal states of mind (Shatz, Wellman, & Silber, 1983). Ricky's first uses of the mental-state verb *know* occurred during this time, but they were limited to only one kind of utterance context, in "I don't know" phrases. Although Ricky seemed to understand (as in Chapter 6) the verb *remember*, he did not produce it, and the same was apparently true for at least one meaning of *think*. Ricky had been building a house with blocks and went to look for some toy people and animals to add to his structure.

R: (Looking in a duffel bag.) Little people.
G: (To Ricky's mother) Are there toys in that bag?
M: Yes, some little people, I think.
R: And a pig, maybe.

*Table 7.1*  Ricky's Verbs at 26 Months

| Action Verbs | | | | Perception Verbs | |
|---|---|---|---|---|---|
| bend | drink | leave | sneeze | feel | read |
| bite | dump | lie | spill | hear | see |
| blow | eat | make | squeeze | look | watch |
| bring | fall | march | stack | | |
| brush | find | mix | stir | *State Verbs* | |
| build | fix | open | stop | be | melt |
| catch | fly | paint | straighten | have | miss |
| chase | give | pick | sweep | hurt | need |
| clap | go | play | swim | know | sleep |
| climb | hang | push | swing | let | wake |
| close | haul | put | take | like | want |
| color | help | ride | talk | love | |
| come | hit | rock | throw | | |
| cook | hold | run | tie | | |
| crawl | hop | share | turn | | |
| cry | hug | shut | wash | | |
| cut | jump | sing | wipe | | |
| dance | kiss | sit | work | | |
| do | knock | skip | write | | |
| draw | laugh | slide | drive | | |
| | | | hammer | | |

Ricky's use of the possibility marker *maybe* in his response to his mother's utterance suggests that he understood she had marked with *think* her degree of certainty about finding dolls in the bag. His ability to assign in context some appropriate interpretations to a few mental-state verbs—and possibly other verbs too—very likely exceeded his productive verb vocabulary.

Other categories of words had grown rapidly as well. Ricky had 10 prepositions, more than a dozen pronouns, and over a dozen modifiers, excluding color and number words. (See Table 7.2.) In total, I had heard him spontaneously produce over 400 different words; this is undoubtedly a conservative estimate of his whole vocabulary, since he very likely produced additional words when I was not in his presence. Even with the conservative estimate, his vocabulary would have more than tripled from 18 to 26 months, with word learning occurring at a rate of one to two new words every day. As at 18 months, about 60% of his vocabulary was composed of nouns.

In Chapter 3, I noted that Ricky may have experienced an early

***Table 7.2*** Word Categories Beyond Nouns and Verbs at 26 Months

| Prepositions/Particles | | Modifiers | Pronouns |
|---|---|---|---|
| in | | tiny | it |
| on | | little | this |
| under | | small | that |
| over | | big | I |
| around | | funny | me |
| up | | cold | mine |
| down | | warm | my |
| out | | wet | you |
| back | | dirty | your(s) |
| off | | messy | he |
| | | other | him |
| | | 'nother | we |
| | | nice | our |
| | Adverbs/Particles | | Determiners |
| more | here | | a |
| almost | there | | the |
| maybe | outside | | |
| later | either | | |
| better | a little bit | | |
| also | yesterday | | |
| now | where | | |

vocabulary spurt. Thereafter, however, his vocabulary growth was more like a rapidly and inexorably expanding mushroom. From 18 months on, he was interested in words and worked on learning them. He often imitated a new word after hearing it, either softly to himself or in conversation. Indeed, at times he seemed like a word sponge, picking up and imitating even the most abstract words that would have been hard for him to understand.

> M: (Talking to G about the inability to recall something.)
>   I can't think of it. I seem to have a mind block.
> R: (Seriously, to G) Mommy has a mind block.

Also, by 2, Ricky would sometimes ask "what?" after hearing a new word so that a speaker would repeat it for him and perhaps even give him an explanation of its meaning. Occasionally, he would persist in asking "what" repeatedly until he had gotten an explanation of the word or phrase that satisfied him.

It is unclear why children follow different patterns and time courses of word learning. The manner of vocabulary growth for an individual child may depend on when the child realizes that words are things to be actively learned. If that insight occurs early, word acquisition may start early and proceed rapidly. If it occurs later, a more mature child may have more cognitive resources, such as better memory skills, for learning many words even more quickly. Although there is much commonality in the content of young children's first 50 or so words (Nelson, 1973), children's vocabularies quickly begin to reflect individual interests. Ricky, for example, had an impressive array of words for different types of trucks.

### Early Lexical Organization

It is unlikely that word acquisition goes much beyond a hundred words without some sort of organization being created for the expanding lexicon. Ricky had already shown with his use of words like *toys*, *animals*, and *clothes* that he had grouped words (or the referents for them) into higher-level categories with their own labels. The basis on which he did so seemed to be the functional or perceptual similarity of the referents. Toys were things to be played with; clothes were things to be worn. Although many of the referents that fell under the term *animal* were perceptually similar (four-legged, furry creatures), some, like fish and birds, were quite different. What they all had in common was spontaneous (nonhuman) animation, and it may have been this characteristic, one commonly noticed by children, that defined animals for Ricky. As discussed earlier, the kind of lexical organization that allowed for groupings of color and number words likely had its roots in discourse, as Ricky was engaged in conversation with questions like "what color" and "how many." Such interactions fostered the development of semantic domains in which words were grouped together, although the specific meanings of the individual words had not necessarily been learned.

Similarly, "where" questions may have encouraged the development of a domain of locative expressions from which replies to "where" questions could be recruited, even though the replies might not be tied to the reality of a situation. One day I was searching for a toy that Ricky had been playing with earlier.

G: Where is the dog?
   (I spot the dog—in Ricky's sight—on the living room floor.)
R: (Quickly) In my room.

Possibly Ricky genuinely believed the dog was in his room, but his quick, almost automatic, reply and the frequency of instances of this sort suggest instead that he was responding either to hold up his end of the conversation or to practice conversation, without a concern to map his reply specifically to the realities of the nonlinguistic world. Despite his blithe indifference to speaking the truth on such occasions, his responses were always appropriate with regard to preserving meaning relations between question and reply. He answered "where" questions with *in*, *on*, or *at* phrases and "where ____ going" questions with *to* phrases. Hence, he could think about formal relations between pieces of discourse abstractly without reference to the concrete reality of specific situations.

One of the conversational maxims that Grice (1975) proposed was that speakers are expected to say only what they believe to be true. Of course, lying is a violation of this maxim, but note that lying works only because the speaker can count on the listener expecting the maxim to be in force. Ricky's violation was different— out of the realm of the maxim altogether. Conversation at times like this seemed like assisted practice at conversation for its own sake. The participation of another person was required, but the rules that typically govern conversation between partners were not in effect. Still, Ricky very likely had at least some understanding of the maxim; indeed, at other times, such as when he argued about the appropriate choice of a label, he seemed to insist on it. Of course, adults also often manipulate the relation between language and reality to create all kinds of nonliteral language for many different purposes. One of the things that toddlers must learn is the appropriate contexts for manipulating the relations between language and reality. Apparently, Ricky knew manipulations were possible, but he differed from adults on the conditions allowing them.

## The Evidence for Grammatical Categories

Like discourse relations, the forms of language itself may also have helped Ricky to organize his lexicon. Categories of word types like noun, verb, and preposition organize an adult's lexicon into groups of words that behave alike in sentences. Words in a single category typically can take similar positions in sentences (e.g., only nouns can follow determiners like *the* and *a*) and similar grammatical markings (e.g., -ed to mark tense on verbs or -s to mark plurality on nouns).

One advantage to having a lexicon organized according to grammatical categories is the ability to make inferences about the characteristics of a new word without having to hear it in many different sentence contexts. Suppose a child hears the word *shovel* for the first time in a sentence like "Give me the shovel." If she notices that the word followed *the*, and she has noticed that words following *the* generally share other characteristics, she can infer with some assurance that she can use modifiers with the word (big shovel) and she can talk about multiple objects (two shovels) without ever having actually heard such constructions. Organization of the lexicon into grammatical categories, then, would give the child considerable inferential power and allow for more rapid progress in language development than if the child had to wait to hear (and remember) every possible variant of each new word in each allowable context. Ricky's lexicon had some semantic categories (e.g., toys) and some discourse-based categories (e.g., color terms). Was his lexicon also organized according to grammatical categories?

Several pieces of evidence suggest Ricky did indeed have something akin to categories based on grammatical information. The first has to do with the way adverbs entered his speech. Despite errors (to be discussed later) that he was making in word order, Ricky was apparently sensitive enough to word order to have noticed that words like *almost, also,* and *maybe* are relatively unconstrained with regard to their placement in utterances—they can usually occur at the beginnings or ends of utterances as well as near the verb. This flexibility of sentence position facilitated his experimentation with such words. By now he had 14 adverbs or adverbial phrases (listed in Table 7.2), almost all of which but *better*[1] had exhibited similar patterns of early usage. For example, during this period he practiced *maybe* at every opportunity, placing it in various positions in his utterances. About three times out of four, his use of the word seemed appropriate as an expression of uncertainty; however, the other inappropriate uses raise doubts about whether he truly intended to mark uncertainty as frequently as he did. Instead, he seemed to be experimenting with the use of a word that could float relatively freely across sentence positions.

This pattern of sometimes semantically inappropriate, over-abundant usage in highly variable utterance positions was observed with other adverbs when he first acquired them, but not with other kinds of words. Because the adverbs so acquired varied considerably semantically, marking notions ranging from time and place (*later*, *there*) to completeness and certainty (*almost*, *maybe*), it is unlikely that meaning similarities among them encouraged common patterns of occurrence. Instead, the syntactic feature of word order, in particular word-order flexibility, seemed to be a basis on which to select a word for this type of experimentation.

Another kind of evidence for grammatical categories came from errors Ricky began to make with grammatical endings. Ricky had been adding -ing appropriately to action words to mark continuous action for some time.

> M: What are you doing?
> R: Reading book.

He had also used the word *building* appropriately as a noun, but he began to avoid using as an object label a word that ended in -ing; that ending was apparently now reserved for action word contexts. We had gone blueberry picking and had started to walk back to the shed to pay for what we had picked. The shed came into sight.

> R: There's the build.
> G: Building. You have to say "building."
> R: (Laughing) Building.

My instruction had little effect, however. Later, when we were reading a book about Babar going to the city, I read "There were many, many buildings in the city." Ricky pointed to the picture of the city and creatively imitated, "Many, many builds."

What is interesting about Ricky's alternative label *build* is that he used that form willingly enough as an action word as well ("Ricky build tower"). Therefore, in some cases at least, a single form could function both as a label and as an action word. Indeed, Ricky had several forms that functioned both ways, including *brush, dance, ride,* and *water.* Rather, it appeared to be the grammatical ending -ing that Ricky wanted to keep only for one class of words. This suggests that he had differentiated grammatical endings from word roots and that he believed they were important features for defining different classes of words; apparently, he preferred exceptionless clues to his word classes.

Ricky's overt marking of irregular plurals could well have been motivated by a related concern. Despite hearing many examples of the correct irregular plural forms, he persisted in adding an -s or -es to sheep and other irregular plurals. Even an immediately preceding example of an irregular plural wouldn't deter him from regularizing plural forms. One day we were reading a book about feet. I had read the word *feet* repeatedly. At the end of the book, I asked Ricky a question.

G: (To R) How many feet do you have?
R: Two foots.

Nor did explicit instruction help. Ricky had been counting his dolls.

R: One person, two persons.
M: People—you can say "people" for more than one.
   One person, two people.
R: One person, two peoples.

Ricky did begin to use the word *people* in the singular, but only when he wanted to refer to a group of individuals as a single whole. In its singular form, then, the word was like *family*—it could refer to multiple persons so long as they were collected into a single entity. When he wanted to express the notion of more than one of an entity type, however, he used an overt plural marker, even when he had no examples for such usage in the speech directed to him.

Ricky's early categories may not have been nouns and verbs as adults recognize and use them, but his creative errors were evidence of two kinds of understanding about the grammatical marking of words that could have formed the basis of grammatical categories. First, he expected the endings appropriate to one set of words not to be appropriate to the other. Second, he expected all the words in one set to take the same endings. Grammatical markings were, then, mutually exclusive between categories and universally applicable within categories—the most dependable system of clues to have for assigning new words to grammatical categories, and possibly, the most straightforward system for producing grammatically marked words. Unfortunately, natural languages tend to be messier than that; Ricky would eventually have to give up his attempt to impose perfect systematicity on the language he was learning and deal with the exceptions, but for now, at least with regard to grammatical markings, regularity was the rule of the day.

There are reports in the literature supporting the notion that toddlers are forming grammatical word classes. Children even under 2 use the presence or absence of determiners to decide whether a new word is a proper name or a common noun (Katz, Baker, & Macnamara, 1974), and 2 year olds who regularly talk in three-word sentences have knowledge of several grammatical categories, including modifiers (Valian, 1986). Indeed, it would be hard to explain how children learn as much language as they do as quickly as they do if one did not grant them the ability to use information about the commonalities and differences among words regarding their positions in sentences and the kinds of grammatical markers they take (Gleitman, 1990; Maratsos, 1982). They have to use whatever relatively consistent characteristics of language they notice to bootstrap their way into learning more (Shatz, 1987). Thus, Ricky exemplifies how children build lexical organization in a variety of ways, using discourse relations, meaning similarities, and grammatical similarities to develop word classes.

## Syntactic Development

The strings of meaningful symbols that languages use to express relationships between things are not arranged arbitrarily. Collations of symbols must be marked systematically to indicate relationships between the things they stand for. Syntax is the part of a language that provides for orderly arrangements with a system of marking devices and their rules of use. The work cited in the prior paragraph shows that toddlers are sensitive to features of order and marking that help them discover word classes. In English, word order is also an important device for differentiating the roles particular words have in a given sentence; for example, "John hit Mary" and "Mary hit John" express two very different relationships between Mary and John by virtue of their differences in word order. The syntax of a language also governs how complex ideas can be combined into single sentences via coordination and subordination. ("John went to Atlanta, and Mary went to visit her mother." "I know that the sky is blue.") It provides means for efficient communication, allowing for the elimination of redundant elements through ellipsis. ("John went to Atlanta and Mary to Phoenix." "Did you bring home the mailing labels? I did.")

Generally children achieve a high level of syntactically appropriate speech by 4 years of age. However, some syntactic constructions are not mastered until much later, and there is considerable controversy among researchers about the nature of children's early syntactic knowledge—for example, whether it is in the form of general syntactic rules. Indeed, children can take a long time to master syntactic constructions, with many months passing between the time of first use and virtually errorless performance. Nonetheless, even in their early utterances, children tend to follow the dominant word order of the language they hear, although their tendency is influenced by how rigid word order is in the language they are learning (Slobin, 1973). Because Ricky already had a good-sized vocabulary and was quite adept at conversation, it is interesting to note that his productive language was not remarkable syntactically. Although he was doing some sophisticated things syntactically, at the same time he continued to produce seemingly low-level errors in word order fairly frequently.

## Word Order Violations

Some word order violations have reasonable explanations. Ricky had an accident one day, spilling some liquid on himself. Assessing the damage, his mother told him his pants were wet but not his underwear. Ricky corrected her.

> R: A little bit underwear wet.

There are two plausible reasons Ricky produced the nonstandard word order. One is that the utterance occurred during the period he was experimenting with the positions of other adverbs and he may have seen "a little bit" as belonging to the same class as *also, more,* and *almost,* words that he positioned freely in utterances. The other is that he may have wanted to foreground the new information for his mother by putting it first in his utterance.

Other word order violations may also have had their roots in communicative concerns. One day, when Ricky was going to take a nap, I suggested he bring a stuffed panda to bed with him. He replied, "teddy bear hold." Even though they never predominated in Ricky's speech, such simple topic-comment utterances were frequent enough that they cannot be explained away as occasional performance errors. They seem like genuine violations of conventional word order—cases where he ignored the regularities of the language he had heard and produced an alternative order. Again, this utterance may have come about because Ricky wanted to foreground his choice of animal and contrast it to mine. More generally, topic-comment utterances may be a consequence of communicative considerations: the child may want to set out the topic for a listener and only then predicate something of it, much like pointing to something and then talking about it. The persistence over many months of such word order errors on simple sentences suggests that patterns of word combination that may be grounded in communicative considerations are not easily overlaid or blotted out by more conventional patterns, even though the child hears only the latter patterns spoken by others.

Other violations occasionally came about when Ricky tried to produce longer, more complex sentences that must have been at the frontier of his syntactic knowledge. He had begun to produce two verb utterances ("I want something to eat"). But, as he went to get dressed one morning, he called, "Help Grandma take off pajamas." His intonation was such that "Grandma" could not have been intended as an attentional expression. Instead, he seemed to be combining his usual way of asking for an action (e.g., "Mommy open it.") with the command "help," apparently not realizing that the meaning of the consequent complex utterance would be inappropriate unless he moved "Grandma" to a position in front of both verbs. Ricky's word order errors, then, seemed to have at least two sources, one having to do with communicative considerations and the other with trying to express in single utterances more complex notions than his syntactic knowledge could readily accommodate.

## Ellipsis

Another of Grice's maxims of conversation is that speakers should say only what is necessary to be understood. At the same time, syntactic rules provide constraints on which elements of a sentence can be eliminated to create grammatically appropriate elliptical sentences. For example, it is appropriate for a speaker, in response to the question, "Are your shoes on the bed or in the closet?" to answer elliptically with "on the bed," but not simply "on," even though, given the form of the question, "on" would be sufficiently informative. "On" is prohibited on syntactic grounds because prepositions are grammatical units that cannot stand alone in response to such questions. Thus, producing grammatically correct elliptical utterances requires sensitivity not only to conversational principles but to syntactic ones as well.

Like most children of this age, Ricky often dropped essential elements of sentences such as subjects, saying for example, "Found Babar back stroller," instead of "I found Babar." Ricky's elliptical utterances in conversation were different from this, including major constituents like subjects when required, while dropping them appropriately at other times.

> G: Do you see the trees have turned yellow?
> R: I see.

On another occasion, subject dropping was allowable.

> G: What are you doing?
> R: Reading book.

Ricky even used the auxiliary *do* in elliptical utterances, although he used no other auxiliaries elsewhere in his speech.

> M: You have to eat some of your pork chop. (Before he could get the dessert he wanted.)
> R: I did.

I heard no errors of ellipsis in Ricky's speech at this time.[2] It is unclear whether Ricky's apparently sophisticated use of ellipsis was based on an understanding of the syntactic rules governing ellipsis or was founded on a set of memorized discourse sequences that he used as models for answering questions. In either case, he had discovered how to create grammatical cohesion across utterances in conversation.

It may seem surprising that Ricky was able to demonstrate in responses some syntactic knowledge that was not regularly in evidence in spontaneous utterances. It is possible that the conversational situations allowing for elliptical responses were ones in which the semantics had been well enough specified in the prior speaker's turn that he could focus most of his energies on the form of his response and its relation to the prior utterance. In any case, conversations are an important place for young children to pick up information about the relations between language form and use. (See Bloom et al., 1976, for a similar argument.)

## Developing a Social-Linguistic Intelligence

Ricky's language development was clearly enhanced by his engagement in conversation. In conversational contexts, he learned new words, argued about their referents, tried out idiomatic phrases, created semantic domains, and practiced narrative, description, and ellipsis. As much as his human capacities for analysis, abstraction, and organization were employed in the task of language acquisition,[3] without a supportive social milieu to motivate him and with which he could engage and practice, it is highly doubtful Ricky's language acquisition path would have taken quite the shape it did. Many of Ricky's strategies for learning language made use of the cooperative people around him, primarily his main caretaker, Alice, and he flourished with her assistance. One can see in his efforts both external influences and internal constraints: his productions were compromises between what he heard in the environment and what he had been able to analyze and systematize, probably with a good bit of random error thrown in.

At the same time as he was using his social world to learn language, he was using language to widen his social world and practice new social roles. For example, the speech he directed to toys and animals showed he realized that different social roles call for different kinds of language. He had begun to recognize that the characteristics of conversational situations could influence what he said and how he said it. He no longer believed he could just create understanding in his telephone caller by creating proximity between the topic of his talk and the telephone. Yet the ease with which he ignored the maxim to say only what he thought true suggested that he still had much to learn about how conversations function to create mutual understanding.

Nonetheless, language had begun to give him the opportunity to express to others a recognition of himself as having both a past and a future.

> (Ricky is looking at a picture of himself and his parents taken when they were leaving the hospital after his birth.)
> R: (To G) Mommy, Daddy, and tiny, little baby.
> G: Who is that little baby?
> R: Ricky.

We had been singing a song about children singing on a bus.

> G: When you go to school on a school bus, you'll be able to sing with the other children.

R: Go on a school bus and a city bus.
Later Ricky do that.[4]

Language and social development, then, while separable, were closely interwoven, each providing learning opportunities for the other as Ricky moved toward the achievement of personhood.

## Notes

1. His first uses of *better* were as utterance-ending comparatives to justify his behavior or preferences. He had been given a dish of frozen yogurt and fresh raspberries; he ate the yogurt, but spit out the berries.

G: You should eat the berries too; they're good.
R: I like the ice cream better.

2. "Read book" would be an error for the last example, as would "did" for the prior one. The omission of determiners like *the* occurred frequently, irrespective of conversational ellipsis and are not considered elliptical errors.

3. One of the major controversies in the field of language acquisition is whether these capacities that show themselves so clearly in early language acquisition are general cognitive ones or are innate, unique specifications for language learning. Regardless of one's position on that question, it is clear that these capacities *are focused at this age* on the all-important task of language learning. Rather than capacities for language learning being innately specified, what may be specified is the focusing of the capacities on the language-learning task at a particular point in development to assure the easy social engagement of others and the early acquisition of basic social competence.

4. "Later" meant "some time in the future" for Ricky, without the connotation of near future that it carries for adult speakers of English. As we were watching a cold September rain fall on the yellowing leaves of the trees, I said to Ricky, "It's fall now, so the leaves are turning yellow. Maybe you can help me rake up the leaves. Would you like that?"

R: Yes.
Later.
G: Oh, yes. After the leaves fall off the trees.

# 8

## *27–28 Months*
## Talking About People
## and Talk

If social-linguistic intelligence is the centerpiece of toddler development, then, as children's abilities to use language grow, one would
expect them to talk about people—their feelings, their knowledge,
and even their language. Indeed, Ricky's talk, and his fantasy play
as well, increasingly dealt with mental life, both his own and that
of others. Also, his frequent comments about language and speech
suggested that he thought a good deal about talk and how people
engaged in it. I discuss first what Ricky was talking about and then
the forms of his talk.

### Inferences and Talk About Mental Life

#### *Talk About Emotional States*

Ricky had come to my house expecting to be left with me while his
parents went shopping, but they never did go on their excursion.
That evening, when they were about to return to their home, Ricky,
disappointed he had not had his promised time alone with me, refused to go home, saying, "Goodbye, Mommy, Daddy. I stay Grandma's house." After much negotiation, Ricky was allowed to stay
overnight. He had trouble settling down to sleep, however, bolting
up in the bed as soon as the light was turned off and announcing, "I
go home now." I finally offered him a pacifier I had at my house,

although a few weeks before, he had thrown his last one at home away. The next morning, when he came into my room, he was in a fine mood.

> G: Well, after breakfast we'll drive you home.
> R: Not yet.
>    I happy at Grandma's house.

Apparently, this was true except for the anxiety over going to sleep.

About a month later, Ricky stayed overnight again. This time, bedtime went more smoothly.

> R: (As the light is turned out.) Where's Mommy?
> G: She and Daddy went out to have fun.
>    You came here so you and I could have fun at my house.
> R: (Settling down) Yep.

Ricky did awake during the night but just called out to me. I went to his room to reassure him all was well, and he went back to sleep. The next morning at breakfast, I told Ricky what the plans were for the day.

> G: So, this morning when we get home, I'm gonna go out with Mommy for a little while and you and Daddy can play together. That'll be fun, won't it?
> R: They miss me.
> G: They miss you? I bet they do.
>    I miss you when you're not here.
>    Do you miss Mommy and Daddy?
> R: Yeah.
> G: Well, you'll see them soon.
>    We'll go home after breakfast.
>    It was very nice to have you here last night.
>    You behaved very nicely. You didn't cry at all.
>    You went to bed very nicely.
> R: (Referring to how he managed his anxiety in the middle of the night.) I cry louder, "Grandma!"
> G: (Laughs)
> R: Like that.
> G: Yeah, that was the only problem, that you woke up in the middle of the night, huh?
> R: (Changing the subject.) Sun shining.

## Exchanging Information with Others

In Chapters 4 and 5, there were already hints that Ricky was sometimes aware that he had information that others did not necessarily share. Now Ricky regularly told people things he thought they did not know. If someone was not physically present during an event, he assumed the person had no knowledge of it. The morning after I had resorted to the pacifier to get Ricky to sleep, I had, unknown to Ricky, relayed the incident to his mother on the phone. When we got back to Ricky's house, Ricky gave her the news himself.

M: I hear you didn't want to go to sleep last night.
R: Grandma gave me a pacifier.

Another day, when I was visiting at Ricky's home, he started off after me when I went to the bathroom. I heard his parents call him back to the living room. When I returned, he told me, "I went looking for you."

Ricky also made inferences about others' knowledge states and needs. I had gone to family day at his gym class and was watching him play on a teeter-tot with another child. I tried to read the other child's name tag, which was covered by her hair.

G: (Softly, to myself) If I can read your name tag, I can say your name.
R: (To G) Talia. (The child's name.)

Ricky correctly inferred that I had no prior acquaintance with the child and, with her name tag covered, couldn't know her name.

Sometimes he was wrong in his evaluation of my knowledge states. There were many things he assumed I didn't know, even though I was an adult. He took me into his kitchen to show me some refrigerator art.

R: We holding up the pictures we made. (They were held up with magnetic letters.)
They don't fall off the 'frigerator.

Ricky also began to go beyond asking what, where, and why questions. Now he wanted to know whether others lived the way he did. At home, he sometimes listened to music or story tapes at mealtimes. One evening, he was having dinner at my house.

R: Grandma have a stereo? (It was covered up whenever he came to visit.)
G: Do you want to hear music?
R: Yes. George tape. (A tape about the character Curious George.)

One day as I was preparing his breakfast, he quizzed me about his grandfather's eating habits.

R: That a bapas eat?

G: Umhmm.

R: That bapas eat? (Points to food G is preparing for R.)

G: Do grandpas eat this?

   Yeah, grandpas eat this.

R: Wow.

G: And some milk. (As G pours milk.)

R: Bapa drink that milk?

G: Yeah, Grandpa drinks that milk. Sometimes.

## Self-Evaluation

Ricky had little opportunity to evaluate his abilities against anyone but adults, and despite the frequent praise of the adults around him, his judgments of his own skills were sometimes harsh. We had been listening to a recording of Scott Joplin music one day.

G: Uncle Jay used to play that music on the piano.
   He could play the piano very well.

R: Ricky play the piano very bad.

G: Maybe you'll play better when you grow up.

R: Ricky no grow up. Ricky stay small.

Another day he had been given a packet of stickers that were difficult to remove from their backing. He had stuck many of them on a blank piece of paper in a haphazard fashion. When I approached him and commented on his getting so many stickers on the paper, he replied in a disgusted tone, "Not good. They all torn."

## Consequences of Knowledge About Mental Life

In sum, Ricky's comments make it clear that he thought of himself and other people as alike in that they all had knowledge, feelings, skills, and habits; but he also recognized that people could differ with regard to the particulars in these areas. In some cases, he made inferences about other people's feelings and knowledge based on what he knew of them and the circumstances. In other cases, he asked whether they were like him or not. In both cases, however, he did not simply assume others knew, felt, or did what he did. He was often wrong in his conclusions about others' mental lives, but his errors were a consequence more of inexperience with adult habits and ignorance about what adults would know than of an egocentric extension of his own inner life to others.

One consequence of Ricky's increased knowledge of differences among people was that he began to understand the nature of relationships between people, and he became more adept at using that knowledge to make his wants known. I had been at his home for a brief visit before going on to the airport, and he was not pleased to hear me say I had to leave. He climbed into my lap, and said, "Take care of me."

Another consequence was that he began to talk about possible solutions to problems that were posed in everyday life. It was as though he had discovered that he could think of alternative actions and then use conversation to get others' feedback on them. The first example I saw of this occurred as we talked about the weather.

R: Sun shining.
G: Umhmm. Yes, it is. A nice day.
   It's cold out though, and there's lots of snow on the ground.
R: I wan shovel all up.
G: Yes. Daddy shoveled some of it last night for us. And if you had some boots, you could go out and play in the snow, but we have to get you some boots before you can go out and play in the snow. You can't play in the snow in your sneakers—your feet will get all wet and cold.
R: I stand on the grass.
G: The grass is all covered with snow now. It doesn't do any good to stand on the grass.
R: Why?
G: 'Cause the grass is all covered with snow. When the snow falls, it falls on the grass, and on the street, and on the sidewalk. It falls everywhere, just like the rain does.
R: We walk on the rain.
G: Sometimes you can take a walk in the rain.
R: We need umbrella.

## Talk About Talking

When at dinnertime a 6 year old answers "yes" and laughs but doesn't move in response to the parental request, "Can you set the table?" the child is demonstrating metalinguistic skill. That is, she has the ability to go beyond using language to looking at its forms and usage objectively; she can see that although her parent's intent was clear, the form of the question is literally a question about ability. Puns, riddles, and double entendre are just some of the language uses that require metalinguistic ability. It is thought to be a capacity that develops slowly, with scant evidence for it during the toddler years (Gleitman & Gleitman, 1979). There are, however, some accounts of 2 year olds self-correcting and commenting on pronunciations of words, suggesting at least that toddlers do monitor the form of their speech productions (Shatz & Ebeling, 1991). By preschool age, children are aware of talk as a social phenomenon and use speech as a marker of others' competence (Rice, 1993; Shatz, 1983a). Ricky's comments about talk, his reporting of the speech of others, and his rehearsing for conversations suggest that, in addition to attending to the form of their own speech, toddlers have some awareness of the centrality of talk in social interactions.

The morning after Ricky had played with a child, Eliza, 6 months younger than he, we began to talk about the toys they had played with. Then Ricky turned the conversation to Eliza's speech, which was less developed than his.

R: Eliza say "hey." "Hey."
G: Did Eliza say "hey?"
R: Yeah.
G: She talks a little bit now.
   She's a little younger than you so she doesn't talk as much as you do, but she's starting to talk.
   She's learning how to talk.
   She says, "sit down" and "Mommy."
R: And "dat."
G: Umhmm. She's a nice girl, Eliza.
R: "Mommy" — and "Papa."
G: Umhmm.
R: "Mommy" and "Grandma."
G: "Mommy" and "Grandma." That's right.
   She said "Grandma," didn't she?

In his toy play, Ricky had his little toy people engage in conversations, and he even talked to his mother and me about their talk. I came into his room one evening as he was playing with some toy people and a schoolhouse.

R: Talkin'. (R is referring to the dolls.)
   Now talking.
G: They're talking?
R: Yeah.
G: What are they saying?
R: (In a high voice, speaking as a doll.) Go to parkie. (R says something unintelligible.)
   Something to eat.
   Now go park.

His mother often overheard him making his dolls carry on such everyday conversations, and occasionally he reported to her what they were saying, "Ernie says to Bert, 'Hi, Bert'," using a different voice as he talked for the dolls.

Ricky's reporting of speech was not limited to his speaking for his dolls. We had gone to a mall so that he could see a "live" version of Babar, one of his favorite storybook characters. One of the stores was having a promotion and had costumed a woman to be identical to the pictorial representation of the elephant king. Ricky had been delighted to see the creature, hugging and kissing it, and offering it a bite of a cookie he had. Babar had declined, saying, "I don't eat cookies; I'm too fat." Back at home, we presented Ricky with a stuffed version of Babar.

> R: Babar say Babar too fat.
> (R holds out the stuffed animal.) This Babar not too fat.

Ricky had been very excited about going to see Babar. On the way to the mall, he sat alone in the back seat of the car, rehearsing the meeting softly to himself.

> R: Knock, knock.
> Babar opens the door.
> "Hi, Babar."
> "Hi."

His mother reported that she had heard him rehearsing for future interactions on other occasions (especially when he was going to see unfamiliar people or people he had not seen in a while) as well as repeating bits of conversations to himself after their occurrence.

Talk, then, was a focus of social interactions for Ricky. Not only did he engage in talk, but he thought about who else engaged in it, how it was carried on, and what it conveyed. At the very least, Ricky had the beginnings of a metalinguistic perspective on talk.

## The Forms of Talk

It is unclear whether Ricky was thinking about conversations earlier but did not have the linguistic skill to reveal his thoughts in speech, or whether his increasing skill with the form of language was encouraging him to think about and find new uses for it. In the following sections, we will see that, although Ricky was indeed increasing his linguistic skills, he was not especially exceptional as a learner of language form, nor did he talk about linguistic forms themselves.

## Increasing Utterance Length

During the 1960s, Roger Brown and his students pioneered the modern study of child language when they did intensive longitudinal research on the language development of three children, focusing on their grammatical, rather than vocabulary or conversational, skills. As one way of characterizing general progress over time, Brown calculated at regular intervals the mean length of a child's utterances (MLU) on samples of 100 utterances; he then organized the children's data into five categories, or stages, bounded by increasing MLUs (Brown, 1973). Instead of counting words per utterance, Brown calculated morphemes, or meaningful units per utterance. For example, the utterance "feed cats" has two words, but three morphemes, because the plural marker -s adds a third meaningful unit to the utterance. Once children begin to acquire their language's grammatical markings, morpheme counts are more sensitive measures of development than word counts.

MLU has become a popular standard measure by which to assess children's progress in language development. It is especially useful because children acquire language at different rates: Brown's work showed that one child could attain an MLU of two morphemes (roughly, talking in two-word utterances) at 20 months whereas another might take 8 or 9 more months to reach that level. With age and MLU data, researchers can assess a child's rate of development relative to other children. A 20 month old with an MLU of 2.0 would be a rapid learner; a 28 month old would not, but both would be within the normal range of ages for achieving that level of development.

The introduction of the MLU measure made it possible to search for commonalities in grammatical development among children who, regardless of age differences, were at the same MLU stage. Up to MLU 3.0, children are fairly similar in the structures and forms they use, with certain forms regularly appearing before others; but divergences become more common thereafter. The nature and quantity of individual differences among children's grammars at various stages of development, particularly the later ones, are still important questions of current research in child language. Moreover, except for studies at the earliest stages of language learning, there are no data on whether children with similar MLUs use their language in similar ways to carry on conversations. MLU, then, is at best a rough measure of overall language development, and even of grammatical development.

Nonetheless, as a way to situate Ricky's language development in a more general context, it is useful to compare Ricky's MLU to MLU data from other children. I did two calculations of MLU on Ricky's audiotaped speech during this period, one at 27 months of age when Ricky and I were playing alone together in his room before bedtime, and one 5 weeks later when he was watching me prepare his breakfast after spending the night at my house. For the first session, Ricky's MLU in morphemes was 3.08; for the second, it was 3.34. One of Brown's (1973) three subjects reached these levels about 3 months earlier than Ricky, but the other two reached them 8 to 10 months later. Ricky's MLU puts him squarely in Brown's Stage III (MLU of 2.75–3.49), a period during which children typically develop question and negative forms. About two-thirds of middle-class children in the United States reach Stage III sometime between 24 and 41 months of age (Miller & Chapman, 1981). By the MLU measure, Ricky could be characterized as a relatively rapid language learner, but he was certainly within the range reported for other children.

## Increasing Utterance Complexity

Another measure of general progress Brown proposed along with MLU was the upper bound, the number of morphemes in the longest utterance produced during an observational session. Brown argued reasonably that MLU calculations might be skewed toward the low end by the relatively high frequency of short utterances children regularly produce in response to questions. Using the upper bound as well gives a fuller picture of a child's ability to create longer, and possibly more complex, utterances.

For Stage III, Brown found that the upper bounds of utterance lengths were 9 to 10 morphemes. In the audiotaped samples used for MLU counts of Ricky's speech, there were several instances of utterances with 7 morphemes, suggesting that utterances about this length were not unusual. ("All the animals is sleeping." "I give that cup for gifts." "I wan' get on my knees.") There was also a marathon utterance that Ricky created by stringing simple coordinate clauses together.

R: (Pointing to places around an empty table) Bubby eat there and Susan eat there and Uncle Jay eat there and Ricky eats there and Grandma eats there.

Coordination, along with *to* complements ("I want someone to go with me"), is among the earliest grammatical devices children use to create complex utterances (Brown, 1973). Ricky's longest and most complex utterances in the four months after his second birthday were examples of these types, but they were still relatively rare, as might be expected for a Stage III child—it is not until Stage IV that complex utterances are expected to appear. However, coordination among phrases ("Grandma and Bapa ride in a airplane like that") was common, despite the rarity of full-sentence coordination.

Ricky's marathon utterance illustrates an important point about his grammatical development. It could be many months from the first time he used a grammatical construction or marker to the time he used it maturely, whenever it was required. For example, even in the same utterance, Ricky variably added the obligatory third person -s marker to "eat." Similar delays from first appearance to consistent usage have been reported for other children. Thus, rapid progress in MLU does not necessarily mean that a higher proportion of utterances are well formed grammatically. It seems instead that the utterances are longer and more complex but still display errors and inconsistencies. Indeed, Ricky, like other children (Shatz & Ebeling, 1991), was even on occasion leaving out of his utterances both required subjects ("Sit down in a tire wheel") and required verbs ("My doll a monkey too.")

As children's utterances grow longer, they have more opportunity to reveal creative efforts at language learning and use. Ricky's negative sentences are good examples of how an individual child's language development exhibits both typicality and originality. When children begin to add negative markers to utterances that are two words or longer, the marker is often placed outside the sentence ("No I tired.") Later, the negative marker moves inside the sentence, but *no* and *not* may be used interchangeably. Ricky exhibited this typical developmental path, but he added a creative twist to it. He began to add an intensifier (with strong stress) to the ends of his negative utterances. One of his most emphatic (and frequent) means of refusal was to say, "No I like it e-der [either]!" *Either* quickly became a standard addition to many of his negatives; he began to use it as a final marker even for negatives where no special emphatic force was intended. I was staying with Ricky one evening when his parents went out to a movie.

> G: Mommy and Daddy went out to dinner, and then they are going to the movies.
> R: I not going to the movies e-der.

Later he showed me his stuffed animals in a little crib.

> R: All the animals is sleeping.
> (Taking one out.) No dis sleeping e-der.

Still later that night, when I suggested it was bedtime, the emphatic function returned.

> R: I play games first.
> No go a sleep e-der!

Presaging a construction that would become popular among older segments of the population a few years later, Ricky had another way of making strong negative pronouncements. On another occasion, as he was just falling asleep while I was reading a story, he jolted himself awake.

> R: I close my eyes NOT!

One area in which Ricky had made remarkably little progress was questions. In English, the standard form for questions requires the use of an auxiliary verb placed at the front of the utterance. This "inverted" form is often preceded by a stage in which children use the auxiliary but do not invert it—for example, "The train can go now?" Ricky asked a great many questions, but he still used only rising sentence-final intonation to mark them. ("Grandma painted that?" "That my juice?" "Me take this flashlight home?") Although he used various forms of the auxiliary verb *do* in declarative utterances ("I did," "They don't fall off the refrigerator"), he did not use them in questions, nor did he use other auxiliary forms such as *be* or *can.*

In a comprehensive investigation of auxiliary verb development, Brian Richards (1990) found that children varied considerably in when and how they learned auxiliary verbs. Ricky's reliance on the simple device of intonation to ask questions despite his overall level of language development confirms that English auxiliary verbs can be a difficult acquisition. One of the reasons that English auxiliary verbs are hard to learn is that they have many irregularities (Shatz

& Wilcox, 1991). For example, some auxiliaries mark third-person singular (*does, has, is*) and others do not (e.g., *can, may, should*). A child who looks for regularity may find all the irregularities of auxiliaries daunting.

## *The Pitfalls of Overregularization*

Ricky's search for regularity led him down several garden paths. His battle with English plurals continued, as he gave up on "mouses" in favor of "mices." He even overmarked a plural he had been using correctly for months, when he said "toyses."

The pattern of moving from a correct usage to an incorrect one as he found new ways to regularize the language also occurred with the pronouns *my* and *mine*. Although he had been using them as well as *yours* errorlessly, he now noticed the -s on *yours* and misanalyzed it as a grammatical morpheme. He then began to apply it to the first-person possessive pronoun, saying "mines" on analogy to *yours*. At dinner one night, Ricky took his analysis one step farther. If "yours" is formed by adding an -s to "your," why not do the same to "my"?

R:  (Asking about his fork.) That mys?
F:  Yes, that's yours.

Possibly his father's response only reinforced Ricky's belief that pronouns in such a construction were marked with -s. In any case, Ricky persisted in drawing on this misanalysis for several months, alternating such usage with correct forms.

## No Talk About Grammar

Interestingly, although Ricky was clearly working on grammatical analysis, he did not talk about it explicitly, even though he could talk about talk. His metalinguistic comments were limited to talk about the sounds of words, names for things, what was said, and who said it; it was not about the forms of language.

There are several possible reasons for this limitation on metalinguistic talk. One is that Ricky simply didn't have the linguistic skills to ask about forms. It is also possible that Ricky did not think the forms of language were a reasonable topic of conversation, whereas who talks and what they say clearly was. As an appropriate conversational topic, the pronunciation of words, too, would rank higher than form, since lack of understanding and misunderstanding often occurred because of poor pronunciation and engendered considerable negotiation about what was being said. Errors of form rarely resulted in misunderstanding. Finally, grammatical analysis may have gone on at a different level of processing than the one that made talk about talk possible. Ricky may not have been aware enough of his own analyses of grammatical forms to comment on them. Regardless of which of these possibilities accounts for the dearth of metalinguistic comments about grammar, Ricky's behavior is typical of 2 year olds. Talk about talk is not typically talk about grammar.

# 9

## 29–30 Months
## Gaining Control over
## a Complex World

### Managing the Social World

*Expanding Social Relationships*

"I turn on the light for you." Ricky's offer to help came after I told him I would interrupt our play for a bathroom break. He ran to the bathroom, got on his stepstool, and flipped the light switch. "Okay," he said, as he exited the room to go back to playing in his bedroom. "Thank you," I replied, touched by his solicitude.

Even infants recognize special "others" in their social world. Bonding to parents and other caretakers occurs very early in a child's life. Infants seem to divide the "others" in their social world into simple dichotomies: caretakers and others, familiar and strange. A broader range of relationships develops during the toddler years as children expand their knowledge of others in their social world on the basis of their increasingly diverse experiences with them. Toddlers recognize more of the differences among family members: Some adults like to tease or roughhouse, others are particularly comforting; siblings have different pet peeves or special needs (Dunn, 1988). Toddlers take account of such differences by increasingly differentiating their behavior toward others in subtle ways. For example, toddlers in day care already show signs of differential friend-liness toward other toddlers (Howes, 1988). This undoubtedly reflects more awareness that their relations with others can take various forms and that their own behavior can influence others.

As Ricky approached the middle of his third year of life, he showed in his treatment of his grandfather and me that, despite the affection he had for each of us, we had different roles in his social world. Ricky's helpful and solicitous behavior was largely reserved for me, and he was more possessive about his things with Richard than with me. When Richard and I came for a visit after several weeks away, he was delighted to see us both. As we ascended the stairs to his apartment, his mother was dressing him and I could hear him exhorting her, "Hurry up! Hurry up!" He rushed to the stairs and greeted us both with enthusiastic hugs and kisses. Yet I was the one invited into his room to see his cache of new toys. Later, he showed me his new snow boots. When I pretended to try to put them on my feet, he made no move to repossess them but said, "Too small." When Richard made the same attempt, he grabbed them away, saying, "That's mines."

Still, a few weeks later, Ricky asked, "Where's Grandpa?" and searched for him on his first visit to my house after Richard had returned to his out-of-state job. Richard's frequent absences were a source of consternation for Ricky. On another occasion, as Ricky, his parents, and I prepared to leave a restaurant, Ricky asked about Richard.

R: Where we going now?
M: Back to Grandma's.
R: We sleep there?
M: No, we have to go home to sleep.
R: Play a little bit first?
M: I don't know.
   We should go home soon because you're tired.
R: (To G) You comin' to our house?
G: I can't. I have to stay at my house.
R: Why? Grandpa comin' home?
G: No, Grandpa's not coming home.
   I have work to do tomorrow.
R: Grandpa comin' soon?
G: Not too soon. Not for a few more weeks.
R: (Disappointed) Oh.

Nonetheless, when we reached home and I lifted the receiver from the phone, Ricky's complex feelings about Richard once again came to the fore.

R: Why you take a telephone?
G: I'm going to call Grandpa.
R: Why?
G: Because I want to talk to him.
R: (Running away and laughing.) Not me!

Ricky delighted in Richard—they teased each other, engaged in Ricky's favorite kind of fantasy play with toy cars, and read books together. Richard was interesting and challenging, but he was also a bit less forgiving than I was, and he was competition for my attention. It may not be surprising, then, that Ricky was not especially solicitous of Richard.

More surprising were those occasions when Ricky was immersed in his own interests and activities but he nonetheless still took the time to show concern for me. We had been visiting Eliza's house and the children had been playing well by themselves, when Eliza's mother offered the children ice cream. They excitedly made their selections, but then suddenly Ricky turned toward me.

R: You want some ice cream too?
G: No, thank you, not right now.
R: Okay.

Although we saw each other frequently, partings were hard. One day, after saying my goodbyes, I was leaving his house; he ran to the stairs as I was about to descend, and he touched my hand gently, stroking my fingers and smiling sadly. Leaving my house to return home one night, he asked whether I would go along.

R: You comin' too?
G: No, I have to stay here.
   This is my house.
R: I be far away.
G: I know, I'll miss you.
   But I'll see you next week.
R: Okay.

## Self-Control of Emotions

Even the best of relationships have their rough moments. Although Ricky was a remarkably calm toddler who rarely threw tantrums or became totally unreasonable, we did occasionally have our disagreements. Ricky had been visiting overnight, and we were waiting for his father to come to pick him up and take him out for supper on the way home. Ricky got hungry and wanted something to eat in the interim. I offered a banana and opened the peel just a little. Ricky's habit was to pull the peel down a bit at a time as he ate the banana, but this night he pulled the peel down too far at once. Annoyed, he tried to throw the banana on the floor, but I intervened. I told Ricky the banana was still good—that it would taste just the same, but he refused to accept it and insisted on another. I said he didn't have to eat the banana—he could have something else, but he wasn't going to have another banana just to play around with. However, there was no compromising. Ricky was angry. He climbed down from his chair and went to stand in a corner, facing the wall. This was his customary response when he wasn't getting his way with his mother. Apparently, it served as a refusal to interact with others when he thought they weren't being fair or good to him. When I ignored him, he took a different tack. He went to climb over to the bunch of bananas on the counter to help himself, but Richard, who was sitting nearby, moved the bananas out of reach. At that point, Ricky announced huffily, "I going upstairs," and he marched out of the kitchen and up the stairs.

After about ten minutes, Richard went upstairs to look for him. He found him lying on the couch in the TV room.

R:  (Grouchily) Don't bodder me. I sleeping.

Richard did as he was told, and left without a word. A bit later, Ricky came back down to the kitchen and announced, "I eat my banana now." He picked off a small piece from the infamous banana, tossed it away, saying, "Yuck," and then ate the rest. His behavior was a remarkably adaptive way to handle his anger, accommodate me, and save face at the same time.

Ricky used his strategy of distancing or disengagement to gain control over other emotions as well. He found a bag of toys that he hadn't seen for about six months. He took out a musical jack-in-the-box that had frightened him when the dog inside it popped out. Apparently, he hadn't forgotten his fear.

G:  Do you want to let the dog out of the box?
R:  First I hide, and you let him out.

Ricky ran into the next room and called to me to start turning the crank on the box. When he heard the dog pop out, he ran back into the living room, laughing. Over the course of the evening, he kept returning to the toy, and we repeated the scenario many times, with Ricky getting increasingly braver. By the end of the evening, he himself was turning the crank until he heard the notes just preceding the pop, at which point he would turn the crank over to me and run to hide not in the next room, but a few feet away under the piano bench, where he could watch the action. During all this, I did only what he told me to, and I offered no suggestions to him as he applied his own behavior modification techniques for getting his fear under some control.

Disengaging was a successful strategy with his young friend Eliza, who became possessive one day at her house whenever he showed especial interest or pleasure in one of her toys. Although he was much bigger, instead of becoming aggressive, he would pick up a toy and run out of the living room into the den, where he quietly played with the toy undisturbed, at least until Eliza became curious enough about his absence to go looking for him. Generally, they did pretty well at sharing that afternoon, but when we returned home, Ricky commented about his interactions with Eliza, "We fighted a little bit."

Ricky was an avid miniature car afficionado. His favorite games involved racing, crashing, washing, and parking cars from his large collection. He rarely left his house without a few cars to amuse him in his car seat, at a restaurant, or at a shop. Many children develop an attachment to a "transitional object," a particular blanket or toy, usually fuzzy, that gives them special comfort. Ricky's attachment to his cars was similar in some ways but different as well. As other children typically do with their transitional objects, Ricky took a car to bed with him each night and had one with him much of the day. But, although he might have a favorite car for a few days (usually his newest), he didn't have a single favorite, nor was there anything fuzzy or soft about the metal toys.

Nonetheless, there was something comforting, almost talismanic, in his devotion to the cars. He would put one in his pocket before going out even though he might not play with it at all. Just having it in his pocket seemed to provide comfort, or maybe even protection from the unknown. One day he had made a relatively rare visit to my lab, where he was happily playing with toys in the waiting room. I suggested we take a walk upstairs to the mailroom. Ricky wanted to go, but only after he had made sure both he and I had a car in one of our hands (we joined hands with our other hands) before venturing out into the strange hallway.

Ricky also gave cars to his loved ones upon their leavetakings from him. When his father went to work, Ricky would give him a car to put in his pocket. As Richard and I prepared to leave his house

Ricky and Eliza

at the end of a visit, he urged a car on each of us. I at first demurred, saying that he should keep it, but he was adamant.

R: I want you to take it home with you.

Reluctantly, I agreed. As I walked out the door with the car in my purse, Ricky wanted to be sure.

R: (Indicating my purse.) You have your car in there?

Giving cars to his loved ones on such occasions was another indication that Ricky may have had a talismanic belief in the power of his cars to comfort and safeguard. Alternatively, it may have simply been a way of maintaining a bond with them during separations. In either case, Ricky's giving of his cars was a creative way to manage the stress of separation.

## Organizing Others

Ricky was as avid a game player as ever, but now he took on more of the role of social director, specifying not only what was to be played but how the play was to proceed. He initiated car play one day, giving Richard and me each a car.

R: Let's take turns.
(R demonstrates how to propel a car across the table.)
(To Gf) After you turns, Grandma's turn.
(Gf propels his car.)
Now 'er turn.

The substance of Ricky's proposals for games changed too. They were more sophisticated in that they explicitly mentioned mental state terms like *guess* and *hide* that presuppose specific knowledge states in the players. He often initiated guessing games by saying, "I want you to guess his name" (referring to a toy animal or a picture in a book) or "Guess his name." Of course, the adults who played this game with Ricky knew either the common or proper names for all the objects, but they would cooperate, proposing incorrect names and giving him the opportunity to respond "No!" with exaggerated intonation. Eventually, the correct name would be "guessed," at which point Ricky would shout "Yes!"

Although Ricky used the word *guess*, I could not tell whether he understood its meaning and whether he believed the adults were "guessing" or whether he realized they actually knew the answers all along and were just feigning ignorance or uncertainty. The origin of the game was unclear. I had on occasion seen his mother make similar requests of Ricky but without using the word "guess."

Hiding games sometimes showed the same conflations between what the participants might actually know and what they would pretend to know in order to play along. One evening Ricky, his parents, and I were all in the living room. Ricky urged me to play with him.

R:  Let's hide, Grandma and me.
G:  You want me to hide with you?
R:  Yes, let's hide from Mommy and Daddy.
     We go into the study and close the doors.

Of course, Ricky's parents had been in the room with us and heard the location of our planned hideaway. For Ricky, the intended object of the game may have been the expected excitement at his parents' reunion with us, and not the inducement of a state of ignorance concerning our whereabouts. It is possible that *hiding* for him meant only "intentionally removing from the sight of another," and that he did not yet realize that it implies the generation of a particular mental state in the other. Even 3 year olds demonstrate little understanding that hiding games require attention to the players' mental states (Peskin, 1992).

Yet it would be a mistake simply to assume that Ricky was ignorant of the presuppositions of all the mental state terms he used. Another incident suggested that he believed that words like *look for* and *find* typically carry presuppositions about states of knowledge. Indeed, he seemed to think that presuppositions of that sort were inviolate, at least in "real-world" situations. I had been playing Ricky's small electric organ and picked out the tune "Mary had a little lamb."

G:  (To R) Do you know what that song is?
R:  Yiddle yamb. (R begins to comb through a music book intently.)
G:  Oh, are you looking for "Mary had a little lamb" in there?
R:  (Annoyed) I KNOW where it is.
     (R locates the appropriate page and points triumphantly to the picture of the lamb.)

Clearly, my use of the term "looking for" had meant to Ricky that I assumed he had no knowledge of the song's location in the book.

Although Ricky possibly believed his playmates in guessing and hiding games were indeed ignorant, it is more likely that he knew they were not, but he believed that their true knowledge state was

Still enjoying Grandma's bike

irrelevant to the game. The whole point of games is that the presuppositions of the real world do not have to hold (Bruner, 1972). Children can be "Daddy" or "Mommy" without having to be an adult. Similarly, people can "guess" without having to be ignorant. Because Ricky played so many fantasy games that defied real-world presuppositions, it would have been reasonable for him to think that guessing and hiding games did not require true states of ignorance from his playmates. They were playing "as if" they were guessing and hiding.

## Means to Acquiring Social Knowledge

Ricky's guessing and hiding games were more like practice of the routines involved in such games than they were the genuine games. The guessing and hiding games of older children are different from those of toddlers. They require the use of problem-solving that often depends on inferring the true mental state of one's opponent. Older children's games still involve practice without real-world consequences; games give them the opportunity to practice tactics for inferring and affecting others' knowledge states, but the knowledge states must be "real." Younger children first have to master the formats and language of the games, irrespective of true knowledge states. Ricky's first primitive routine for hiding, his "where" game of more than a year earlier, had some of the essentials correct—physical and visual separation and reunion. A year later, Ricky used the hiding game to practice a more sophisticated vocabulary, but his view of the goal of the game apparently had not changed much. Practicing the linguistic framework for such games, Ricky was building a skeletal foundation for more mature games that would eventually incorporate strategies for actually influencing others' mental states.

There was some play involving internal states that allowed Ricky to gain direct information about others. Now able to realize that others could have different states from his own, he began to ask direct questions to discover what their internal states were and to make games out of such questioning opportunities. Ricky was pretending that he was going to the grocery store.

> R: I buy Coke and orange pop.
> G: Oh, I like orange pop.
> R: You like Coke?

After my reply, he began to poll everyone else in the room to discover their beverage preferences.

Ricky modeled, modified, and transformed social behaviors to extend his social repertoire. He loved playing with the telephone. He would pick up the phone, punch in a series of numbers, and then say, "35, please," in imitation of his mother, who, after dialing the number, would request his father's extension at work. Ricky would also practice saying a string of letters into the telephone, in apparent imitation of his parents' often spelling their name on the phone.

Ricky's turning his face to the wall and refusing to interact when he was angry probably had its source in some transformation of observed or imposed behavior. One possible source is his parents' imposition of "time-outs," time spent quietly in his room when he had misbehaved; this may have been the genesis of the idea of social disengagement when relations with others became troubled. However, he had never been made to stand in a corner. It is possible that this way of disengaging himself from the social world was his own invention, or he may have gotten the idea from one of his many children's books, without realizing that standing in the corner typically is an involuntary punishment and not a voluntary act.

Ricky did at times try out some of the behaviors of fictional characters he read about in books. He was fascinated by a book by Maurice Sendak (1962) about a child named Pierre, who refused to comply with any requests of his parents. Saying repeatedly, "I don't care," Pierre almost meets a grisly end when his defeated parents leave him home by himself and a lion comes along to eat him. One day, about three blocks from home, on a walk back from the park, Ricky settled down on the sidewalk and refused to continue walking or to be carried. Uncharacteristically, he turned a deaf ear to reasoning and pleading, saying stolidly, "I want to stay here all by myself." In desperation, I left him in Richard's care, hoping that he would decide eventually to return to his beloved grandmother's presence. After much cajoling, Richard finally got him home.

> G: What would you have done if Grandpa had left you?
> R: I don't know.
> G: Would you have been able to find your way back here?
> R: Yes.

When I recounted the incident to Alice, she told me Ricky had been playing out little scenarios similar to those in *Pierre* for several weeks. Possibly Ricky was fascinated with Pierre because the character was so different from Ricky's usually reasonable self. At times like these and when he teased about misbehavior, pretending, for example, that he was going to push the buttons on the dishwasher after being warned not to, he seemed to be experimenting: He was gathering information about how the social world would react to other ways of his being.

Practicing, questioning, modeling, and experimenting, then, were all means Ricky had at his disposal for gaining information about the social world and expanding his repertoire of social behaviors. In other words, they were the means to the end of making an increasingly complex social world comprehensible and manageable. In order for these devices for learning to work, Ricky had to have an active social life. He needed models, varied experiences, and attentive adults who would respond to his overtures and questions. Much of his social learning went on without overt comments about his behavior from those around him; his parents rarely explicitly told him how to behave or not behave. Instead, his acquisition of social knowledge was much like his acquisition of language—both were the consequence of active participation with attentive adults in the business of daily living.

## Managing the Conceptual World

### *Representations of Reality*

Mental representations of the world allow people to gain control over the world. With a mental representation, an individual can develop expectations, consider alternatives, and plan actions. Even infants create mental representations of the world around them. Infants can be surprised when objects undergo unusual transformations, showing that they have already developed some expectations about the way objects ought to look and to behave (Spelke, 1985). Toddlers have two new tools for elaborating their mental representations. They can use language to discover aspects of the world they do not experience directly, and when they realize the difference between thinking something may be the case and knowing that it is the case, they can begin to reflect on the certainty of their own knowledge states.

As with social learning, Ricky used language more and more to fill in his representations of reality. He often asked questions of others when he had no direct access to the information he needed to fill out his mental picture. In a book Ricky and I were reading was a picture of a helicopter.

G: Grandpa and I rode in a helicopter like that.
R: You be in the back?

Not only did he use language to get more information for himself, but in a phone conversation with me about Christmas trees, Ricky showed once again that he used it to convey information that was directly inaccessible to others.

R: We have a Christmas tree!
G: You do!
R: Ornaments on it.
G: It has ornaments on it?
   What ornaments does it have?
R: Yights and aminals.
G: What?
R: Yights! Binking yights—bink, bink, bink.
G: Oh, Blinking lights.
R: Grandma have a Christmas tree?

Ricky was becoming more aware of his own thought processes and ability to make inferences and draw conclusions. The word *think* is often used in American English to indicate some degree of certainty about one's inferences. There were many instances of Ricky using the word that way by this time. We had gone on a tour of a partially finished house I was considering buying. Ricky had never been in an unfinished house before, and he delighted in rushing from room to room and declaring what the room would be. When he entered a room with a vinyl floor and cabinets but no appliances, he said, "I think this is the kitchen." Another day, he had been playing with the phone so much that his mother finally unplugged it from its socket. The next time Ricky picked it up, he was dismayed to discover the change.

R: No noise here.
   This phone not working.
M: Is it broken?
R: Maybe it is broken.
   I think it was broken.

It is possible that *think* was a marker for probable but not certain states of affairs, simply a synonym for *maybe*; alternatively, Ricky may have understood that it explicitly marked his own internal state of knowledge. Another interaction suggests he did understand that his own mental state was involved.

> M: Do you remember where we are going next Wednesday?
> R: I'm thinking.
> G: What are you thinking about?
> R: Where we're going next Wednesday.

In fact, Ricky didn't remember and had to be prompted by his mother.

> M: Roller-skating.
> R: (To G) Roller-skating.

Nonetheless, his clear reference to his own mental activity suggests he understood that he had the ability to represent information internally.

Ricky also was able to use new information to evaluate his inferences. He had wanted to watch *Sesame Street*, but it was past the starting time, and I wasn't sure of the correct channel. I flipped the dial until I found something that looked like a good bet—a lesson about the letter *t* in Spanish.

> R: Maybe this *Sesame Street*.
> G: Maybe.
> (After a few minutes, Big Bird appeared on screen.)
> R: It IS *Sesame Street*!

## Tying Conceptual Categories to the World

One means of managing the conceptual world is to organize it into categories of entities that are similar in important ways. Ten months earlier Ricky had used "top down" learning to develop separate domains of knowledge having to do with color and number terms. He had created categories of number and color terms without actually being able to map particular terms correctly to their real-world referents. Now Ricky showed that he was indeed tying terms in those categories to the real world.

Earlier, Ricky had been unable to relate the cardinal and ordinal aspects of number. (See Chapter 4.) Now he was working on that relation. One day he told me he had two cars and then began to count. He would now count an array when asked "How many?" and regularly would arrive at the correct number. In preparation for play, he passed out cars to Richard and me.

R: (Holding one car.) And one for Ricky.
G: So, how many is that?
R: One, two, three. (Holding up a finger for each number term spoken.)

Ricky was now also mapping color terms to appropriate referents, spontaneously describing the color of objects, and sometimes
asking when he wasn't sure about a particular hue.

R: (Pointing to a purple block.) That purple?

Nonetheless, he felt confident enough of his color-term knowledge
to instruct his younger friend Eliza who mislabeled orange as green
one day when they were painting.

G: Show Eliza where the green is.
R: (Pointing to the green paint.) This is green.

At the same time, Ricky was developing another descriptive
category. He had begun to describe objects by the materials they
were made of. As with color and number, his answers were not
necessarily accurate. However, unlike number and color terms, the
first uses I noticed of his material terms were spontaneously gener-
ated and not in response to questions. In the case of color particularly, his first uses offered no evidence that he even knew which
characteristic the term *color* referred to.[1] In the case of material
terms, he seemed at least to have an idea of what the domain was,
so that even when he was wrong, he seemed to be referring to the
characteristic of materials of real-world objects. One morning, I had
set out juice cups on the breakfast table for the family, giving Ricky
his usual plastic cup. Ricky used an incorrect material term to contrast (appropriately) a set of cups with the plastic one he regularly
used.

R: (Indicating the cups for the adults). I want one of these too—a metal
one.
G: That's not metal, it's ceramic.
R: Ceramic.
G: You want one of those?
R: Yeah.
G: Okay, here's one for you.

He also used a material term to make a note of an unusual material.
When we had been walking through the partially built house, Ricky
had noticed that the stair spindles were made of lucite and not
wood.

R: Plastic poles!

In response to my asking whether Ricky and she had been talking about materials, Alice couldn't recall doing so, but her ensuing dialogue with Ricky suggests that perhaps a question about materials was not unfamiliar to him.

M: (Pointing to the dining-room table.) What's this made of?
R: Wood.

Whether the descriptive category of materials develops in a "bottom-up" way, with children first noticing differences in materials and then trying to find words to describe them, or in a "top-down" way, through discourse, is a question that needs to be answered by examining the development of other children.

## Levels of Knowledge in a 30 Month Old

A common view in the field of child development is that children's language ability develops far more quickly and effortlessly than other skills. Such a claim is grounded in the belief that certain domains of knowledge, such as syntax or number, can be characterized by structural (formal) descriptions and that an individual's development can then be assessed in terms of the amount of structural knowledge acquired. Yet the claim is meaningless because it is impossible to compare levels of knowledge across domains. There is no metric whereby one can equate a level of skill in one domain with a level of skill in another. For example, is a 2 year old who can produce two-clause sentences but cannot pass a Piagetian conservation task more advanced in language than cognitive development? Is an 18 month old who can tease a sibling but cannot yet produce mental-state verbs more advanced in social development than language? Only a relative developmental benchmark measures a child's performance in each area—how well a child compares in a given area to other children of his or her age. An analogy to height and weight is useful here: We would say of a child who is taller and thinner than average that she is tall for her age and, possibly, underweight; but we would not say that the child is more advanced in height than in weight.

Moreover, there is no way to assess whether there is more to learn overall in one area than in others. Nor have we quantified adult knowledge so that we can say what proportion of that knowledge a child has acquired by a certain time; thus, we cannot say whether a child by age 3 has acquired 80% of adult linguistic knowledge but only 60% of adult social knowledge. Indeed, because adults keep acquiring many kinds of knowledge throughout life, attempts of this sort would be pointless.

A focus on language acquisition as the unique achievement of a child by age 4 ignores the fact that a toddler like Ricky makes very real advances in social and cognitive understanding, such as gaining the abilities to control one's emotions and to make inferences about others' knowledge. Consequently, it overlooks the interrelations among areas that form the basis of a developing social-linguistic intelligence. This is not to say that the domains have a common *structural description*—there are some good reasons to believe in somewhat separate descriptions (Keil, 1981). Rather, the *processes* of acquiring knowledge in the three domains are often similar; sometimes knowledge acquisition in one area requires reference to knowledge in another. In other words, the domains are not completely autonomous. Human beings, after all, are not just vessels for compartmentalized knowledge. Just as the organs of the body, with different structures and functions, must work together to support a living organism, so humans interrelate different domains of knowledge both to produce appropriate behavior and to continue to learn.

Most important, close examination of one child's development in the three domains suggests that no area seems easy or effortless. In all three, Ricky had procedures for learning: he sought information, practiced, and actively worked at organizing his knowledge. Sometimes his analyses in each of the domains were incomplete or inaccurate, but he often used his partial knowledge in one area to participate in the world around him and to gain more information in doing so. Thus, even toddlers demonstrate that integrating and interrelating one's knowledge is an essential aspect of human behavior and fundamental to human development.

## Note

1. In an ongoing series of studies, we have as yet been unable to find clear evidence that children under age 2 understand which characteristic the term *color* refers to, even if they produce one or more color terms (Shatz, Backscheider, & Loken, in preparation).

# 10

## *31–32 Months*
## Preparing for
## Second-Order Thinking

Second-order thinking—thinking about the thoughts of others—is the core of mental life and social action in adult humans. Politicians pick their words to accord with what they think the voters want to hear, lovers worry about how they look to their beloved, students try to predict what information their teachers think is important enough to test, and athletic coaches plan strategies to counter what they think their opponents are planning. Second-order thinking depends on a theory of mind—it requires understanding that actions are based on internal states and that others' internal states can be different from one's own. Successful second-order thinking involves still more—the accurate assessment of others' internal states. Adults use their accumulated experience of how they themselves and others behave in various situations to infer the mental states of others. They, of course, can be unsuccessful at second-order thinking when they misjudge what others know or intend, or they miscalculate how others will react; but they seem to know the importance of engaging in it, and they do it regularly.

Generally, successful second-order thinkers are astute observers of human behavior. They can identify others' emotional states, they compare and evaluate people's behaviors, and they use those comparisons and evaluations to predict future behavior. That is, they develop a sense of what is possible or even probable for themselves and for others.

We expect children to be less successful second-order thinkers than adults. There are three reasons why this might be so. At the very least, they have less experience than adults; they may not recognize some situations as calling for second-order thinking, and they should not be as knowledgeable or skillful at determining the particulars of others' states. They also have fewer resources for drawing on their experience; they have to use more time or mental energy just to represent the basic circumstances of a situation and hence have fewer resources for comparing the present situation to previous ones. The more unfamiliar or demanding the circumstances, the harder it should be for children to engage in second-order thinking at all, let alone to be successful at it.[1]

The third and most controversial reason is that children under the age of 4 lack an essential understanding of how mental representations relate to the real world. Namely, they may not understand that people can unintentionally *misrepresent* reality—that they can have false beliefs. As discussed earlier, understanding false belief is central to a mature theory of mind, and it is necessary for successful second-order thinking in many situations.

To think about false beliefs, a child may have to be able to reflect on and relate the notions of pretense, knowledge, and intention. When 18 month olds engage in pretend play, they indicate they can free themselves from the concrete reality of the here and now. They can intentionally act "as if" another reality pertained. However, they may not be able to reflect on their actions and recognize them as dependent on their own intentional mental representations of an alternate reality. Moreover, as noted in Chapter 5, children have to discover that both knowledge and pretense involve internal representations, one of reality and one of nonreality. Generally, toddlers appear to understand this sometime in the third year, when they begin to check whether they and their interlocutors are both operating in the same world, either the real or the pretend.

Children must also see that, although they and others can both be working in the same world, their *representations* of that world can differ (Flavell, 1988). And they have to understand that there are two possible reasons for differing representations. One is that two perceivers can have two different perspectives on reality, as with visual perspectives;[2] the other is that one representation is not of reality at all—it is simply wrong. To achieve this level of understanding, children must realize that pretense is only a subset of possible representations of the nonreal—the intentional kind. People represent nonreality unintentionally as well; indeed, they *think* they are representing reality when they in fact are not—they have false beliefs. For example, I think I left my keys on the table, but when I go to get them, they are not there and I must search for them. When children realize that representations can be either accurate or inaccurate, it is a natural consequence to wonder how accurate representations of reality are reached and hence to show interest in sources of knowledge.

A review of Ricky's progress toward mature second-order thinking supports the idea that the capacity develops gradually, and involves the acquisition of several different skills and kinds of knowledge. At 18 months, Ricky had begun to understand that people could have different visual perspectives from his and that he had to take account of those perspectives; for example, he turned books around to face his listeners. At 21 months, his pretense with the pacifier suggested he understood that both he and others could disengage from concrete reality. At 24 months, he began to justify his actions to others by making his intentions more explicit, suggesting that he believed they had no direct access to his intentions. By 30 months, the knowledge that others' internal states were not necessarily the same as his and that he sometimes knew things they did not, and vice versa, seemed well established. He asked many *why* questions and queried people about their preferences. Moreover, he had a growing vocabulary of terms to describe mental states that he often used appropriately.

Nonetheless, Ricky still had more to learn: he did not seem to understand all the presuppositions of his mental-state terms (like *guess* and *hide*), his social experiences were still quite limited, and he had not yet shown that he had the idea of false beliefs. In the next few months, Ricky would make more strides toward mature second-order thinking. For one, he continued to work at learning about people. Like many children, he was a close observer of others' behavior, and he continued to evaluate his own actions relative to others. He began to think about how knowledge was acquired; and his talk about pretense showed that he was not just doing it, he was thinking about it, particularly about when it was being engaged in. Importantly, he gave his first explicit indication of some understanding of false belief—at least with regard to his own mental state.

## Attending to Mental States and Abilities

Ricky's references to his own and others' internal states were increasingly frequent. One day we were reading about Curious George's adventures in a baseball stadium. Looking very distressed, George was pictured atop a light pole, where he had been chased by angry players after he had disrupted the game. Ricky pointed to George and told me, "He scared." Another time he mimicked a look of consternation on his mother's face and then said to me, "Mommy does this all the time." He described his own state, as he lay on the floor, looking tired.

G: Are you going to take a nap?
R: I just relaxing a little bit.

Ricky regularly got annoyed when people told him things he already knew, suggesting he expected them to know he knew them. He had been playing in my lab/playroom one day and found a plastic replica of a stagecoach and horses.

R: I take this home?
G: Yes, if you want.
   That's a stagecoach.
R: Stagecoach. (R repeated the word three or four times.)
   (Pointing toward the harness.) Airhop.
G: What?
R: Airhop.
G: What's airhop?
   (R did not reply, but continued to play with the toy.)
R: (Several minutes later) Airhop.
G: That's a STAGECOACH.
R: (Annoyed) I KNOW that's a stagecoach.

I never did find out what "airhop" meant; even Alice could shed no light on it when I asked her about it upon returning to Ricky's house.

Ricky referred to knowledge states in arguments and as justifications for behaviors—or lack of them. After he threw a block toward the fireplace, I reminded him he was not supposed to play near it. As he continued to do so, I said "No, don't do that!" Annoyed at being reproached, Ricky said "I know that!"

G: Then why did you do that?
R: I don't know.

We were talking one day about an impending trip to the circus. Selecting from things we had seen at a circus the year before, I asked what he expected to see.

G: Will you see clowns?
R: Yes.

G: And elephants?
R: Un-huh, elephants.
G: And dancing dogs?
R: No.
G: No? No dancing dogs?
R: No dogs know how.

He was more aware of the differences between fact and possibility, and began to mark his own inferences with the word *probably*. We had come back to his house to discover that someone had parked in his mother's parking place. She went off to try to discover whose car it was. Ricky turned to me and said, "It probably Denise's." (Denise was a neighbor.) Another day we talked about possible fits for things.

R: (Trying on my glasses.) Why these not fit on me?
G: Because my head is bigger than yours.
   (R puts on his fireman's helmet.)
   Your hat fits on you though.
   Do you think it will fit on me?
R: I think it probably too small.

For the first time, I heard him ask about the source of another's knowledge. We were taking a walk when Alice noticed some snow stuck high up on a tree trunk.

M: Look at this tree with snow on its side!
R: How you know that?

Ricky's question was not appropriate by adult conversational standards, since it was clear that Alice knew the tree had snow clinging to it because she had looked at it. On the one hand, Ricky may have meant to ask a different question, such as "How did you happen to notice it?" or even "How did it happen?" On the other hand, he may have discovered that there were different ways to gain knowledge, and he was just practicing asking a question that would tell him something about how a particular piece of knowledge was acquired. His not-quite appropriate question was reminiscent of his early overuse of adverbs like *maybe*.

A few months earlier, I had noticed the beginnings of self-evaluations (Chapter 8). Ricky continued to evaluate his own accomplishments relative to those of the adults around him. He was especially glad to see Richard one day and invited him into his bedroom to play. When I went into the room a bit later, I found them at the two-sided easel.

R:  We painting.
    Grandpa and I are painters.
G:  Oh, that's nice. What are you painting?
R:  A cat. (As R draws a series of circles.)
    (R walks around the easel to look at Gf's drawing.)
    What you drawing?
Gf: A cat.
R:  He needs a stomach. (Making swirls on Gf's cat.)
G:  What's in that stomach?
R:  A baby. (R's mother was three months pregnant.)

Ricky walked around to his side of the easel, ripped his picture from it and handed it to me.

R:  This is a rotten cat.

Another day, as I was talking to Alice on the phone, I heard Ricky in the background, rustling newspaper and calling to her.

R:  Teach me, teach me.
M:  What do you want me to teach you?
R:  This. (M told G that R was pointing to the crossword puzzle—his parents were avid puzzle doers.)
M:  First you have to learn a lot of words and what they mean.
R:  a, b, c, d, e, f, g. . . . (R sings the whole alphabet song.)

There were times when Ricky knew something—or thought he did—that adults did not, and he seemed to enjoy the opportunity to teach others. Alice told me Ricky liked to play the card game Uno (albeit with the players' cards face up), and we all decided to play together. I told Ricky I didn't know the game, and he would have to teach Richard and me. To my surprise, he took up the challenge and began to give us a reasonably coherent set of instructions, although at a very basic level.

R:  You have to use these. (Holding up the cards.)
    You have to put them in here. (Taking the card holder from its box.)
    You have to deal the cards.
G:  How many?
    (R holds up four, then five fingers.)
G:  Four? Five?
M:  Yeah, Five.
R:  You have to do this. (R splits the deck in half, and makes as if to shuffle the cards.)

I had to leave the scene to get more paper to continue writing all of this down. When I returned, Ricky was still instructing his grandfather on how the colors on the cards had to be matched. We played a game, and then Ricky picked up the cards in preparation for the next round.

R: (To Gf) You know how to shuffle, Grandpa?
   We will show you.

Ricky knew what shuffling was but didn't have the dexterity to do it. Possibly realizing that, he promptly handed the cards to me!

## Looking for Causes of Behavior

One way Ricky learned more about people was to ask what motivated their actions. More and more, he began to ask others to explain or justify their actions or refusals to act. At a barbecue one day, Alice had put a charred hot dog on her plate, and Ricky asked her, "Why you take a dirty one?" Another day, when I was noting down something he'd said, he asked me why I was writing.

R: Why you got a pen?
   To write how many words there are?
G: (Distractedly) Yes, I'm writing lots of words.
R: For me to learn?
   How many words there are?
G: Lots and lots.
R: In the alphabet?
G: Well, there are letters in the alphabet. Twenty-six letters.
   You can make lots of words with those letters.[3]

Ricky tried hard to get justifications from others when they would not accede to his requests. He had wanted to reinstitute a game we had played earlier in the day in which I went out into the front hall while he shut the doors from the living room, pretending to lock me out. I refused to play.

R: (Argumentatively) You was out there earlier.
G: Yes, we were, but now it's too cold out there.

Stubbornly, Ricky opened the door and went out himself to check the temperature in the hall, but he apparently agreed with me and didn't press me any further.

## Developing Social Categories

To facilitate second-order thinking, adults generalize from experience with individuals and groups to predict behavior. They expect that, in similar circumstances, people will behave the way they behaved before. Also, they make inferences about people on the basis of similar others they have known. People who are alike in some ways are expected to behave alike in other ways. That is, adults have social categories. If you know a teenager who likes loud rock music, you might expect other teenagers to like it as well. Social categories give people at least some information on which to base their second-order thinking when they have to make inferences about relatively unfamiliar others or in relatively unfamiliar circumstances.

During toddlerhood, children begin to create social categories; gender is one dimension on which children categorize early (Martin & Little, 1990). Ricky had become very attentive to gender distinctions. We were taking a walk one day when he stopped to watch two cars go by and to categorize their drivers.

> R: A man driving that car.
> A woman driving that one.

I was drawing pictures to amuse him in a restaurant, and had drawn a house with a path leading up to it.

> R: Now draw someone walking all the way up to the house.
> G: Okay, here's a boy walking home. (G draws a boy.)
> R: Now draw his girlfriend.

Looking out the window, I noticed a woman walking her dog, and I called them to Ricky's attention.

> G: Look at the person walking her dog.
> R: Is that a boy or a girl?
> G: The dog or the person walking the dog?
> I don't know whether . . . (G hesitates.)
> R: . . . the dog barks or not.
> G: (Laughing at Ricky finishing my sentence)
> Well, I'm sure the dog barks.
> Were you asking me about the dog being a boy or a girl?
> Is that what you meant?
> R: The DOG, I meant.

Another day, we were trying to fix the timer on the exercise bicycle that Ricky liked to pretend was his motorcycle.

> G: It has a screw here.
> R: You have a screwdriver?
> G: I'm not sure I have a little enough one.
> R: Grandpa own one?

Ricky's use of the verb *own* is interesting. Possibly he thought it likely that a male would own a tool like a screwdriver. Even if he had not yet developed the usual stereotypes for males and females, they were, despite his mothers' best efforts at nonsexist education, to surface not much later. After just a few months in nursery school, he told me, when he was a bit past 3, that he didn't play with girls at school but that he liked the girls "because they wear pretty dresses." (According to Alice, he often played with girls at school, and they just about never wore dresses.)

## Metalanguage About Reality and Nonreality

Sometime after age 30 months, children begin to comment explicitly on the distinctions between reality and nonreality (Woolley & Wellman, 1990). Ricky's frequent comments about nonreality, particularly pretense, suggest that he was becoming increasingly reflective about it and its relation to reality.

I had arrived at Ricky's house for dinner. No sooner was I in the living room than he pointed to his red sneakers on the floor.

R: Those are my fireman's boots.
G: (With disbelief) Those are fireman's boots?
R: I USE them as my fireman's boots.
G: Oh, that's a good idea.

One day, Ricky had come to my house with his mother. Soon after their arrival, we were preparing to go out for lunch when Ricky headed for the refrigerator, took out a coffee yogurt (his favorite), put it in a little basket he was carrying, and said he wanted to go on a picnic. I did not realize Ricky was just playing, and I protested, saying we were going to a restaurant for lunch. Ricky corrected my misunderstanding by making his intent explicit, "Let's pretend first." We had to have several rounds of "picnicking" in each of the bedrooms before Ricky would agree to leave for the restaurant.

Ricky regularly made explicit the distinction between reality and nonreality. It was as though he wanted to be sure both he and his conversational partners were operating in the same realm of discourse. At dinner one evening, he wanted to hear an audiotape of a story about Corduroy Bear. His mother refused, saying it was nicer to talk together since his grandparents were present. Ricky persisted and, to distract him, I asked him about the tape.

G: What is the story of Corduroy Bear?
R: He lost a button. (Fingering his shirt.)

Gf:  (With concern in his voice.) He lost his button?

R:   This just tells about it. (Meaning it is just a story and nothing to be really concerned about.)

Not just with stories, but with teasing as well, Ricky did not want to leave mutual knowledge about the real world too far behind. He wanted to be sure I was well aware of the reality of his love of ice cream after I had pretended otherwise and he had willingly taken up the pretense with a look of disgust.

G:   I know you don't like ice cream.
     You NEVER eat ice cream.

R:   Yeah. (R says this in an exaggerated tone while making a face of disgust.)
     A little bit. (R's voice and face become more natural.)

G:   Oh, you like it a little bit?
     When do you eat ice cream?

R:   At Eliza's house.

Ricky engaged in what might be called second-order pretense when he attributed the mental act of pretending to one of his dolls. He had been playing with a Matchbox car and a Little People doll, pretending to have the doll open the car doors. As I watched him, I thought he was about to try to put the much larger doll into the car.

G:   Isn't that doll too big for that car?
     (Ricky did not respond, but continued his action.)

G:   Can that person fit in there?

R:   He's pretending.

In all these instances, Ricky was explicitly attending to the real-ity-pretense distinction. Toddlers prior to that age can engage in pretense and hence know something about the difference between it and reality. But as they become more aware of others' mental states, they think consciously about the distinction; they want to check more often on whether conversation is about reality or fan-tasy, and whether they are sharing a common world with their in-terlocutors. Even though there is more conscious attention to the nature and conditions of pretense by age 3, a recent experimental study showed that children under 5 do not always appreciate that one can be said to be pretending only if one is willfully representing some nonreality (Lillard, 1993b). More work is needed, however, to determine just how fragile young children's understanding of pre-tense is.

## The Beginnings of a False Belief Theory of Mind

Ricky had initiated a game of hide-and-seek. When it was my turn to hide, I went into the study, on the first floor. Ricky headed for the stairs to look for me upstairs. Alice gave him a hint, saying, "I don't think Grandma went upstairs." Ricky turned around and began to look for me on the correct floor, locating me rather quickly. When he saw me, he reported his false belief, "I think you upstairs."

Ricky did not just tell me he had started upstairs. Instead, he used the phrase "I think" to describe explicitly his prior state of mind and implicitly contrast it with the actual state of affairs, suggesting that he understood his mental representation had been in error. Admittedly, Alice had used "think" in her utterance to tell him, rather subtly, that he was heading toward the wrong location. That may have facilitated his use of the word. Nonetheless, she was telling him about *her* belief—he still had to make an inference about my actual location and then convey to me what *he* had been thinking.

Contrasts between prior (incorrect) beliefs and actuality have been noted in the spontaneous speech of other children about Ricky's age (Shatz, Wellman, & Silber, 1983). At least in natural situations, some children in the second half of their third year have enough of the skills needed to understand and begin to talk about prior false beliefs. Still to come was clear evidence that Ricky understood two people could simultaneously hold differing beliefs about a single event.

Even a beginning understanding of the idea of false belief opens up many new possibilities for second-order thinking in social interactions. Children who understand that misrepresentations of reality occur unintentionally try to speak in ways that influence their listeners' representations of reality. Lies, of course, are the most flagrant attempts to misrepresent reality to others. There are less grievous ways to manipulate others, by subtle choices of words that bend the truth just enough to enhance speakers' chances of getting what they want from a listener. Soon after I first heard Ricky make a statement about false belief, he began to try to mask his true intentions in words he thought more palatable to his listeners.

His first attempt was poorly disguised. Much to Ricky's dismay,

Alice and I were engaged in conversation and ignoring him. After several rejections, he picked up his beloved Babar, waved it before me, and said, in his Babar voice, "I need someone to talk to me."

Another attempt was more subtle. Ricky loved playing at my desk, where he was allowed to use pencil and crayons to draw. When boredom set in, he noticed the cup of pens that were off limits.

R: I need a pen too.
G: I don't think you NEED a pen.
R: I WANT one, IN CASE I need it.

I had caught Ricky in his subterfuge, and he knew it; but, needless to say, I was disarmed by his quick-witted retort, and he got his pen. The innocent toddler who had stated his wants simply and who had admitted blithely to his transgressions was fast transforming himself into a wily second-order thinker.

## The Other Side of the Coin

So far this chapter has focused on Ricky's expansion or acquisition of new skills needed for mature second-order thinking, but there was another side to Ricky's behavior during this period. One of the characteristics of new skills is that they are inconsistently displayed; only with practice do they become reliable. There were occasions when it was easy to see that, despite his growing sophistication, Ricky was still something of a novice at second-order thinking. In a game of hide-and-seek with his mother, Ricky copied Alice's prior (easy to discover) hiding place when it was his turn to hide, but he covered his own eyes—apparently to make himself harder to find! This immature behavior was followed on his next turn by a much better choice—crouching behind the bed where he could not be seen by anyone entering the room.

Also, Ricky misunderstood that I was using the word *say* in a nonliteral way, when we met a friendly cat on the street one day.

G: It's saying "hello" to us.
R: No it saying hello.
G: It's not saying hello?
R: (R shakes his head from side to side.)
G: What's it saying then?
R: Meow.
G: Well, it doesn't talk our language, but that's its way of greeting us. Greeting means saying "hello."

To understand my use of the word *say*, Ricky either would have had to know that *say* does not have to introduce only exact quotes, or he would have had to recognize one of the important conventions governing conversational understandings (Grice, 1975; Searle, 1975): When a speaker's statement would obviously be wrong if taken literally, then the speaker very likely intends those words to mean something else. Because I, too, had heard exactly what sound the cat had made, a more knowledgeable second-order thinker would have recognized that I could not have meant to state that the cat actually said "hello," and would have inferred that I meant something else.

The ease of second-order thinking is undoubtedly facilitated by knowledge of a broad range of adult conventions. Sometimes Ricky's lack of such knowledge led him to try to engage adults in inappropriate ways that they found funny but that he could see no humor in, and he was at a loss to understand their responses to him. He had been playing with Alice at delivering "luggage"—a telephone book—on my luggage carrier.

R: Let's pretend there are words in there.
M: There ARE words in there. Haven't you heard me reading them? (M had been reeling off a list of names every time R had brought her the book.)
R: Let's pretend the words are pictures. (R meant "Let's pretend this is a storybook.")

A few minutes later, Ricky tried to deliver the book to Richard.

R: (To Gf) Here's a book for you.
Gf: I never read that book.
R: You never read this book?
Gf: I never read the telephone book.
R: You want to read this book?
Gf: No, I never read it.
R: You WANT to read it?
Gf: No, I don't want to read it.

Ricky never did realize that the telephone book was not a typical book. He finally gave up on his grandfather and, amid laughter from the adults, he again offered the book to his mother.

R: (To M) You wanna come on a airplane with me?
M: Yes, I'd love to go on an airplane.
R: Take your book and let's go.

Despite his failures due to ignorance or lapses in applying what he knew, Ricky was determinedly making progress toward the development of a belief psychology that he could use to interact with others. In the next few months, he would show even more clearly that he understood the idea of false belief, with regard to others' beliefs as well as his own.

### Notes

1. The same is very likely true of adults, but adults may recognize how essential second-order thinking is and hence apportion their resources somewhat differently from children, giving up on such thinking only when absolutely necessary. Nonetheless, at least for some communication tasks requiring that speakers take listener knowledge into account, increasing the cognitive demands on adults can indeed make them perform like children. (See Shatz, 1978, for a discussion.)

2. We have seen that children under age 2 can sometimes adjust their behavior to take account of others' visual perspectives, but they may not reflect on the relation between different perspectives on reality and different internal representations of it.

3. It is unclear how aware Ricky was of my interest in his language development. I never discussed it with his parents in front of him, but certainly he and I spent considerable time talking about language, as did he and his mother. Although I was often jotting down notes when we were together, this was the only time he asked me to explain what I was doing. Although Ricky may have been sensitive to language because of the frequent literacy activities in both my household and his, I doubt that my notetaking per se influenced his behavior.

# 11

## *33–34 Months*
## The Emergent
## Preschooler

### Preschool Readiness

Ricky was reaching a new stage in his life. He started going to
preschool two mornings a week. Beginning school represents a sig-
nificant step toward growing up for any child. Even preschools that
do not emphasize academics offer major opportunities to acquire
new skills and exercise emotional maturity. For many children, preschool is the first time they have to deal on a regular basis with
adults who are not primary caretakers and whom they do not know
well. It is also, except for children from large families or group day
care, the first regular experience at being just one of a group. How
well would Ricky, an only child and first grandchild, who had obviously received a great deal of attention from the adults around him,
fare when he was not the center of attention?

Several things made the transition to school easy for Ricky. He
loved being with other children but had few opportunities for peer
play in his neighborhood, so school represented a reliable, new avenue to play with other children. Because Ricky had spent many overnights with me away from his parents, he was less concerned about
separation from them than he might otherwise have been. Third, he
typically relished achieving more mature forms of behavior. Ricky
had weaned himself, had been the instigator of toilet training and

sleeping in a bed, and was enthusiastic about going to school, especially so because a few of his friends already did.

The one potential negative was his continued relative shyness with strangers. As noted in Chapter 6, Ricky typically was reluctant to approach unfamiliar children; almost a year later, he still was, although he at least seemed more aware of the various responses he might get to his possible overtures. Just a few weeks before he started school, we went to the park, where he saw a child playing in the sand with bulldozers, pails, and shovels. Ricky lounged on the monkey bars, watching the other child attentively.

> R: (Quietly) I want to play with that bulldozer.
> G: Well, ask the boy if you can play with him.
> R: Grandma ask him.
> G: No, I'm not the one who wants to play.
>    You are. You have to ask him.
>    I'll go over with you though.
> R: (Shyly, almost to himself.) I want to play with that.
> G: Well, ask him if you can play with him.
> R: And he say "yes" or "no"?
> G: That's right; he'll say "yes" or "no."
> R: (After a few minutes more of hesitation.) Grandma, come with me.

We walked over to the boy, but Ricky stood frozen in silence; it was I who ultimately had to break the ice, after which the two children played very nicely together, along with several other children who happened by.

Of course, when the stakes were high enough, Ricky could forget his shyness and approach a strange child. We had been shopping in a large store where Ricky had immediately discovered the toy section and had taken possession of a child-sized, bright pink convertible. He had been driving up and down the aisles happily, but abandoned the car momentarily to run over to me in a nearby section. He dashed back to it when he spotted a little girl begin to climb in. "Only one driver in here," he announced authoritatively as he gently but firmly muscled her away from the enticing car. Ricky's boldness may have been engendered by his sense of possession about the car. He probably felt as though he hadn't really relinquished it; yet his justification suggests he also recognized he didn't have genuine ownership rights to it either.

Ricky's diffidence at initiating social interactions with unfamiliar children is not uncommon in children around age 3. In the park I had watched a newly arrived boy who wanted to join the other children but hung back as Ricky had. His strategy was to badger his mother to go home to get his own pail and shovel so that he would have something to bring to the group. She had a hard time convincing him he could participate without the paraphernalia. It would be interesting to know whether young children are more comfortable about negotiating group inclusion in other societies where people orient more toward community and less toward personal property and individual rights. Of course, it is possible that in such societies young children would be less likely to meet up with unfamiliar others, and the degree to which 3 year olds are familiar with their peers very much affects the nature of their interactions (Doyle, 1982).

Negotiating group inclusion is apparently one of the skills children in the United States practice in preschool (Newman, 1978). Indeed, it seemed to be a skill Ricky acquired there. After his first few days at school, I asked Ricky about his experiences.

G: Do you know any of the names of the children yet?
R: No. I don't talk to any of them.
G: No? Why not?
R: They changed their minds not to talk to me.
G: Oh, I don't think they decided not to talk to you. You have to talk to them first. Just try that.

Within a year, I observed very different behavior from Ricky on our trips to the park. He regularly approached other children, often with invitations to play with him or with suggestions for some novel activity. He had learned his lessons on initiating interactions well.

Despite his initial shyness, Ricky's transition to school was remarkably smooth. There were no crying episodes at school and no behavioral or sleep disturbances at home. Ricky did report that he had not used the bathroom at school because it was inhabited by some sort of monster. When I asked what it looked like, he replied, "A red cookie monster." The monster turned out to be the spectre of having to ask the teacher to help him with his clothes.

## Second-Order Thinking

That Ricky attributed to his classmates a decision not to talk to him was an instance of his increasing use of psychological states to explain others' behaviors. He was on his way to my house for the weekend when he became too warm in the car and began to unzip his jacket. I helped him with the zipper.

R: My teacher zipped it all the way down.
G: Oh, did she unzip it for you at school?
R: (Nodding his head.) Her thought me was warm.

The first night of his visit, Ricky had an accident; in the morning his pajamas and bedding were wet. I changed the linens without comment. The morning after his second night at my house, he appeared at my door naked. I asked where his pajamas were, and he replied, "In the bathroom." I suggested we get him a shirt and some underpants, but he refused. With skepticism, I asked, "Do you want to put your pajamas back on?" Ricky nodded. I retrieved the — to my surprise — dry pajamas from the bathroom and, without a word, began to dress him. Ricky said, "You thought these were wet." Based on the prior day's events, I had indeed had that false belief.

Ricky was not always so capable of accurately inferring the mental states of others. Particularly with regard to adults' likes and dislikes, he sometimes wrongly assumed that the things that gave him pleasure would give them pleasure too. It was Richard's birthday the weekend of Ricky's visit. Ricky saw some of my preparations for it and wanted to wrap a present for his grandfather. I suggested we go out to buy something, but he said no, that he wanted to give him one of his prized miniature cars. He picked one out and wrapped it. The next day, Ricky couldn't contain his excitement about the birthday, telling Richard, "I got you a car." Richard nonetheless made a great fuss about it when he opened Ricky's package. When Ricky's parents' arrived with a gift of their own, Ricky told them he had already given Richard a gift of a car, "He opened the car up and he yoved [loved] it!"

Ricky may have thought the car was an appropriate gift because he and Richard often played with the cars together. Also, Richard's warm enthusiasm for the gift did nothing to suggest otherwise. However, that same weekend there was another instance of misjudging others' preferences that cannot be explained away quite so easily. In my continuing quest for a new home, we had gone to another open house. At the house, there was a spectacular collection of baseball caps atop the owner's canopied bed. Ricky, who was obsessed with hats at the time, was captivated by them. About an hour later, as we were driving home from a stop at a park, Ricky asked me about my plans.

R: You movin'?
G: Maybe, I haven't decided yet.
   What did you think of that house?
R: You would like wearing those hats.

Some research with children in a laboratory setting suggests that 3 year olds are better able to infer others' likes and dislikes than their false beliefs (Flavell, Flavell, Green, & Moses, 1990). At least in some instances, Ricky's inferences about others' belief states were more accurate than his inferences about others' preferences. He could explain others' actions by making inferences about their belief states; and, as in the pajama example, he could do this even when their states of knowledge were different from his and their belief states were different from reality.

In what kinds of situations did Ricky think appropriately about others' beliefs? In some cases, Ricky himself had very likely experienced similar thoughts while engaging in similar activities—for example, you unzip your jacket when you feel warm (or you help someone unzip his jacket if he looks warm). In this case, any person could be expected to behave the same way under similar circumstances—no information about the particular person other than the fact of their unzipping behavior need be considered. In the same way, the counterfactual "you thought these were wet" required a chain of inference based on our sharing the previous day's accident, his appearing naked, and my response to it, but Ricky could have made the same inference about any caretaker's belief under those circumstances. He had to consider nothing particular about my past history or the idiosyncracies of my thought patterns to arrive at his conclusion. In other words, to explain others' behavior, apparently Ricky reasonably attributed to others the sorts of inferences he—or anyone else—in such knowledge states would have made in those situations.

The claim that at least some toddlers use belief states to explain others' behavior gains plausibility in light of a recent experimental study with slightly older children. When asked why Jane, who wanted her cat, searched for it under the piano (when it was under the couch), 3 year olds recruited false belief explanations, responding, for example, "because she thought it was under the piano" (Bartsch & Wellman, 1989). Thus, young children attribute rational motives to others to explain their observed behaviors.[1]

However, second-order thinking that requires considering the idiosyncratic experiences, dispositions, or reasoning patterns of individuals (or groups) should be more difficult for young children. For this reason, it may have been hard for Ricky to assess adults' preferences accurately; he probably had little direct experience with them (except at the dinner table). Having passed through a life stage helps a child go beyond his or her personal preferences: Four year olds tend to be better at picking out birthday presents for peers or younger children than they are for older children (Shatz, 1978). As we might expect, experience plays an important part in whether children's inferences about others will be accurate.

Also, to the extent that people who are alike in some way tend to behave alike, categorizing people based on similar characteristics can be helpful in making inferences about how they will think or behave. Toddlers are in the process of creating categories of people based on characteristics like gender or age, but those categories may not yet be well enough established to support many inferences about the individuals who belong to them.

Ricky did seem to know he needed more information about others' preferences and opinions. He frequently asked his listeners "What you think?" after giving his own opinion or preference. And he would ask questions about others' intentions and preferences when he didn't understand why they were behaving as they did. We had been out shopping and were making a stop at home to drop my mother off so that she could take her daily rest as she watched her favorite soap opera. Ricky wasn't familiar with soap operas, and he wanted clarification about what he had overheard.

R: Why we leave Bubby at home?
G: She's tired. She wants to rest.
R: And she wants to watch some kind of movie?
G: Yes, she wants to watch a videotape.
R: About what?

Although toddlers are sometimes inaccurate, thinking and talking about the beliefs and interests of others is a major accomplishment long thought to be beyond their ability. Piaget, for example, would not have expected that such young children, in accounting for others' behavior, were able to think beyond their own view of reality to how the other must be seeing the world differently. In many ways, Ricky showed that he was working hard trying to understand not just the relation between reality and nonreality, but other kinds of perspective problems as well.

## Perceptual Perspective-Taking

It had been more than a year since I had first observed Ricky turn a book appropriately for another viewer. Such adjustments now were commonplace. Ricky had tried on a new shirt that was decorated with paw prints, and his mother told him what sorts of animals made the prints. Ricky then turned his back to us and asked, "What's on the back?"

Still, adjusting to another's perceptual perspective did not always happen automatically. At times he showed he thought consciously about the problems of perceptual perspective. We were on the porch having lunch. On the porch rail sat, turned sideways to us, a ceramic frog with shiny brown spots on its side.

R: How many spots on that frog?
G: I see three.
R: On the other side too?
G: I don't know. I would guess there are as many on one side as the other.
R: You see spots on the other side?
G: Can I see the other side from where I am?
R: (Shakes his head no.)
G: Where would I have to be to see the other side?
R: Down there. (R points appropriately beyond the railing.)

Another day Ricky switched on a lamp on a table at which we were sitting. I moved the lamp a bit to keep its light out of my eyes. Ricky then moved it to the other side of the table, saying, "I move it back." The cord was now in a dangerous place, so I moved the lamp once again.

R: You move it cause it's blocking baseball thing?

(The lamp, I realized, had been in my line of sight had I been watching the baseball game on TV. I had inadvertently moved it a bit into Ricky's line of sight of the TV.)

G: Uh, yes.

Ricky let me know my action had now blocked *his* view of the TV.

R: So, I move it back here and it not block baseball.
(R moves the lamp to clear his view of the TV.)

Ricky did not understand why I had begun the lamp-moving, but he inferred that it had something to do with my line of sight to the television screen. The full realization that unobstructed straight lines of sight are necessary for visual perception is not accomplished until later in the preschool years (Yaniv & Shatz, 1990; Flavell, Green, Herrera, & Flavell, 1991). By then, children have also realized that people (with normal hearing) in the same room hear the same things.

In the den with Alice, Ricky was sitting on my exercise bike, playing with the timer.

R: I think this (the timer) is still on.
M: I don't know, I can't hear it.
R: (R turns the timer until it starts to tick.) Now you can.
M: How do you know that Ricky?

Ricky, unable or unwilling to try to explain his inference, made no reply. Still, these examples all show that he was aware of others' perceptual capacities, generally recognizing when he shared their percepts and when others' perspectives were different from his.

## Thinking About the Self and Possible Selves

One kind of perspective-taking involves being able to consider oneself objectively and imagine oneself in situations other than the present. This ability seems central to many positive behaviors such as empathy and generosity. Also, being able to view oneself in different roles makes setting and achieving goals easier (Markus & Nurius, 1986). Children often talk about what they will be when they grow up, picking professions that seem exciting (fire fighter) or fun (baseball player). Usually, they are quite fickle about their choices, choosing whatever seems most appealing or salient at the time. Ricky, although he loved pretending at many occupations, especially fire-fighting, nonetheless, was consistent about how he saw his future. He was interested in all sports, undoubtedly because several family members enjoyed playing and watching sports on TV, but he talked about himself only becoming either a baseball player or a bike or car racer.

Ricky was watching a golf match on TV with his grandfather. As Jack Nicklaus sank a putt, Ricky, who had experienced the difficulty of swinging a club, said in admiration, "That guy turned into a golfer!"

G: When you get bigger, are you going to turn into a golfer?
R: No, when I get bigger, I'm gonna play baseball. I have a bat, but no more ball, so I use my eggs, and I hit my eggs. (R had plastic, baseball-sized ovals.)

Still another day, Ricky saw a man dressed in racing silks and asked about him. His grandfather explained he was a jockey who rode race horses.

R: I wish I can be an airplane driver.
G: What?

R: (Correcting himself to be consistent with other occasions.) I wish I can be a bike racer.

Ricky also spontaneously commented on his own behaviors regularly. On Richard's birthday, he sang the birthday song to him, and then sang "Happy Birthday to Ricky." When he finished, he said to me, "I sing 'Happy Birthday' to myself." Self-evaluations of his productions had been occurring for some time. Now he proudly demonstrated his new achievements. When his parents came to pick him up from an overnight visit, he excitedly showed them that he had discovered a new way to ride his tricycle—by putting one foot on the back platform and scooting it along with his other foot.

F: Wow!
R: You didn't see me did this before?
F: No, I never did.

He considered it very much his province to describe his own internal states, and he corrected others when they inaccurately attributed a state to him. I had napped while keeping Ricky company as he watched a videotape of Babar. As we walked back downstairs, I made a casual comment.

G: We almost fell asleep up there.
R: Who did?
G: Uh, me, I almost fell asleep.
R: Not I!

Possibly one reason why Ricky's transition to school was so smooth is that he was able to recognize his own individuality and that of others. Research with older children has revealed that there is a positive relation between the ability to take account of others' perspectives and the quality of one's social relationships with peers and the quality of social adjustment more generally (e.g., Chandler, 1973; Feffer & Sutchotliff, 1966). The same may be true of toddlers; indeed, whether young children show an interest and some ability in perspective-taking may be a good test of preschool readiness.

## The Language of the Emergent Preschooler

### *Acquiring a Language of Modality*

The realization that the contents of one's mind are not necessarily identical either to reality or to the minds of others has an important consequence for communication. Talk becomes the child's chief means of telling others what is in her mind. To do so, the child

The expert trike rider

must learn the particular devices her language has for expressing relations between the speaker's mind and reality. All languages have such devices, although the particular relations between mind and reality—as well as the kinds of devices used to encode them—differ across languages. The elements of a language that indicate these relations between mind and reality are called modal elements.

Utterances are typically made up of two segments: a proposition, such as JOHN COME, and a modal element that indicates the speaker's mental stance on that proposition. For example, a speaker may want to know whether John is able to come (CAN John come?) or may want to convey John's obligation to come (John MUST come) or his belief that John is likely to come (I THINK John is coming). Modal elements are crucial if speakers are to convey clearly their own ideas about propositions to their listeners.

In English, sentence modality is perhaps the most straightforward kind of modality. Speakers indicate whether they are seeking information, making an assertion, or making a demand by using question, declarative, or imperative sentence forms. Even very young children differentiate their utterances by intonation, if not by standard grammatical markings, into these three categories.[2] Modal verbs are common devices allowing for more sophisticated and varied expressions of speaker stance. These include the modal auxiliaries like *must, may, can, should,* and *ought,* as well as mental-state verbs such as *think, wish,* and *hope.* Adverbials such as *maybe, probably,* and *certainly* also are modal expressions.

In recent years, researchers with interests in either language development or the development of theory of mind have studied children's acquisition of these modal expressions. (See Shatz & Wilcox, 1991, for a review.) Not surprisingly, given the kinds of ideas they encode, children acquire such expressions slowly, with the first instances of modal terms occurring as early as age 2 or shortly before, and the understanding of them increasing throughout the elementary school years.

Ricky's use of modal expressions mushroomed in these months. I observed the first uses of *wish, hope,* and *must,* all used appropriately. For example, Ricky didn't like the whirring sound his tape recorder made, and as I turned mine on, he said, "I hope it not make noise-ee." He also continued to use *think* to mark relative certainty. He was home from preschool with a cold, and we had been talking about his being sick when he brought up his friend: "I think Jonathan is a little bit sick also, I think." Indeed, his first utterance tags were of this sort, using the word *think.*

Many of his uses of *think* now marked his belief about the truth of the propositional content of his utterance. In these cases, "I think" could be glossed as *I believe it's the case that* . . . , and "I don't think" as *I believe it's not the case that.* . . . I had been trying to convince him to use the bathroom before we started out for the airport. He justified his refusal by saying, "I think there are toilets at the airport." When he couldn't find something he was searching for, he had this interchange with his mother.

R: I don't think we have it anymore.
M: Oh, I think we still do.
R: (Perturbed) Then, where IS it?

He also began to use questions and tag questions with *think* to ask others about their opinions as well—for example, "They gonna race again, you'll think?" or "What you think?" Thus, before age 3, Ricky was using *think* to express a range of mental-state meanings as do adults, including describing mental actions (Chapter 9) and characterizing levels of certainty and states of belief.

In laboratory studies, preschoolers have shown that many of the subtler distinctions among terms expressing mental stance escape them, although they can interpret some mental-stance terms appropriately (e.g., Moore, Bryant, & Furrow, 1989; Wilcox, 1990/1991), and they can distinguish reality from dreams and imagined states (Wellman & Estes, 1986). When Ricky increasingly marked his utterances appropriately with modal expressions, he demonstrated that he was thinking about how his mental state related to reality. Other toddlers approaching age 3 are beginning to do so as well, at least in spontaneous conversations (Shatz, Wellman, & Silber, 1983).[3]

### Continuing to Practice Language

Ricky began to use the expression *not really*, and, as with many other newly learned modifiers, he inserted it wherever he could, even when it may not have been appropriate. As we returned to my house from a trip to the supermarket, Ricky brought up his grandfather, who was in California.

R: Maybe Grandpa be at home now.
G: Well, Grandpa won't be home now, but he'll be here in a few days. He's coming on Friday. Do you miss him?
R: Not really.

Maybe at that moment Ricky did not miss Richard, but he'd had no contact with him since a conversation of just a few weeks earlier when he had expressed very different sentiments. Ricky told me he had tried to phone Richard with no success.

G: Do you miss Grandpa?
R: I miss him a yot and a yot. [A lot and a lot.]
G: Well, I'm going to talk to Grandpa on the phone later. Why don't you give me a kiss for him, and I'll give it to him later? (R makes kissing noises.)

Ricky's expression "a yot and a yot" may have been the result of an incorrect inference about the expression "lots and lots" that I had used a few weeks earlier. During the same time Ricky had been focused on intensifying his modifying expressions, and duplication was a favorite device. He produced "It's real, real sharp," "Turn on this nice, nice light," and "Oh, that works very right!" all in one afternoon. A few weeks later, during this period, *not really* had replaced intensifiers as the expression to be practiced.

Language practice went beyond just using new expressions repeatedly. Ricky also practiced expressing particular semantic relations with different expressions. One day he walked around the bathroom, commenting on possession: "This is Grandpa's towel, this is your towel." Then, out spilled a whole string of pronouns, spoken in a soft sing-song voice to himself, "I, me, my, you, your, he, him, her, she, we, ours." Apparently, Ricky had organized the personal pronouns into a separate list—maybe even a class—of words. Like his list of opposites (see Chapter 4), the basis of the pronoun grouping seemed relatively abstract: It included not just possessive pronouns, which might have been elicited by his focus at that moment on the possession of towels, but other pronominal forms as well, indicating that he had a general category of words that could stand for names of animates in a variety of semantic circumstances and syntactic contexts.

### Comprehension and Production Monitoring

There are many anecdotes about the difficulty of getting toddlers to attend to corrections of their grammar. Children are also poor monitors of their understanding of what is said to them (Markman, 1981a). On occasion, I had tried to make corrections to Ricky's speech, only to see his eyes glaze over in boredom and his interests turn elsewhere. Most often, as in the deer example of Chapter 5, I didn't even try to give an explicit reason for why he and I differed in our speech. However, one day, he listened quietly as I corrected with an explanation his misuse of the objective pronoun *her* for the nominative *she*, an error I had observed in other young children. "You can say 'she', just like 'he.' 'She' and 'her' are like 'he' and 'him.'" A few hours later, Ricky said, "Her want me to come down," but then corrected himself, saying, "She want me to come down." Thereafter, *her* and *she* shared nominative roles for some time, suggesting that my explanation had some impact. Still, the fact that both forms coexisted for some time, even though *she* was the only form being reinforced by what Ricky heard, shows how slow to change children's language systems can sometimes be, even when the children do attend to corrections.

Ricky kept a close watch for opportunities to learn new words. When he saw an object for which he had no label—for example, a rubber-tipped gum massager—he would say, "I don't know what this is." He also asked for clarification when he couldn't identify a referent from another's speech. We had been playing hide-and-seek, and Richard and Ricky were searching for me. Richard and I habitually referred to the series of upstairs rooms in my house by the colors of the rugs, but Ricky didn't know that. Nonetheless, he picked the terminology up quickly.

Gf: Now I'll look in the green room.
R: (Whispering) Which room is that?

Later, after Richard had explained the naming system to him and it was their turn to hide, Ricky said, "Let's hide in the green room."

Ricky's monitoring of speech included assessing the veridicality of what was said to him, and he would question statements for which he didn't find corroborating evidence. I was in the kitchen, when he called to me from the living room, where he was playing with my mother. She gave him a reason why I couldn't join them just then.

B: Grandma is washing the dishes now.
R: I don't hear the water running.
B: Well, right now, she's putting something away in the refrigerator. Then she'll wash the dishes.

Previously Ricky had corrected others when they had said something he thought was wrong, or he had given them information he thought they lacked. This challenge to another's language had a different character. In questioning whether I was indeed washing the dishes, Ricky asked Bubby about the evidence for the truth of her claim. At least in this instance, he seemed to be following the Gricean principle that speakers have some obligation to say only what they believe to be true. Making that kind of demand on his interlocutor showed just how far Ricky had progressed in 19 months from the toddler who imitated words from others' prior utterances to the active participant who took his turn in a conversation.

## Strategies for Language Learning

Ricky's devices for learning language were varied. He showed more evidence of organizing his lexicon in fairly sophisticated, abstract ways (e.g., his pronoun list). He practiced new words (such as adverbial modifiers) and new constructions (such as tags) in multiple situations, often using them more profusely than was appropriate, and he practiced semantic relationships (like possession) with a variety of lexical items, often in contexts where there was no communicative value to his talk. Thus, much talk seemed to be for talk's sake, primarily to practice language. Other techniques seemed more directed at getting additional information about language, such as his asking questions about labels for things or asking "what" when he heard an unanticipated construction. Most of these devices had been part of Ricky's repertoire since the beginnings of overt language production. They were just used over time on different words, constructions, and relations. Thus, in part, language learning seems to be a recursive process, with many of the same strategies recruited repeatedly over time.

Other people were obviously crucial to Ricky's language learning, but it is very clear that they could not directly control its course. Although he heard massive amounts of well-formed language and he would occasionally take up explicit corrections (the "she" example), his errors would often persist even in the face of such input. Along with the evidence already presented for categorization, regularization, and generalization, his consistent errors are proof that he was actively working on organizing the data into a systematic whole. Only gradually would he be able to achieve a coherence that would adequately capture both the regularities and the idiosyncracies of the language he was learning.

### Notes

1. However, Wellman (1990) reports that the children who did best on the Bartsch and Wellman task were the older 3 year olds.

2. Of course, no system created by humans is ever quite so simple. There are indirect ways of expressing questions, assertions, and demands as well. (See, for example, Ervin-Tripp, 1977, and Searle, 1975.) Children have to learn these indirect means in addition to the direct grammatical forms (Shatz, 1978a).

3. Children who at age 3 use mental terms to refer to their mental states are likely to have mothers who used the terms relatively frequently to refer explicitly to mental states when the children were 2 year olds (Furrow, Moore, Davidge, & Chiasson, 1992).

# 12

## 35–36 Months
## Preschooler Paradoxes

### Changing Social Behaviors

Three year olds are typically more cooperative than 2 year olds. As they leave toddlerhood behind, children have learned something about the rights and limitations of a separate self, and they head out into the larger world of preschool enthusiastic for new experiences and new friendships. There are times when the newly confident preschooler sometimes shows an impatient, critical side that presages the teenager-to-be. At other times, the preschooler reveals how much he or she still has to learn about the complexities of the social world.

### Three Going on Thirteen

Ricky was generally an endearingly affectionate and warmly generous preschooler; still, there were occasions, during bouts of impatience or recalcitrance about adult demands, when he seemed more like 13 than 3. Like most children, Ricky was not especially good at cleaning up his toys, but at my house he was usually cooperative about being tidy. One day, however, when he had cut up scraps of paper that were scattered all over the floor, he argued with me in response to my request that he pick them up.

R: I'm not a garbage boy!
G: Well, I'm not a garbage Grandma!
R: Yes you are!
G: Oh, no! It's not my job to clean up YOUR mess.

A few months earlier, Ricky had begun to complete sentences for adults who sometimes groped for words or took too long to finish what they had started to say, but he had always done it good-naturedly. Now, a new response joined his repertoire. When his adult interlocutors talked down to him or got too long-winded, he would, with some impatience, say "Right," and try to move on to another topic. Once, when his grandfather began to give him a long explanation of something he thought he understood, he said, "Right, right, right," in a tone of bored resignation worthy of any teenager forced to listen to an adult lecture.

Like a teenager, he was also quick to correct or question adults' statements—although he was sometimes wrong as well. As I watched him complete a successful turn at a video game, I praised him.

G: Oh, good! You set off the firecrackers.
R: (To me) No. (To himself) What are they called?
   Oh. (To me) Fireworkers.
G: FireWORKS. Firecrackers are a kind of fireworks.

One day, he saw an ad on TV showing a fantastic dragon lolling on a raft in a swimming pool. At first, he was impressed with the picture, but then called it into question.

R: I didn't know creatures went on floats in pools.
   I don't think creatures swim in pools.

Ricky's added knowledge of and attention to the emotions and mental states of others made for increasingly sophisticated teasing and subtler attempts to manipulate others for his own ends. One day, when he was pretending to be a monster, he teased me with a threat to make Richard feel bad.

R: I'm going to eat you all up!
   And I'll tell Grandpa you died.
G: You will! And will he be happy or sad?
R: Sad.

Ricky was an avid eater of chocolate ice cream. One day, when he had already had his allotment of ice cream and knew he would not get any more with a direct request, he tried a new tactic on his mother, who had not yet had her treat.

M: I'm going downstairs to have ice cream.
R: Can we share?
  You take a lick and I'll take a lick, and that's how we can share.

One fine summer evening, Richard, Ricky, and I had gone to a park for some exercise. When we got into the car to return to my house, Ricky must have been struck by a desire for a stop at the ice cream shop. However, he had become too circumspect to ask for it directly, although he did back down quickly when his ruse was called into question.

R: My mommy gives me chocolate ice cream every day.
G: (Disbelieving) Every day?
  I don't believe she gives it to you EVERY DAY.
R: Sometimes she does and sometimes she doesn't.
G: Well, I guess you can have some today.

Despite his circumspect request, Ricky had no reservations about directly expressing his gratitude at having his desire fulfilled or about making a bit of a joke about his earlier indirectness. Back at the house, we dished out the goodies Richard had stopped to buy on the way home.

R: (Handing Gf a dish.) This one yours?
Gf: Thanks.
R: Thanks for buying it for me.
Gf: What?
R: Thanks. [overlap]
Gf: [overlap] Is that good?
G: Thanks for what? Buying it for you?
  Is that what you were saying to Grandpa?
  (R nods.)
Gf: Oh, well, you're welcome, sweetheart.
  I get so pleased when I see that you're having what you—what you like.
  You really like that, don't you?
R: Every day.
Gf: How many times a day?
  (R holds up two fingers.)

Generally, Ricky's social behaviors were taking on a more mature cast. He had always been eager to share his possessions with his beloved family members, but now his generosity was couched in more adult language. I had commented as I was saying goodbye to him after a visit to my house that he had a lot of miniature cars to play with on the way home.

R: You want to borrow one?
G: Okay.
R: Here they are. Take whatever you want.

He had been something of a problem solver earlier; now he offered plans of action whenever the adults were slow to decide on possible activities. We were dithering about how to arrange the timing of an evening of swimming and dinner, when Ricky offered the following plan, "We can go swimming; when the pizza comes, we are getting out of the pool, and eating our pizza!"

Ricky's interests in play activities were maturing too. His devotion to video games grew although he knew his mother largely disapproved of them. As she was telling me that she prohibited some of the games Ricky's father had bought because they were too wild and violent for Ricky, he located one such tape on the table and brought it to me, saying, "This is MUCH wild." He then demonstrated his skill with an allowed tape. "I went through the whole pattern," he excitedly announced when he had completed a section. Later, when he was disappointed that he hadn't gotten farther in a sequence, he lamented, "I thought I was going up the stairs!"

## Forays into a Rule-Governed Social World

It was easier for Ricky to play tirelessly against the screen in a video game than to engage for very long in games with adults that had rules or required much athletic skill. Although he would badger adults to play with him, he would quickly forsake even simplified rule-governed games of croquet or baseball for the less structured enjoyment of swinging bats or mallets at balls. He stubbornly insisted one day on trying out tennis racquets that he saw in the trunk of my car, despite Richard's warning that tennis was a very hard game. When he realized the difficulty of hitting the ball over the net with a full-sized racquet, he grew bad-tempered and gave up. I suggested that a child-sized racquet would be easier. A few days later, he told me he had tried a more appropriate size, "I tried it out and it was very great!"

Just as in sports, Ricky's interest in the world of social relations often exceeded his competence. Despite his sophisticated phrases, his talk revealed his naiveté about adult social relations. Richard and I had been visiting at Ricky's house on the Fourth of July. Ricky and his parents were going to go to a fireworks display, but Richard demurred. I tried to explain to Ricky that Richard was tired and we would not join him, but he was adamant about my participation, saying, "I want to go with you." With my allegiance split, I suggested to Richard that he stay at home while I go on to the show. Overhearing the conversation, Ricky apparently thought I had to have Richard's permission, because he said, "Can you come by yourself?"

Months later, while he and his 27-year-old visiting uncle watched cartoons together, he again displayed his naiveté about the nature of others' social relations.

U: I like watching Mario Brothers' cartoons.
R: (Incredulously) Your mother lets you?

Ricky clearly knew what permissions were, but he did not understand much about authority relations among adult family members, and he just drew analogies from his own situation. Possibly, 3 year olds with older siblings or a larger family unit would be more sophisticated about who has authority over whom in families.

More likely, coming to understand a culture's authority relations requires considerable effort from any preschooler. Going to school introduces children to a whole new set of rules and expectations. Ricky discovered that the appropriate application of those rules was not always obvious. A few weeks after he had started school, Alice had come to pick him up, but they made a trip to the bathroom together before leaving the school. When she went to turn on the hot water faucet, Ricky became visibly upset, telling her that only the teachers were allowed to do that. Apparently, to prevent the children from being burned, the teachers had cautioned the children that only the teachers could turn on the hot water. A teacher finally had to assure Ricky that his mother was "like a teacher" in order to calm him down.

Ricky's attempt to apply social rules to everyone is reminiscent of his attempts to overregularize language. In both the social and the linguistic domain, he seemed to see that there were some general rules, but he tried to make them apply without exception to all cases. Exceptionless rules can be learned and used with less mental effort than rules with exceptions. They offer predictability and control over the world with a minimum of effort. Little wonder toddlers favor them.

The 3 year old's social behavior is paradoxical in that it can be both sophisticated and naive. Young preschoolers are capable of second-order thinking; they can be indirect and subtle. They are increasingly aware that various kinds of rules and regulations govern social relations between people. Yet they are ignorant of many of the criteria that define status relations between people, and they have yet to learn which social rules vary with the context. As the preschooler's world expands beyond the home, these are undoubtedly some of the things learned in the early school years.

## Complex Language Skills

### *Growing Preliteracy Skills*

By age 3, Ricky could recognize most letters and was learning to write them. He could write the letter R, and, on his birthday, he showed me he could write his name. His first foray into writing had been the word *HI*, which was relatively easy since it required no curves. He loved playing with a small chalkboard I had, and one day he wrote both *HI* and *IH*, and then read both correctly to me, indicating he understood that the sequencing of the letters mattered. He would sometimes point to particular words in books or magazines and ask, "What does that word mean?" He knew that words beginning with the same letter started with the same sound, but he was not especially accurate at matching sounds and letters or identifying the first letters of words from their sounds. It would be some time before he had the knowledge of sound-letter correspondences that presages fluent reading, although he was increasingly aware of the sounds of words. He told me the name of a videotape he had watched, "Horton hears a who," and then said under his breath, "That's a hard thing to say."

The first few days in school initiated a new game at home: playing school. Ricky got anyone he could to be the students while he played the teacher, although he would graciously offer to switch roles after a time. "Real" school was a lively, informal place with virtually no lessons; "pretend" school, however, almost always involved writing lessons, and a rather formal atmosphere of instruction. It was difficult to see where Ricky's fantasies about school were coming from or how his actual experiences in school were influencing his play. Possibly, his focus on the more formal aspects of schooling were consequences of his interest in literacy and his newfound attention to rule-governed social behaviors. After a year of being assured he would learn to read and write in school, he may even have been a little disappointed that it was not happening overnight.

## Sophistication and Naiveté in Language

Like his social behavior, Ricky's language skills were paradoxical. Both his lexicon and sentence structure were remarkably sophisticated. Yet there were very common aspects of grammar, like question forms, that had eluded him up to now.

Ricky used words like *slice, someone, waterfall, pattern, heal,* and *always* correctly, and one day he impressed the whole family with his vocabulary when he commented, as we sat down for dinner at the porch table laden with freshly grilled food, "There's a lot of food on the table for this feast." He produced many kinds of complex sentences, including ones with subordinate clauses and all sorts of complementizers and conjunctions. (See Table 12.1 for examples.)

Ricky now had a large set of modal auxiliaries, including *can, could, must, may, would,* and *will.* Children have typically been reported to use modals first in their deontic, or social regulation, senses (e.g., for permission) and only later in their epistemic senses (having to do with beliefs, attitudes, and knowledge states). (See Shatz & Wilcox, 1991, for a review.) Several possible reasons have been proposed for this. Children may not understand enough about the difference between certainty and probability or they may not monitor their mental states well enough to mark certainty. Alternatively, children may use other means to mark the degree of certainty, such as words like *maybe* and *think.* They may prefer to keep the modals for deontic uses only, which apparently would be in keeping with what they hear. Although more research is required, preliminary findings show that mothers tend to use pri-

---

*Table 12.1*  Examples of Ricky's Complex Sentences at 36 Months

---

I tried it out and it was very great!
This is a picture of when I was running through the water with Mommy.
Where you are going when I go to the fireworks with Mommy and Daddy?
I didn't know creatures went on floats in pools.
I don't think creatures swim in pools.
I thought it was just a little, little slice. (Talking about the full moon.)
I think he wants some.
We can always pretend we have another one.
And the teacher put it up on the counter so no one could reach it. (Toy racer he'd taken to school.)
I really want to keep it (a basketball) while we're at the park.
You need to get your own ball if you want to play "hit the tree."
When I grow up and I'm a baseball player, I'll have my baseball hat, and I'll put it on, and I'll play baseball.

---

marily deontic modals in talk directed to their toddlers (Shatz & Wilcox, 1991).

In Ricky's case, however, I observed him use one modal auxiliary, *may*, in its epistemic sense before I heard it with a deontic sense. Two months before, Ricky had been playing in my lab with a toy that was similar to one he had at home.

R: Is this mine?
G: No. That one's not yours.
   I think you have another one at home, don't you?
R: (Persistently) It MAY be mine.
G: I don't think you brought any of your little people here.

Ricky's use of *may* to express possibility shows that at least some children learning English can use modal auxiliaries in their epistemic senses by late in their third year. Of course, Ricky had been using other terms like *think, know, probably,* and *maybe* to describe his beliefs about possibility and degrees of certainty for some time, showing that he had the cognitive understanding necessary for the epistemic senses. Since both his mother and I used *may* in the epistemic sense on occasion, Ricky also had examples of it in his environment. Confirming that epistemic expressions are not beyond the cognitive capacities of toddlers, Choi (1991) found that Korean 2 year olds use epistemic markers that are required by the language before they express some deontic distinctions. Therefore, the frequency of the expressions in the language the children hear may be a major factor determining when epistemics appear in their speech.

Within two months after turning 3, Ricky began to combine his knowledge of modals and complex sentences to produce many examples of another construction long thought beyond the ken of young children—hypotheticals. In the space of a short afternoon visit, I heard, "If I had a ladder, I would climb up it and change that light bulb"; "If I had a fishing pole, I would go fishing and catch a fish"; and "If I was in a spaceship, I would fly right up to them" ("them" being fireworks). Clearly, Ricky's hypothetical worlds knew few bounds. Kuczaj and Daly (1979) have reported on other children's hypothetical constructions about the age of 3 years. Preschoolers' ability to create such sentences suggests that they have more capacity to engage in hypothetical thinking than previously believed.

Despite this conceptual sophistication, the common practice of asking questions by inverting auxiliary verbs and subjects (e.g., *Can you open this? Where are you going?*) had eluded Ricky. Just before his third birthday, Ricky was still asking uninverted questions. For example, when he thought we would not accompany him to the Fourth of July fireworks, he asked, "Where you are going when I go to the fireworks with Mommy and Daddy?" Ricky certainly had not lacked for information on conventional question forms. By this time, he must have heard thousands of examples of inverted questions from his interlocutors. Moreover, he had never exhibited any difficulty recognizing inversions as questions or responding to them as such. Indeed, it is very likely that he had noticed the inverted position of the auxiliaries in others' questions. Still, noninverted forms persisted in his own questions.

It is possible Ricky thought that both the inverted and the noninverted forms were allowable. One question that has plagued language acquisition theorists is how children manage to recover from such conclusions once they draw them (Bowerman, 1983). Apparently, adults give little direct feedback to children when they use ungrammatical constructions like uninverted questions. Possibly, they rarely overtly correct their young children's grammar because they are so often ignored when they attempt to do so. As a more indirect method of recovering from incorrect inferences, children may search the speech they hear for examples of alternate constructions they think are allowable. If they always hear one alternative but not the other, they will eventually drop the unheard type in favor of the exemplified one (Pinker, 1984). Unfortunately, this suggestion does not account for why Ricky persisted in his uninverted usage despite an overwhelming number of examples favoring the other alternative.

Nonetheless, one incident suggests that Ricky was sensitive to the information about inversion and noninversion that was in the language addressed to him. One day, when I used a noninverted verb in a "what" exclamation, Ricky immediately asked, "What?" as he often did when he did not understand a word or phrase addressed to him. He had been licking his lips with his tongue when I made my exclamation.

G: What a long tongue you have!
R: What?
G: What a long tongue you have!
R: What?
G: (Slowly) What a long tongue you have!
R: Say it again.

At this point, I realized it was not the words but the exclamatory construction I had used that was giving Ricky trouble. Utterances beginning with *what* were questions for Ricky, but this *what* utterance was difficult to interpret as a question on several grounds. One was that he had not heard me use the uninverted form before to ask a question, another was that the meaning of the question seemed anomalous, and, moreover, the intonation was different from a question. I tried to explain to Ricky what the intention behind my utterance had been by rephrasing it.

G: I'm exclaiming that your tongue is very long.
   I'm saying, "My, you have a long tongue!"
   Did you think I was asking you a question?
R: Yes. (R nods his head.)
G: Oh, then I would have said, "Do you have a long tongue?"

Just a few days after this, I heard Ricky produce a flurry of inverted auxiliaries in questions: "Can I go down there," "Can we share," and "May I see?"

My little grammar lesson was very likely not solely responsible for Ricky's finally capitulating to grammatical convention, but it may have helped. I had given him a way of interpreting my noninverted what-sentence so that it would not have to be interpreted as an anomalous question. But, in so doing, I had created another problem for him. Utterances of his like "What you are doing?" would now be potentially ambiguous—they could be questions or exclamations. Since there is some evidence that young children try to avoid having one form express two meanings (Karmiloff-Smith, 1979), there was now a reason to invert verbs when questions were intended—the results would be unambiguous.[1] Ricky may have inferred that the inverted forms were therefore preferable, if not required, ways for him to ask questions. In any case, inversions quickly became the more frequent form in his speech.

Considering further why Ricky resisted auxiliary inversion for so long, despite its frequency in the speech he heard, offers some insight into the language acquisition process. Possibly Ricky's frequent use of noninverted forms provided the necessary feedback to maintain the error. Children do hear what they themselves say, after all, and some research confirms that children's own errors can be self-perpetuating (Platt & MacWhinney, 1983).

Why some errors are self-perpetuating and hard to correct whereas others are not is a question researchers need to answer. Possibly, errors become established when alternatives to them do not readily fit with the way the child is thinking about her language. Such a possibility seems reasonable in the case of auxiliary inversion. Inversion in English is based on rather abstract structural principles and requires on occasion the inclusion of the "dummy" element *do*, which carries no meaning of its own. Ricky's creation of grammatical categories suggests some ability to deal with language abstractly, but he was also especially attentive to words and their meanings, and he tried to make the language he was learning simpler and more regular than it is. Dealing with a "dummy" element as well as all the irregularities of the auxiliary system apparently was hard for him. Recent research suggests that children differ in the ways they approach the language-learning task, with some using an analytical approach more often than others (Bretherton, McNew, Snyder, & Bates, 1983; Richards, 1990). Another child who thought somewhat less about meanings of linguistic forms and who patterned her language more readily on examples she heard might have had an easier time adapting to the more conventional question form.

Perhaps the best examples of Ricky's paradoxical blend of sophistication and naiveté come from his attempts to use and understand expressions of time. Such expressions would occupy him for months to come, as he struggled to use in conversation a set of terms tied to a dimension of reality that he could not calibrate. Ricky may have known what dimension time words referred to, but he did not know how to measure time. Thus, he developed a lexicon of time words, much as he did for color terms, which he used in a top-down fashion. He answered time questions with time words, but his answers were only categorically appropriate, not correct. For example, his mother was making him an egg for breakfast and wanted to know whether he wanted it soft or hard boiled.

M: How long should I cook this egg?
R: Ten months.

At least the meanings of time words were easier to ask about directly than were the meanings of color words. I had told Ricky I would love him forever. He asked, "Forever is a long, long time? Like when you don't want to go to sleep?"

## Why the Paradoxes?

Several times in previous chapters, the notion of inconsistency in children's behavior has come up. It is frequently the case that new toddler skills appear in one instance only to be missing in the next. Such inconsistencies may be a phenomenon of skill acquisition throughout development. Often their occurrence can be attributed to the contexts in which the new skill is required. In familiar or simple circumstances that require little else of the child, a new skill can be expressed. In more demanding contexts, children's energies and resources are stretched farther; they find it harder to demonstrate new skills and may fall back on more immature modes of behavior. (See Shatz, 1978b, 1983a, for discussions of this phenomenon with regard to communication tasks.) Because so many things are new to toddlers, more contexts are going to be demanding for them; hence, they are more susceptible to inconsistent behavior than older children. With practice, new skills become increasingly easy to access and execute, and gradually fewer contexts generate "overloads" on the child's cognitive processing resources.

The preschooler paradoxes described here are based on a different sort of developmental phenomenon. Children between 3 and 5 have learned a great deal and can be sophisticated about many things; but their sophistication, while real, may be "local," limited to particular spheres of knowledge. Unlike the problem of consistency, which seems more a matter of limitations in short-term processing capacity—the child at that moment in that context simply does not have the resources to perform the new skill—paradoxical behaviors seem to be a consequence of lack of knowledge.

In the language domain, producing hypothetical sentences seems sophisticated, producing uninverted question forms seems unsophisticated. Although there is no logical reason why a child at age 3 should control both the grammatical constructions appropriate to hypotheticals and to questions, it seems somewhat surprising that Ricky did not. When we see some mature behaviors in a domain like language, we expect to see them throughout the domain. Yet we are gradually discovering from research into the preschool period that paradoxes of the sort seen in Ricky are not unusual. For example, based on casual observation of preschoolers, Noam Chomsky argued that, by age 4, children had essentially acquired adult-like competence with grammar. However, careful experimentation and observation have revealed numerous instances where full grammatical understanding is acquired only long after age 4 (e.g., C. Chomsky, 1969; Karmiloff-Smith, 1986). Some seemingly sophisticated skills can precede others that on the surface may seem no more complex, or even simpler, but that in reality require deeper analysis or revision of earlier, simpler organizations as the child, with increasing experience and knowledge, discovers that the prior organization can no longer account for new understandings (Bowerman, 1982).

There are undoubtedly similar phenomena in the social and cognitive domains. Ricky seemed attuned to social rules and authority relations, but he defined them in terms of his limited experience. Surely his knowledge would be expanded and reorganized as he gained more experience with others in a variety of social roles. An example of change in the social domain is the finding that, although preschoolers have some general notions of how they and others behave across time, they don't organize these into dispositional notions of people until several years later (Eder, 1989). In the perspective-taking domain, too, 3 year olds can take account of others' mental states in many circumstances, making them seem quite sophisticated. Yet they have trouble predicting, in the face of reality, others' incorrect actions based on false beliefs. (Some of them may have less trouble using false belief, as Ricky did, as a post-hoc explanation for others' incorrect actions; see Bartsch & Wellman, 1989, and Moses & Flavell, 1990, for differing views on 3 year olds' competence.) The paradox of coexisting sophistication and naiveté is not limited, then, to the language domain.

Why is what can be described as "local" learning noteworthy? There are two reasons. First, as adults, we expect a certain level of performance from each other in all spheres. We expect, for example, that people who look like adults will also behave like them. There is no logical connection between relatively large size and mature behavior, but the probability of co-occurrence is high; our expectations are based on that. Indeed, our expectations are so deep-seated that children who are big for their age often are subject to age-inappropriate demands even from those who know their age. Unsurprisingly (but unreasonably), when we see relatively high levels of sophistication in some areas, we expect to see them in others.

The second reason has to do with phenomena that *are* logically related. Much research in cognition and language is based on the belief that knowledge can be described in terms of general structures (e.g., Piaget, 1970). If people have such structures, they should be able to solve a broad array of problems so long as the problems are structurally alike. For example, as noted in Chapter 5, Leslie (1987) has proposed that children who pretend can also be expected to have the capacity to understand false belief because the phenomena seem logically the same. However, the idea that there are structural bases to knowledge that organize all the information in a single domain, or even across several domains, has been called into question. Recent findings suggest that even adults are far less able spontaneously to apply their knowledge across all structurally similar circumstances than had previously been assumed. For example, adults are not especially good at generating analogies that would allow them to apply the solution from a problem in one content area to another structurally similar problem with a different content (Gick & Holyoak, 1980). If cognitive scientists are to maintain the claim that abstract structures generally characterize human knowledge, we will have to explain why knowledge so often seems to be acquired locally and applied variably.

In sum, there are several reasons why children can appear sometimes sophisticated and sometimes naive. For one, their knowledge may not be put to use when a task is just too demanding for them. For another, it may be that their knowledge is still incomplete and requires further elaboration and reorganization as a function of experience. Finally, they may be just like adults, sometimes unable to see readily that structurally similar problems have common solutions.

## Note

1. Note, however, that children do not always avoid one-form-to-multiple-meaning mappings. Ricky used *may*, for example, in two senses, to mean *be allowed to* and *is possible that*.

# 13

# *The Path from Infancy to Childhood*

## How Persons Develop

We experience ourselves as having inner lives, with emotions, desires, thoughts, and beliefs about which we can reflect. Moreover, we feel that others do not have direct access to these inner selves; for them to know about us, they can at best make inferences on the basis of our overt behavior, or we must convey in language what they cannot observe. One of the greatest puzzles about the human condition concerns these inner experiences; for centuries philosophers, and, more recently, social scientists, have speculated about them. Are they a consequence of our language and social systems or a precondition of them? Do we indeed have direct understanding of our own inner experiences, or do we acquire an understanding of self only as a function of others' views of us? Is our folk psychology merely epiphenomenal in that we may not need it to describe how the brain "causes" behavior?

Such questions go beyond the scope of this study; yet the description of how a human becomes a person is relevant to them. This book began with the claim that the period in a human's life from roughly 15 to 36 months of age is crucial for becoming a person—that is, for developing a self that has the means to understand and be understood by others in common terms. When I introduced Ricky, he had a fragile sense of himself as a distinct individual, and he was a one-word speaker dependent on verbal imitation and repetition to maintain engagement with others. When we left him, he was a rather adept social being, one who could express his own thoughts, justify his behavior, make inferences about others, and attempt to influence them in subtle, indirect ways. As Ricky traversed toddlerhood, he acquired the language of his community and learned to use it to carry out such social activity. By the age of 3, he shared with others a dominion of rationality that provided common assumptions about the ways (in both language and action) people behave and how those behaviors can be explained reasonably.

Participating in a dominion of rationality is what makes a person. It is what validates and makes our inner lives comprehensible even to ourselves. Probably we could experience ourselves in the total absence of a community of others, but the experience would surely be more chaotic and less interpretable. For some, the inculcation of the infant into a linguistic culture may be imprisonment, a loss of freedom; instead, I see it as a flowering, the emergence of a coherence that otherwise would have no hope of fully realizing itself.

It is in this sense, then, that the changes we observed in Ricky during toddlerhood are a crucial part of human development. What accounts for the changes? Are Ricky's accomplishments mainly a consequence of acquiring his community's language, or did his conceptual capacities lead the way? How important was the environment to his development, and how important were characteristics internal to him? Should the toddler years be defined as a stage of human development somehow discontinuous with the periods prior to and following it? Or have we opened a window onto a larger, essentially continuous process of growth over time from birth through childhood?

Questions like these—about language and cognition, nature and environment, continuity and discontinuity—have been among the foundational questions of the field of developmental psychology. No study answers them definitively. Indeed, any simple answers would almost surely be wrong, because the forms of the questions are wrong: Forcing developmental questions into the terminology of dichotomies ignores the complexities of the factors affecting development (Shatz, 1983b). How, then, should questions about development be reformulated?

As I said in the introduction, a case study can best be used, not as a proof of a theory, but as a basis for generating ideas about the nature of an adequate theory of development. In this sense, Ricky's story is valuable for a variety of reasons. It reminds us that development occurs in context, as the living organism tries to cope with the opportunities and challenges provided by its environment. For example, Ricky's development of self-awareness was facilitated by experiences, both with other humans and with animals, that allowed for processes of comparison. In addition, Ricky's story shows us that, although different sorts of knowledge may have different structural properties, there is an individual acquiring those kinds of knowledge, using whatever processes and capacities are available and bootstrapping one kind of knowledge with another. Language, however primitive, is a prime example of how one sort of knowledge helps in the acquisition of other kinds. Also, the account of Ricky's progress over time encourages an appreciation of the continuity of development. However, this is not because careful observation in the early months revealed the same competencies as in the later ones, but because it revealed an ongoing process of organizing and integrating pieces of knowledge into increasingly complex knowledge systems. Ricky's ongoing efforts to expand and organize his lexicon are an example of this. Questions about development, then, must be reformulated to consider how change occurs in context, how acquiring some skills facilitates the acquisition of others, and how change is promoted and extended over time.

In the next three sections, I address several issues that have hovered in the background throughout the book. The first harks back to the question posed in the Preface by my sister's bird, Wafoo: What is it that makes human children different from other animals? The second elaborates on the role the environment plays in development, and the third concerns the relation of the toddler years to the age periods bracketing them.

## The Potential to Be a Person

In Chapter 1, I argued that only humans have the potential to become persons. That potential inheres in several capacities. I list three here that are important for distinguishing human potential from that of other animals, and then I argue that these capacities are crucial for the kind of learning that toddlers do.

Obviously, one important capacity that humans do not, as far as we know, share with any other species is the ability to acquire a complex language (either spoken or manual), replete with a grammar. Recent work with other primate species has revealed more sophisticated communicative behavior than was previously granted them, but, nonetheless, the ability systematically to relate abstract symbols to other symbols, which characterizes human languages, has not yet been demonstrated in other animals.

Ricky was fairly typical of human children in his development of language, including grammar. Although language acquisition seemed to be a more demanding task than some linguistic theorists would have us believe, his efforts at it were largely self-directed, utilizing vast amounts of experience but needing little of the overt training that other animals require for much less language learning. For example, with no special encouragement, Ricky created abstract grammatical categories of pronouns and adverbial modifiers on the basis of what he heard. Sometimes, for long periods of time, he would ignore aspects of grammar (like auxiliaries) he did not understand, or he would choose to modify what he heard to make it more consistent (as in his overregularization of plurals). Taken together, these sorts of spontaneous, constructive behaviors suggest that Ricky's process of acquiring linguistic knowledge cannot be characterized as strictly dependent either on maturation or environmental influence; rather, he abstracted, categorized, and systematized data from his experiences to create a coherence that he continued to test against input and to refine. Ricky was producing "local" pockets of organization in his grammar, even as he learned it. Early on, he did not have a complete picture of the language he was acquiring, but as much as he understood, he tried to make consistent. Early organizations, as of plurals, had to give way eventually to later ones that could incorporate conflicting data and, perhaps, increasing tolerance for the irregularities in language.

Another capacity that may be particular to humans is self-reflection. Although chimpanzees can recognize themselves in mirrors (Gallup, 1970), suggesting that there is some capacity for self-awareness among nonhuman primates, mirror recognition is surely not the best indicator of an essential kind of self-knowledge. More important is the ability to reflect spontaneously on one's own behavior, evaluate it, and modify it. I know of no evidence that other animals either evaluate their own behaviors relative to others or spontaneously self-correct in the absence of feedback or external reinforcement. In contrast, Ricky, like other toddlers, did both. He showed by spontaneous self-repairs that he at least occasionally monitored and corrected his own language, and he made evaluative comments about other skills like drawing.

A third capacity that is hard to demonstrate in other animals is the ability to think about internal or mental states, especially the belief states of others. There is some evidence that animals can dissemble; for example, a chimpanzee can intentionally misrepresent reality to a disliked trainer (Premack & Woodruff, 1978; also see Mitchell & Thompson, 1986). However, one can question whether this behavior should count as "lying" and entail an understanding of mind on the part of the perpetrator (Premack, 1988). As noted in Chapter 5, one need not grant animals an understanding of belief to explain their seemingly sophisticated behavior. Instead, animals may simply have the capacity for planful action based on knowledge of complex behavioral contingencies built up from simpler contingencies such as "if x happens, then y happens." The dog that barks at the door when he wants to sit in the chair that his master is occupying may not have the idea to fool his master into thinking he wants to go out. He only has to have the idea that barking at the door results in his master coming to open it. Since his master cannot be in two places at once, the chair will be free and he can then jump into it (Dennett, 1978).

The evidence that Ricky has an understanding of mind is based on more than this sort of dissembling behavior and, overall, is more difficult to dismiss with an account based on observable response contingencies. His regular references to his own internal states, as when he said he was "relaxing" or "thinking," as well as his attributions of internal states to others, suggest that he considered internal states to be central to explanations of behavior. As reported in Chapter 11, his spontaneous attribution to me of a false belief about his pajamas ("You thought these were wet") is especially compelling evidence for a fairly sophisticated understanding of mind. Still, even a human child had to be closely observed up to age 3 to provide enough converging evidence across different situations to grant him this much understanding.

Why are these three capacities so crucial? I argued that the toddler acquires in language a powerful tool for learning. By coupling language with the self-reflectiveness and the attention to internal states that have begun to manifest themselves, the toddler can learn in new ways about new things. She can get from others information not based on immediate experience, and she can compare her own experience of feelings and thoughts with the statements of others about theirs. Thus, the world becomes many-faceted, beyond immediate experience and limited perspectives.

## Environmental Supports for the Developing Person

The role of others in realizing the potential to be a person is essential. At the very least, a child needs others to provide data on language and for self-other comparisons. Even more, recent studies have revealed a positive relation between the frequencies of mental terms in maternal speech and in later child speech (Furrow, et al., 1992), as well as an association between mother-child talk about feelings and causality and later performance by 40-month-olds on false-belief explanation tasks (Dunn, Brown, Slomkowski, Tesla, & Youngblade, 1991).

Still, the child very much controls the developmental progress toward becoming a person. Ricky often ignored information made available to him on others' initiation. In contrast, he regularly sought information from others by questioning, and often took up their answers, trying to incorporate them into his understanding of things. An environment responsive to his information-seeking and supporting his attempts at learning and practice very likely encouraged him to continue his efforts and may even have influenced the speed with which he acquired knowledge; yet even an environment essential to the process does not necessarily control it. The content of what Ricky learned was determined by those around him; how he learned it was determined by the capacities he brought to the learning situation. Those capacities are gradually realized in a sociocultural environment; they have undoubtedly evolved with it and cannot emerge without it. Similarly, the most supportive of social environments will not result in birds, or even chimpanzees, behaving like persons, although they may occasionally give good approximations.

There is some similarity between my view of the role of the environment and the one put forth by Rogoff (1990, 1993). For both of us, development cannot be explained without reference to the embeddedness of the child in a sociocultural context. Moreover, we agree that the child is an active participant in the process of becoming a mature member of a society. Rogoff's notions of apprenticeships in thinking and guided participation aptly characterize many of the examples from Ricky's interactions with family members— for example, the way (described in Chapter 6) he recruited his mother to provide the content, but not the actual response, in his conversations with others.

Where we disagree, I think, is in the characterization of the mind. Rogoff (1993) argues that the mind itself is a social construction, a social object located not in the individual but in interactional space. For me, the mind is an internal entity, admittedly dependent for its full realization on external influences but nonetheless separably identifiable from them. In my view, the individual mind emerges from the interplay between external forces and internal states, resulting in the recognition that one's self is alike and yet different from other persons. It is this that makes human individuals unique, and both self-awareness and perspective-taking so essential to the mature social behavior of persons.

## Situating Toddlerhood in the Course of Development

How to relate the toddler years to the broader course of development is the third issue deserving more comment. I have argued that the toddler years are a crucial period for the development of personhood, when the potentials for language, self-reflection, and an understanding of mind flower. Despite my focus on this period, I do not advocate a sharp discontinuity between the toddler years and the years surrounding them. On the contrary, the detailed longitudinal approach taken here reveals the many small achievements that contribute to ongoing change over time, and suggests that, overall, development is relatively seamless. Indeed, one of the main characteristics of early childhood is the variable occurrence of more advanced behaviors. For example, across a spectrum of domains, from plural usage to visual perspective-taking, Ricky's behavior vacillated for long periods between immature and sophisticated.

Instances of variable performance so frequently observed in early childhood are by and large embarrassing to theorists favoring either structural developmental or nativist theories of cognition that predict more consistent performance. Piaget, arguing for a general, logical structure that underlies all cognitive skills at a given age, proposed "horizontal decalage" as a way to account for the fact that children performed variably in tasks with different content but the same putative underlying structure.[1] In essence, he argued that differential levels of experience or familiarity with content areas affected the likelihood that the structural capacity would be displayed. Nativists have taken a different but related tack, proposing that "performance" constraints (e.g., memory or computational limitations) in complex situations block the display of underlying structural "competence" (e.g., Fodor, 1992).

These approaches to variability are problematic. One difficulty is that variability in behavior is not limited to occurrences across content areas or levels of complexity. Sometimes child behaviors fluctuate even within a content area or at the same level of complexity (as Ricky's plural and pronominal expressions did). Structuralist solutions do not explain such cases well. Another problem is that strategies or heuristics that are proposed as aspects of performance rather than competence often seem ad hoc, and require an explanation in their own right, which is rarely forthcoming. It is undoubtedly true that situational factors can affect the display of competence; I have used that sort of argument myself to explain variable communicative performance in both children and adults (Shatz, 1978b). Yet, the frequency of variable behavior and the range of content areas in which it occurs during toddlerhood suggest that it is more a central datum of development than a bothersome consequence of circumstance. As such, it deserves a more satisfying theoretical account. My proposal is that children are continually organizing and reorganizing their knowledge, as they acquire more of it and discover new interconnections among spheres of knowledge. New organizations do not instantly replace old; instead, children try them out, adjust and readjust, as they gain feedback from the environment and examine their systems for coherence. Only gradually is consistency achieved.[2]

Nonetheless, children at various ages are different from one another; on the whole, 3 year olds do not think like 1 year olds. Hence, it is reasonable to characterize older children as being at different stages from younger children so long as we recognize that the characterizations of such stages depend on the gradual accrual, organization, and integration of competencies across a broad spectrum of domains of knowledge and contexts of use. Even language, which I have argued provides an immensely powerful tool for acquiring knowledge across a variety of knowledge domains, is acquired over a period of years and exerts its influence on other domains gradually.

## *Before Toddlerhood*

Throughout the book, I have noted that learning about language, about self, and about others has its roots in infancy. Certainly, infants demonstrate the capacities to engage socially and to remember, differentiate, and organize their experiences of events and entities in their world (Mandler, 1988, 1992; Sroufe, 1990). The exercise of these capacities during infancy provides the toddler a foundation on which to build a social-linguistic intelligence: at the very least, a nascent awareness of self as a separate entity nonetheless closely allied to other humans, a recognition of some of the differences between animate and inanimate entities, and expectations about event contingencies (e.g., when the key is turned, the car starts). The potentials are further realized as toddlers develop and expand their ability to learn from and compare themselves to others as they begin to use a conventional language.

Even while Ricky was learning the rudiments of language, he began to tease nonverbally, to modify his behavior to violate another's expectations. His pretending to go down rather than up the stairs (Chapter 4) seemed to be an attempt to surprise me; his coy behavior suggests he had a sense that I had some internal state that might be jolted by his action and that this jolt would influence my demeanor, if not my direction of stair-climbing. To use Dunn's (1988) words, on some "practical" level, he appeared to have a preliminary understanding of my state of mind. Undoubtedly, young toddlers compare their own emotional states to those overtly signalled in others even before language; the stair-climbing incident suggests that very early they begin to think about others' expectations as well. What language does is label, legitimate, and make salient other states for comparison that are not so overtly signalled by action or emotion, such as knowledge and belief states. In a bootstrapping fashion, children move among language, broadening social experience, and self-reflection to expand their understanding of internal states and to discover how they can relate the behavior of themselves and others to states of mind. Thus, social, cognitive, and linguistic experience and knowledge converge and combine to achieve an increasingly sophisticated level of social competence throughout the first three years of life.

## Beyond Toddlerhood

Despite all their progress toward personhood, 3 year olds obviously do not display all the social sophistication of adults or older children. Ricky, for example, had yet to learn the scope of social rules such as those governing the watching of TV. To illustrate how development goes on beyond toddlerhood, I discuss in this section three phenomena that show how social reasoning continues to change after age 3. The first phenomenon involves the characterization of persons; the second concerns the predictions of others' actions, and the third addresses the relations between mind, reality, and language.

*Using Dispositional Explanations.* In characterizing other people, older children tend to rely more on enduring dispositional traits like kindness and selfishness than do younger children (Eder, 1989). However, this developmental trend is not universal. Miller (1984) found that children in the United States were much more likely than children in India to cite dispositions as causes for behavior, suggesting a cultural influence on the use of dispositional explanations. Still, one can ask why dispositional explanations become more frequent relatively late in childhood even in cultures that favor them. Possibly it is uncommon (as it was in Ricky's household) for adults to talk to very young children about dispositional traits; hence, an explicit dispositional view of persons may develop later after exposure to dispositional language.[3] It is also possible that young children, who see themselves and other young children changing so rapidly, find it difficult to believe in enduring traits that would operate across situations. Toddlers, after all, behave very differently from babies, and for them changes in overt behaviors may be much more compelling than subtler continuities. Nonetheless, children in preschool shun unusually aggressive children, and this fact suggests that possibly by then they have developed expectations about consistent behavior in individuals, at least across time within similar situations.[4] A community's use of dispositional language probably codifies such experiences for children and sanctions dispositional thinking as causally explanatory.

*Predicting Behavior Based on False Beliefs.* Three year olds are notoriously bad at what is known as the standard false belief task, which requires them to predict where another child (say, Max) who wants something will look for it after it has been moved from the location where Max last saw it to a different one. Having seen the object moved to the new location, 3 year olds incorrectly predict Max will look for the object in its actual place, whereas 4 year olds correctly predict that Max's now faulty belief about the location will lead him to its former one (Wimmer & Perner, 1983). There is some controversy over how to account for the differences in the performances of younger and older children. Do younger children have an essentially different understanding of belief from older children (e.g., Perner, 1991)? Or do they have essentially the same understanding but simple response strategies that sometimes result in incorrect answers in complex situations (e.g., Fodor, 1992)? There are also disagreements about whether children actually hold theories about others' minds (Gopnik & Wellman, 1994) or just have working models of others to which they make analogies from their experiences of their own internal states (Harris, 1994).

We must take into account both the findings on the standard task and Ricky's data in considering what toddlers have accomplished and what they have yet to attain. Before his third birthday, Ricky explicitly explained his teacher's and my actions with comments about our beliefs; indeed, he appropriately attributed a false belief to me. His statements are evidence that even 2 year olds have the rudiments of a belief psychology. Thinking about belief states, even others' false belief states, is within the bounds of children under age 3. Nevertheless, we do not know how generally Ricky could have applied his belief psychology. He made no spontaneous predictions about behavior based on false beliefs; nor did I try to elicit any from him. Therefore, how he would have responded on the standard false belief task is unknown. The fact that most 3 year olds who pass a false belief explanation task still fail the standard prediction task (Bartsch & Wellman, 1989; Dunn, et al., 1991) suggests that Ricky likely would not have done well on it either.

One reason for the relative difficulty of the standard task may be that it involves both an actor about to look for something he hopes to find and an actual location for the object known to the child observing the action. Some 3 year olds can make accurate predictions based on beliefs when, instead of an actual location, two possible locations are specified, and hence it is not known whether the actor's belief is true or false (Wellman & Bartsch, 1988). However, in the standard task, a unique location is specified, and it is the only choice with which the actor can satisfy his desire for the object. If children give priority to the actor's satisfaction of his desire state, they will ignore the actor's belief state and predict incorrectly that the actor will look in the actual location.

Two proposals have been offered to account for the priority of desire over belief. One is that a desire psychology is a more fundamental aspect of the early understanding of mind (Wellman & Woolley, 1990) and, in cases of conflict, takes precedence over considerations of belief states (Bartsch & Wellman, 1989). The second is that desire satisfaction motivates a simple computational heuristic young children use to arrive at responses to questions about motives for behavior in complex situations (Fodor, 1992). Essentially, if the child can find a single way to satisfy the actor's desire, the child will choose that way without even considering what the actor believes.[5]

Neither of these accounts implies that predictions using false beliefs are *inherently* more difficult than false belief explanations. Therefore, in tasks in which the desires of the actor are not involved, young children should be able to predict behavior based on false beliefs as easily as explain it. For example, consider the case from Chapter 11 of Ricky appearing at my bedside naked. If he had thought that I would incorrectly believe his nakedness to be the result of another nighttime accident, Ricky should have been able to predict (as well as explain) my surprise at his expressed intention to put his pajamas back on.

Alternatively, prediction using false beliefs may be inherently harder than explanation because it requires the child *to anticipate* an actor's acting on a belief state different from the child's own and different from reality as well. In the explanation task, the problem facing the child is to account for the fact of an incorrect behavior; in the prediction task, it is to name a future behavior for the actor that will prove to be incorrect, given reality. As yet, there is no research providing evidence to decide between the priority of desire and the inherent difficulty explanations for the poor performances of 3 year olds on the standard prediction task. In any case, the ability to recruit notions of false belief to predict behavior continues to develop beyond the age of 3.

*Mind, Reality, and Language.* In thinking about false beliefs, one must compare an internal state (either experienced or inferred) with some assessment of reality. As a toddler, Ricky began to understand the relation between mind and reality. At the start of toddlerhood, he was already engaging in simple pretend play, suggesting that even then he recognized that he could intentionally manipulate reality in some ways. By the time he was 3, he knew that people's minds were not mirrors of reality. He recognized not only that people could lack knowledge of reality but that they could have a false impression of it. Yet the story is not quite so straightforward as that, nor does it end quite so early. Although young children can distinquish reality from nonreality in many situations (Wellman & Estes, 1986), even preschoolers still give evidence of appearance-reality confusions (Flavell, Green, & Flavell, 1986). And Ricky at times showed a remarkable disregard for the constraints of reality, especially on those occasions when he seemed content to answer questions with linguistically appropriate answers that were untroubled by reference to real-world conditions. Apparently, mind-reality relations are still relatively unstable at the end of toddlerhood.

One cause for the long period of instability can be language itself. Although language is an important—indeed crucial—tool for learning, it may be a source of confusion as well. Language provides a conventional means for organizing the world and communicating one's experience of it, but it allows organizations that go beyond the expression of the perceptually obvious—indeed, that is one of its great strengths. When we say, as Alice did in Chapter 5, that the panther *is like* a tiger, even though it *looks like* a cat, we propose that reality cannot be known on the basis of perceptual information alone; perceptual data may even on occasion be misleading. Infants rely heavily on perceptual information for their early, preverbal organization of the world; language initiates the transition to thinking about reality as less perceptually accessible.

Language also can be used to distort or ignore reality. There are many ways to use language unconstrained by direct relation to reality; teasing, jokes, fantasies, and songs are several modes to which young children are exposed. Children have to learn when in their culture reference to reality is important in language use and when it is not. As a toddler, Ricky tried his hand at less constrained modes of language, with teasing, jokes, and little stories. He also sometimes checked explicitly on the mode of discourse in which he was engaging, to be sure he and his interlocutor were in the same mode. Both of these kinds of behavior suggest that as they acquire language, toddlers recognize the complexity of the relations among mind, language, and reality. However, learning how to manage them across a full range of situations extends beyond toddlerhood.

## Summary

A theoretical perspective on human development emerges from the story of Ricky and other toddlers. Unique among species, human beings become persons as they use their capacities to self-reflect and compare themselves to others. Language is central to the process; it allows toddlers to go beyond immediate perceptual experience to gain information about unobservable states and motivations. Communication in a sociocultural context is a crucial avenue to such information. Finally, the process of becoming a person is an ongoing one, requiring the young child to bootstrap cognitive, linguistic, and social knowledge into an increasingly organized and integrated system for generating, predicting, and understanding social behavior.

The end of toddlerhood is not, of course, the culmination of the development of personhood. However their culture defines rational personal behavior, children continue to develop in their ability to act in accordance with that definition, as they expand their social world beyond the family, sharpen their understanding of the ways language is used for various purposes, and become more adept at thinking about complex situations. Nonetheless, Ricky's journey through toddlerhood is evidence that, as the toddler years draw to a close, the major components have converged to create a functioning person with the means to continue to grow.

## Notes

1. For example, because the solutions to both problems recruit the same logical operations, assessing whether the amount of water in a glass stays the same when poured from a short, wide glass into a tall, narrow one should be equivalent to assessing whether the number of buttons close together in a row stays the same when the row is spread out. Nonetheless, children often cannot pass these and logically similar "conservation" tasks simultaneously.

2. As in the natural sciences, psychology is beginning to explore and develop the idea of self-organizing systems (Thelen, 1989, 1992). At a preliminary level, my approach seems compatible with a dynamic systems framework that takes variability in behavior as evidence of an unstable organization, either as a consequence of different sources of information competing for priority or as a result of a transition between one organization and another as new kinds of information are incorporated into the system. Variability, then, is an expected feature of development in dynamic systems theory.

Dynamic systems approaches seem to account well for aspects of motor development (Thelen, Kelso, & Fogel, 1987) and perceptual development (Edelman, 1993). Researchers are beginning to suggest that they provide an appropriate framework too for the acquisition of "higher-order" mental capacities like language (e.g., Bates, 1993; Tucker & Hirsh-Pasek, 1993). It remains to be seen whether they will be adequate to such tasks, as well as to the equally daunting one of accommodating to the notion that higher-order capacities like language themselves function not only as knowledge bases but as the very means of further development.

3. However, there may be broad family or subcultural differences in the kind of language used to describe persons discussed at home. Goldfield and Snow (1992) report on parents who tutor their toddler on the kinds of interactions she can expect to have with different family members. In contrast to the kind of talk about relations Ricky heard (Chapter 5), their focus is more on relatives' dispositions than on features of lineage, gender, or age.

4. See Eder, 1989, for yet another explanation based on changes in memories that occur between ages 3 and 7.

5. This heuristic is basically a restatement of the phenonmenon. Fodor gives no explanation for why 3 year olds use this strategy (and older children do not) other than to say that on probabilistic grounds, it is relatively successful — it fails only in false-belief cases.

# EPILOGUE

Ricky's story, of course, is an ongoing one. As a kindergartner, he is learning all sorts of new skills. He enthusiastically practices writing, has just learned to swim, and loves computer lab at school. He has had much to adjust to: A brother arrived two months after his third birthday. There have been problems in the family; he has moved twice in the past two years, and he has attended different schools each year. He has grown more circumspect; it is harder to know what he is thinking. Still, throughout his fourth year, he continued to display his thoughts about language, mind, and reality with the openness that had first encouraged me to document his development as a toddler. Although I had stopped taking regular, extensive notes a month after his third birthday, I still occasionally, during his fourth year, wrote down the details of an especially appealing comment or an incident particularly revealing of his thoughts and interests. Those sporadic notes disclose an increasing sophistication about language, mind, and reality. As eight of us were sitting down to a holiday dinner, he said "I'm thinking this is called a 'group.'" When his uncle exclaimed, "There you are!" as a greeting upon Ricky's return to the living room after a short absence, Ricky made an inference about the motivation for his uncle's utterance and decided to check it, asking "You were wondering where I was?" He fell on the sidewalk one day, and after allowing me to fuss over what I thought was a wounded knee, he quietly and matter-of-factly set the record straight by saying, "Actually, I didn't hurt my knee. I hurt my toe."

Despite his attention to truth in such cases, he still easily engaged in fantasy. At the end of a visit to my house, we traded stuffed animals, Ricky taking home the panda I usually kept for him and leaving Babar in my care. As he walked out the door clutching the panda, I called after him, "Do I need to know anything about taking care of Babar?" Ricky tossed his reply over his shoulder, "He likes all kinds of grains."

Yet the events of the real world were not far away. Ricky had begun to take an interest in the wider world; by kindergarten, discussions of current events like the presidential election of 1992 stimulated him to raise such topics with me. Even before then, when he was a 3 year old, there was no escaping the fearful questions provoked by wartime. One day I was telling Ricky about my paternal grandmother's long hair, which, unbraided, reached almost to the floor.

G: Hannah is my grandmother's name.
    She was very old. She's not living now.
R: She's dead?
G: Yes.
R: She got killed by bombs dropping on her?
G: No, nobody dropped bombs on her. She just was very old. She'd lived a long, happy life.
R: They drop bombs on people in Iraq.

Ricky somewhat anxiously asked about the progress of the war almost every day and was as relieved as any adult when it ended.

Finally, the young toddler whose sense of his self-image had been so tentative that he had to check on whether he had a tail (Chapter 5) was now beginning to understand that, despite the mental and physical changes wrought with time, he would remain, nonetheless, a single entity. Ricky and I were in my kitchen the day after his brother was born. Alice and the new baby were still in the hospital. I was loading my camera in preparation for a visit to see them the next day. Ricky asked whether I was going to take pictures of the new baby. I replied that I would, just as I had taken pictures of him as a baby. The child who at 21 months had been reluctant to name himself in a photograph, now (at 38 months) suggested, "Why don't you take a picture of me holding a picture of me (as a baby)?" A toddler's life had become the life of a person.

Ricky holding a picture of himself

# REFERENCES

Abrahamsen, A. A., Cavallo, M. M., & McCluer, J. A. (1985). Is the sign advantage a robust phenomenon? From gesture to language in two modalities. *Merrill-Palmer Quarterly, 31,* 177–209.

Allen, R., & Shatz, M. (1983). "What says meow?." The role of context and linguistic experience in very young children's responses to *what* questions. *Journal of Child Language, 10,* 321–335.

Andersen, E. S. (1990). *Speaking with style.* London: Routledge.

Avis, J., & Harris, P. L. (1991). Belief-desire reasoning among Baka children: Evidence for a universal conception of mind. *Child Development, 62,* 460–467.

Backscheider, A. G., & Shatz, M. (1993, April). *Children's acquisition of lexical domains.* Paper presented at the Parasession on conceptual representations, Regional Meeting of the Chicago Linguistic Society, Chicago, IL.

Backscheider, A. G., Shatz, M., & Gelman, S. A. (1993). Preschoolers' ability to distinguish living kinds as a function of regrowth. *Child Development, 64,* 1242–1257.

Baillargeon, R. (1986). Representing the existence and the location of hidden objects: Object permanence in 6- and 9-month old infants. *Cognition, 23,* 21–41.

Banigan, R., & Mervis, C. B. (1988). Role of input in young children's category evolution II: An experimental study. *Journal of Child Language, 15,* 493–504.

Bartlett, E. (1978). The acquisition of the meaning of color terms: A study of lexical development. In R. Campbell & P. Smith (Eds.), *Recent advances in the Psychology of Language* (pp. 89–108). New York: Plenum.

Bartsch, K., & Wellman, H. M. (1989). Young children's attributions of action to beliefs and desires. *Child Development, 60,* 946–964.

Bates, E. (1976). *Language and context: The acquisition of pragmatics.* New York: Academic Press.

Bates, E. (1990). Language about me and you: Pronominal reference and the emerging concept of self. In D. Cicchetti & M. Beeghly (Eds.), *The self in transition* (pp. 165–182). Chicago: University of Chicago Press.

Bates, E. (1993, March). Nature, nurture, and language development. Invited address presented at the biennial meeting of the Society for Research in Child Development, New Orleans, LA.

Benedict, H. (1979). Early lexical development: Comprehension and production. *Journal of Child Language, 6,* 183–200.

Bloom, L., Hood, L., & Lightbown, P. (1974). Imitation in language acquisition: If, when, and why? *Cognitive Psychology, 6,* 380–420.

Bloom, L., Rocissano, L., & Hood, L. (1976). Adult-child discourse: Developmental interaction between information processing and linguistic knowledge. *Cognitive Psychology, 8,* 521–552.

Bowerman, M. (1982). Reorganizational processes in lexical and semantic development. In E. Wanner & L. R. Gleitman (Eds.), *Language acquisition* (pp. 319–346). Cambridge: Cambridge University Press.

Bowerman, M. (1983). How do children avoid constructing an overly general grammar in the absence of feedback about what is not a sentence? *Papers and Reports on Child Language Development, 22,* 23–34.

Branigan, G. (1979). Some reasons why successive single word utterances are not. *Journal of Child Language, 6,* 411–421.

Bretherton, I., McNew, S., Snyder, L., & Bates, E. (1983). Individual differences at 20 months: Analytic and holistic strategies in language acquisition. *Journal of Child Language, 10,* 293–320.

Brown, R. (1973). *A first language.* Cambridge, MA: Harvard University Press.

Bruner, J. S. (1972). Nature and uses of immaturity. *American Psychologist, 27,* 1–28.

Bruner, J. S. (1983). *Child's talk.* New York: Norton.

Butterworth, G. (1990). Self-perception in Infancy. In D. Cicchetti & M. Beeghly (Eds.), *The self in transition* (pp. 119–137). Chicago: University of Chicago Press.

Callanan, M. A., & Markman, E. M. (1982). Principles of organization in young children's natural language hierarchies. *Child Development, 53,* 1093–1101.

Carey, S. (1985). *Conceptual change in childhood.* Cambridge, MA: MIT Press.

Cazden, C. B. (1976). Play with language and metalinguistic awareness: One dimension of language experience. In J. Bruner, A. Jolly, & K. Sylva (Eds.), *Play—its role in development and evolution* (pp. 603–608). New York: Basic Books.

Chandler, M. (1973). Egocentrism & antisocial behavior: The assessment and training of social perspective-taking skills. *Developmental Psychology, 9,* 326–332.

Choi, S. (1991). Early acquisition of epistemic meanings in Korean: A study of sentence-ending suffixes in the spontaneous speech of three children. *First Language, 11,* 93–119.

Chomsky, C. (1969). *The acquisition of syntax in children from 5 to 10.* Cambridge, MA: MIT Press.

Chomsky, N. (1975). *Reflections on language.* New York: Pantheon Books.

Clark, E. V. (1973). What's in a word? On the child's acquisition of semantics in his first language. In T. E. Moore (Ed.), *Cognitive development and the acquisition of language* (pp. 65–110). New York: Academic Press.

Dennett, D. C. (1978). *Brainstorms.* Ch. 11, Conditions on personhood. Cambridge, MA: Bradford Books.

Doyle, A. B. (1982). Friends, acquaintances, and strangers: The influence of familiarity and ethnolinguistic background on social interaction. In K. H. Rubin & H. S. Ross (Eds.), *Peer relationships and social skills in childhood* (pp. 229–252). New York: Springer-Verlag.

Dunn, J. (1988). *The beginnings of social understanding.* Cambridge, MA: Harvard University Press.

Dunn, J., Brown, J., Slomkowski, C., Tesla, C., & Youngblade, L. (1991). Young children's understanding of other people's feelings and beliefs: Individual differences and their antecedents. *Child Development, 62,* 1352–1366.

Dunn, J., & Shatz, M. (1989). Becoming a conversationalist despite (or because of) having a sibling. *Child Development, 60,* 399–410.

Eckerman, C. O., & Didow, S. M. (1989). Toddlers' social coordinations: Changing responses to another's invitation to play. *Developmental Psychology, 25,* 794–804.

Edelman, G. (1993, March). *Population thinking and psychological theory.* Invited address presented at the biennial meeting of the Society for Research in Child Development, New Orleans, LA.

Eder, R. A. (1989). The emergent personologist: The structure and content of 3-1/2-, 5-1/2-, and 7-1/2-year-olds' concepts of themselves and other persons. *Child Development, 60,* 1218–1228.

Ervin-Tripp, S. (1977). Wait for me, roller-skate. In S. Ervin-Tripp & C. Mitchell-Kernan (Eds.), *Child discourse* (pp. 165–188). New York: Academic Press.

Feffer, M., & Suchotliff, L. (1966). Decentering implications of social interactions. *Journal of Personality and Social Psychology, 4,* 415–422.

Feldman, H., Goldin-Meadow, S., & Gleitman, L. R. (1978). Beyond Herodotus: The creation of language by linguistically deprived children. In A. Lock (Ed.), *Action, symbol, and gesture: the emergence of language* (pp. 351–414). New York: Academic Press.

Fernald, A., & Kuhl P. (1987). Acoustic determinants of infant preference for motherese speech. *Infant Behavior, 10,* 279–293.

Fernald, A., & Morikawa, H. (1993). Common themes and cultural variations in Japanese and American mothers' speech to infants. *Child Development, 64,* 637–656.

Flavell, J. H. (1988). The development of children's knowledge about the mind: From cognitive connections to mental representations. In J.

Astington, P. Harris, & D. Olson (Eds.), *Developing theories of mind* (pp. 244–267). New York: Cambridge University Press.

Flavell, J. H., Flavell, E. R., Green, F. L., & Moses, L. J. (1990). Young children's understanding of fact beliefs versus value beliefs. *Child Development, 61,* 915–928.

Flavell, J. H., Green, F. L., & Flavell, E. R. (1986). Development of knowledge about the appearance-reality distinction. *Monographs of the Society for Research in Child Development, 51* (1, Serial No. 212).

Flavell, J. H., Green, F. L., Herrera, C., & Flavell, E. R. (1991). Young children's knowledge about visual perception: Lines of sight must be straight. *British Journal of Developmental Psychology, 9,* 73–87.

Flavell, J. H., Shipstead, S. G., & Croft, K. (1978). Young children's knowledge about visual perception: Hiding objects from others. *Child Development, 49,* 1208–1211.

Fodor, J. A. (1992). A theory of the child's theory of mind. *Cognition, 44,* 283–296.

Foster, S. H. (1979). From non-verbal to verbal communication: A study of the development of topic initiation strategies during the first two-and-a-half years. Doctoral dissertation, University of Lancaster.

Fremgen, A., & Fay, D. (1980). Overextensions in production and comprehension: A methodological clarification. *Journal of Child Language, 7,* 205–211.

Frye, D., Braisby, N., Lowe, J., Maroudas, C., & Nicholls, J. (1989). Young children's understanding of counting and cardinality. *Child Development, 60,* 1158–1171.

Furrow, D., Moore, C., Davidge, J., & Chiasson, L. (1992). Mental terms in mothers' and children's speech: Similarities and relationships. *Journal of Child Language, 19,* 617–631.

Fuson, K., Pergament, G., Lyons, B., & Hall, J. (1985). Children's conformity to the cardinality rule as a function of set size and counting accuracy. *Child Development, 56,* 1429–1436.

Gallagher, T. M. (1981). Contingent query sequences within adult-child discourse. *Journal of Child Language, 8,* 51–62.

Gallup, G. G. (1970). Chimpanzees: Self-recognition. *Science, 167,* 86–87.

Garnica, O. K. (1977). Some prosodic and paralinguistic features of speech to young children. In C. Snow & C. A. Ferguson (Eds.), *Talking to Children* (pp. 63–88). Cambridge: Cambridge University Press.

Garvey, C. (1977). *Play.* Cambridge, MA: Harvard University Press.

Gelman, R. (1990). First principles organize attention to and learning about relevant data: Number and the animate-inanimate distinction as examples. *Cognitive Science, 14,* 79–106.

Gelman, R., & Baillargeon, R. (1983). A review of some Piagetian concepts. In J. H. Flavell & E. M. Markman (Eds.), *Cognitive Development* (Vol. 3, pp. 167–230, of P. H. Mussen [Gen. Ed.], *Handbook of child psychology*). New York: Wiley.

Gelman, R., & Spelke, E. (1981). The development of thoughts about animates and inanimates: Implications for research on social cognition. In J. H. Flavell & L. Ross (Eds.), *Piaget and the foundations of knowledge* (pp. 43–66). Hillsdale, NJ: Erlbaum.

Gelman, S. A., & Markman, E. M. (1986). Categories and induction in young children. *Cognition, 23,* 183–209.

Gelman, S. A. , Coley, J. D., & Gottfried, G. M. (1994). Essentialist beliefs in children: The acquisition of concepts and theories. In L. A. Hirschfeld & S. A. Gelman (Eds.), *Mapping the mind: Domain specificity in cognition and culture* (pp. 341–365). New York: Cambridge University Press.

Gentner, D. (1982). Why nouns are learned before verbs: Linguistic relativity versus natural partitioning. In S. A. Kuczaj II (Ed.), *Language development: Vol. 2. Language, thought, and culture* (pp. 301–334). Hillsdale, NJ: Erlbaum.

Gick, M. L., & Holyoak, K. J. (1980). Analogical problem solving. *Cognitive Psychology, 12,* 306–355.

Gleitman, H., & Gleitman, L. R. (1979). Language use and language judgment. In C. J. Fillmore, D. Kempler, & W. S-Y. Wang (Eds.), *Individual differences in language ability and language behavior* (pp. 103–126). New York: Academic Press.

Gleitman, L. R. (1990). The structural sources of verb meanings. *Language Acquisition, 1,* 3–55.

Goldfield, B. A., & Reznick, J. S. (1990). Early lexical acquisition: Rate, content, and the vocabulary spurt. *Journal of Child Language, 17,* 171–183.

Goldfied, B. A., & Snow, C. E. (1992). "What's your cousin Arthur's mommy's name?": Features of family talk about kin and kin terms. *First Language, 12,* 187–205.

Golinkoff, R. M. (1993). When is communication a "meeting of minds"? *Journal of Child Language, 20,* 199–207.

Gopnik, A., & Wellman, H. M. (1994). The theory theory. In L. Hirschfeld & S. A. Gelman (Eds.), *Mapping the mind: Domain specificity in cognition and culture* (pp. 257–293). New York: Cambridge University Press.

Grice, H. P. (1975). Logic and conversation. In P. Cole & J. L. Morgan (Eds.), *Speech acts: Vol. 3. Syntax and semantics* (pp. 41–58). New York: Academic Press.

Halliday, M. A. K. (1975). *Learning how to mean: Explorations in the development of language.* London: Edward Arnold.

Harris, P. L. (1991). The work of the imagination. In A. Whiten (Ed.), *Natural theories of mind* (pp. 283–304). Oxford: Basil Blackwell.

Harris, P. L. (1994). Thinking by children and scientists: False analogies and neglected similarities. In L. Hirschfeld & S. A. Gelman (Eds.), *Mapping the mind: Domain specificity in cognition and culture* (pp. 294–315). New York: Cambridge University Press.

Hobson, R. P. (1990). On acquiring knowledge about people, and the capacity to pretend: Response to Leslie. *Psychological Review, 97,* 114–121.

Hoff-Ginsberg, E. (1985). Some contributions of mothers' speech to their children's syntactic growth. *Journal of Child Language, 12,* 367–385.

Hoff-Ginsberg, E., & Shatz, M. (1982). Linguistic input and the child's acquisition of language. *Psychological Bulletin, 92,* 3–26.

Horton, M. S., & Markman, E. M. (1980). Developmental differences in the acquisition of basic and superordinate categories. *Child Development, 51,* 708–719.

Howes, C. (1988). Peer interaction of young children. *Monographs of the Society for Research in Child Development, 53* (1, Serial No. 217).

Huttenlocher, J., Haight, W., Bryk, A., Seltzer, M., & Lyons, T. (1991). Early vocabulary growth: Relation to language input and gender. *Developmental Psychology, 27,* 236–248.

Jespersen, O. (1922). *Language: Its nature, development, and origin.* London: Allen & Unwin.

Kagan, J. (1981). *The second year: The emergence of self-awareness.* Cambridge, MA: Harvard University Press.

Karmiloff-Smith, A. (1979). *A functional approach to child language.* Cambridge: Cambridge University Press.

Karmiloff-Smith, A. (1983). Language development as a problem-solving process. *Papers and reports on child language development, 22,* 1–22.

Karmiloff-Smith, A. (1986). Some fundamental aspects of language development after age 5. In P. Fletcher & M. Garman (Eds.), *Language acquisition* (pp. 455–474). Cambridge: Cambridge University Press.

Katz, N., Baker, E., & Macnamara, J. (1974). What's in a name? A study of how children learn common and proper names. *Child Development, 45,* 469–473.

Keil, F. (1981). Constraints on knowledge and cognitive development. *Psychological Review, 88,* 197–227.

Kuczaj, S. A., II. (1983). *Crib speech and language play.* New York: Springer-Verlag.

Kuczaj, S. A., II, & Daly, M. J. (1979). The development of hypothetical reference in the speech of young children. *Journal of Child Language, 6,* 563–579.

Landau, B., & Gleitman, L. R. (1985). *Language and experience.* Cambridge, MA: Harvard University Press.

Lempers, J. D., Flavell, E. R., & Flavell, J. H. (1977). The development in very young children of tacit knowledge concerning visual perception. *Genetic Psychology Monographs, 95,* 3–53.

Leslie, A. M. (1987). Pretense and representation: The origins of "theory of mind." *Psychological Review, 94,* 412–426.

Leung, E., & Rheingold, H. (1981). Development of pointing as a social gesture. *Developmental Psychology, 17,* 215–220.

Lewis, M., & Brooks-Gunn, J. (1979). *Social cognition and the acquisition of self.* New York: Plenum.

Lillard, A. S. (1993a). Pretend play skills and the child's theory of mind. *Child Development, 64,* 348–371.

Lillard, A. S. (1993b). Young children's conceptualization of pretend: Action or mental representational state? *Child Development, 64*, 372–386.

Macnamara, J. (1982). *Names for things*. Cambridge, MA: MIT Press.

Mandler, J. M. (1988). How to build a baby: On the development of an accessible representational system. *Cognitive Development, 3*, 113–136.

Mandler, J. M. (1992). How to build a baby: II. Conceptual primitives. *Psychological Review, 99*, 587–604.

Maratsos, M. P. (1973). Nonegocentric communication abilities in preschool children. *Child Development, 44*, 697–700.

Maratsos, M. P. (1982). The child's construction of grammatical categories. In E. Wanner & L. R. Gleitman (Eds.), *Language acquisition* (pp. 240–266). New York: Cambridge University Press.

Markman, E. M. (1981a). Comprehension monitoring. In W. P. Dickson (Ed.), *Children's oral communication skills* (pp. 66–84). New York: Academic Press.

Markman, E. M. (1981b). Two different principles of conceptual organization. In M. E. Lamb & A. Brown (Eds.), *Advances in developmental psychology* (pp. 199–236). Hillsdale, NJ: Erlbaum.

Markman, E. M. (1987). How children constrain the possible meanings of words. In U. Neisser (Ed.), *Concepts and conceptual development: Ecological and intellectual factors in categorization* (pp. 255–287). Cambridge: Cambridge University Press.

Markus, H., & Nurius, P. S. (1986). Possible selves. *American Psychologist, 41*, 954–969.

Martin, C. L., & Little, J. K. (1990). The relation of gender understanding to children's sex-typed preferences and gender stereotypes. *Child Development, 61*, 1427–1439.

Mead, G. H. (1934). *Mind, self, and society*. Chicago: University of Chicago Press.

Meier, R. P., & Newport, E. L. (1990). Out of the hands of babes: On a possible sign advantage in language acquisition. *Language, 66*, 1–23.

Mervis, C. B., & Crisafi, M. A. (1982). Order of acquisition of subordinate-, basic-, and superordinate-level categories. *Child Development, 53*, 258–266.

Miller, J. (1984). Culture and the development of everyday social experience. *Journal of Personality and Social Psychology, 46*, 961–978.

Miller, J. F., & Chapman, R. S. (1981). The relation between age and mean length of utterance in morphemes. *Journal of Speech and Hearing Research, 24*, 154–161.

Mitchell, R. W., & Thompson, N. S. (Eds.). (1986). *Deception: Perspectives on human and nonhuman deceit*. Albany: State University of New York Press.

Moore, C., Bryant, D., & Furrow, D. (1989). Mental terms and the development of certainty. *Child Development, 60*, 167–171.

Morford, M., & Goldin-Meadow, S. (1992). Comprehension and production of gesture in combination with speech in one-word speakers. *Journal of Child Language, 19,* 559–580.

Moses, L. J., & Flavell, J. H. (1990). Inferring false beliefs from actions and reactions. *Child Development, 61,* 929–945.

Nelson, K. (1973). Structure and strategy in learning to talk. *Monographs of the Society for Research in Child Development, 38* (1–2, Serial No. 149).

Nelson, K. (1974). Concept, word, and sentence: Interrelations in acquisition and development. *Psychological Review, 81,* 267–285.

Nelson, K., Benedict, H., Gruendel, J., Rescorla, L. (1977, February). *Lessons from early lexicons.* Paper presented at the biennial meeting of the Society for Research in Child Development, New Orleans, LA.

Newman, D. (1978). Ownership and permission among nursery-school children. In J. Glick & A. Clarke-Stewart (Eds.), *Studies in social and cognitive development* (pp. 213–219). New York: Gardner Press.

Newport, E. L. (1990). Maturational constraints on language learning. *Cognitive Science, 14,* 11–28.

Ninio, A., & Bruner, J. S. (1978). The achievements and antecedents of labelling. *Journal of Child Language, 5,* 1–15.

Orlansky, M. D., & Bonvillian, J. D. (1984). Sign language acquisition: Language development in children of deaf parents and implications for other populations. *Merrill-Palmer Quarterly, 31,* 127–143.

Perner, J. (1991). *Understanding the representational mind.* Cambridge, MA: MIT Press.

Peskin, J. (1992). Ruse and representations: On children's ability to conceal information. *Developmental Psychology, 28,* 84–89.

Petitto, L. A. (1988). "Language" in the pre-linguistic child. In F. S. Kessel (Ed.), *The development of language and language researchers* (pp. 187–221). Hillsdale, NJ: Erlbaum.

Piaget, J. (1926). *The language and thought of the child.* New York: Harcourt, Brace.

Piaget, J. (1952). *The origins of intelligence in children.* New York: Norton.

Piaget, J. (1954). *The construction of reality in the child.* New York: Basic Books.

Piaget, J. (1962). *Play, dreams, and imitation.* New York: Norton.

Piaget, J. (1970). Piaget's theory. In P. H. Mussen (Ed.), *Carmichael's manual of child psychology* (3rd ed., Vol. 1, pp. 703–732). New York: Wiley.

Pine, J. M. (1991). Maternal style at the early one-word stage: Re-evaluating the stereotype of the directive mother. *First Language, 12,* 169–186.

Pinker, S. (1984). *Language learnability and language development.* Cambridge, MA: Harvard University Press.

Pinker, S., & Bloom, P. (1990). Natural language and natural selection. *Behavioral and Brain Sciences, 13,* 707–784.

Platt, C. B., & MacWhinney, B. (1983). Error assimilation as a mechanism in language learning. *Journal of Child Language, 10,* 401–414.

Poulin-Dubois, D., & Shultz, T. (1988). The development of the understanding of human behavior: From agency to intentionality. In J. W. Astington, P. L. Harris, & D. R. Olson (Eds.), *Developing theories of mind* (pp. 109–125). Cambridge: Cambridge University Press.

Premack, D. (1988). "Does the chimpanzee have a theory of mind?" revisited. In R. Byrne & A. Whiten (Eds.), *Machiavellian intelligence* (pp. 160–179). Oxford: Clarendon Press.

Premack, D., & Woodruff, G. (1978). Does the chimpanzee have a theory of mind? *Behavioral and Brain Sciences, 1,* 515–526.

Rescorla, L. (1980). Overextension in early language development. *Journal of Child Language, 7,* 321–335.

Reznick, J. S., Kagan, J., Snidman, N., Gersten, M., Baak, K., & Rosenberg, A. (1986). Inhibited and uninhibited children: A follow-up study. *Child Development, 57,* 660–680.

Rice, M. (1980). *Cognition to language.* Baltimore, MD: University Park Press.

Rice, M. (1993). "Don't talk to him; he's weird": A social consequences account of language and social interactions. In A. P. Kaiser & D. B. Gray (Eds.), *Enhancing children's communication* (pp. 139–158). Baltimore: Brookes.

Richards, B. J. (1990). *Language development and individual differences: A study of auxiliary verb learning.* Cambridge: Cambridge University Press.

Rogoff, B. (1990). *Apprenticeship in thinking.* New York: Oxford University Press.

Rogoff, B. (1993). Children's guided participation and participatory appropriation in sociocultural activity. In R. Wozniak & K. Fischer (Eds.), *Development in context* (pp. 121–153). Hillsdale, NJ: Erlbaum.

Ruffman, T., Olson, D. R., Ash, T., & Keenan, T. (1993). The ABCs of deception. Do young children understand deception in the same way as adults? *Developmental Psychology, 29,* 74–87.

Scaife, M., & Bruner, J. (1975). The capacity for joint attention in the infant. *Nature, 253,* 265–266.

Schieffelin, B., & Ochs, E. (1986). Language socialization. *Annual Review of Anthropology, 15,* 163–191.

Schnur, E., & Shatz, M. (1983). The role of maternal gesturing in conversations with one-year-olds. *Journal of Child Language, 11,* 29–41.

Searle, J. R. (1975). Indirect speech acts. In P. Cole & J. L. Morgan (Eds.), *Speech acts: Vol. 3. Syntax and semantics* (pp. 59–82). New York: Academic Press.

Sendak, M. (1962). *Pierre.* New York: Harper and Row.

Shatz, M. (1978a). On the development of communicative understandings: An early strategy for interpreting and responding to messages. *Cognitive Psychology, 10,* 271–301.

Shatz, M. (1978b). The relationship between cognitive processes and the development of communication skills. In C. B. Keasey (Ed.), *Nebraska symposium on motivation* (Vol. 25, pp. 1-30). Lincoln: University of Nebraska Press.

Shatz, M. (1982). On mechanisms of development: Can features of the communicative environment account for language development? In E. Wanner & L. R. Gleitman (Eds.), *Language acquisition* (pp. 102-127). New York: Cambridge University Press.

Shatz, M. (1983a). Communication. In J. H. Flavell and E. M. Markman (Eds.), *Cognitive development* (Vol. 3, pp. 841-889, of P. Mussen [Gen. Ed.], *Handbook of child psychology*). New York: Wiley.

Shatz, M. (1983b). On transition, continuity, and coupling: An alternative approach to communicative development. In R. M. Golinkoff (Ed.), *The transition from prelinguistic to linguistic communication* (pp. 43-55). Hillsdale, NJ: Erlbaum.

Shatz, M. (1985). An evolutionary perspective on plasticity in language development: A commentary. *Merrill-Palmer Quarterly, 31,* 211-222.

Shatz, M. (1987). Bootstrapping operations in child language. In K. Nelson & A. VanKleeck (Eds.), *Children's Language* (Vol. 6, pp. 1-22). Hillsdale, NJ: Erlbaum.

Shatz, M. (1992). A forward or backward step in the search for an adequate theory of language acquisition? *Social Development, 1,* 151-154.

Shatz, M. (1993, July). *Ways to words: Early strategies for building a lexicon.* Paper presented at the Sixth International Congress for the Study of Child Language, Trieste, Italy.

Shatz, M., & Backscheider, A. (1991, November). *Toddlers' understanding of the normal concepts of color and number.* Paper presented at the annual meeting of the Psychonomic Society, San Francisco, CA.

Shatz, M., Backscheider, A., & Loken, E. (In preparation). Do toddlers know the dimension to which "color" applies?

Shatz, M., & Ebeling, K. (1991). Patterns of language learning related behavior: Evidence for self-help in acquiring grammar. *Journal of Child Language, 18,* 295-313.

Shatz, M., & Gelman, R. (1977). Beyond syntax: The influence of conversational constraints on speech modifications. In C. E. Snow & C. A. Ferguson (Eds.), *Talking to children* (pp. 189-198). Cambridge: Cambridge University Press.

Shatz, M., Grimm, H., Wilcox, S. A., & Niemeier-Wind, K. (1989, April). *The uses of modal expressions in conversations between German and American mothers and their 2-year-olds.* Paper presented at the biennial meeting of the Society for Research in Child Development, Kansas City, MO.

Shatz, M., & O'Reilly, A. (1990). Conversational or communicative skill? A reassessment of two-year-olds' behaviour in miscommunication episodes. *Journal of Child Language, 17,* 131-146.

Shatz, M., Wellman, H. M., & Silber, S. (1983). The acquisition of mental terms: A systematic investigation of the first reference to mental state. *Cognition, 14,* 301-321.

Shatz, M., & Wilcox, S. A. (1991). Constraints on the acquisition of English modals. In S. A. Gelman & J. Byrnes (Eds.), *Perspectives on thought and language: Interrelations in development* (pp. 319–353). New York: Cambridge University Press.

Singleton, J. L., & Newport, E. L. (1987, April). *When learners surpass their models: The acquisition of American Sign Language from impoverished input.* Poster presented at the biennial meeting of the Society for Research in Child Development, Baltimore, MD.

Slobin, D. I. (1973). Cognitive prerequisites for the development of grammar. In C. A. Ferguson & D. I. Slobin (Eds.), *Studies of child language development* (pp. 175–208). New York: Holt, Rinehart, & Winston.

Sorce, J., Emde, R. N., Campos, J. J., & Klinnert, M. (1985). Maternal emotional signalling: Its effect on the visual cliff behavior of 1-year-olds. *Developmental Psychology, 21,* 195–200.

Spelke, E. (1985). Perception of unity, persistence, and identity: Thoughts on infants' conceptions of objects. In J. Mehler & R. Fox (Eds.), *Neonate cognition: Beyond the blooming buzzing confusion* (pp. 89–113). Hillsdale, NJ: Erlbaum.

Sroufe, L. A. (1990). An organizational perspective on the self. In D. Cicchetti and M. Beeghly (Eds.), *The self in transition* (pp. 281–307). Chicago: University of Chicago Press.

Steffenson, M. (1978). Satisfying inquisitive adults: Some simple methods of answering yes/no questions. *Journal of Child Language, 5,* 221–236.

Teale, W., & Sulzby, E. (1986). *Emergent literacy: Writing and reading.* Norwood, NJ: Ablex.

Thelen, E. (1989). Self-organization in developmental processes: Can systems approaches work? In M. Gunnar (Ed.), *Systems in development: The Minnesota Symposium on Child Psychology* (Vol. 22, pp. 77–117). Hillsdale, NJ: Erlbaum.

Thelen, E. (1992). Development as a dynamic system. *Current directions in psychological science, 1,* 189–193.

Thelen, E., Kelso, J. A. S., & Fogel, A. (1987). Self-organizing systems and infant motor development. *Developmental Review, 7,* 39–65.

Tomasello, M. (1992). The social bases for language acquisition. *Social Development, 1,* 67–87.

Tucker, M., & Hirsh-Pasek, K. (1993, March). *Dynamical systems and language: Theoretical implications.* Paper presented at the Biennial Meeting of the Society for Research in Child Development, New Orleans, LA.

Valian, V. (1986). Syntactic categories in young children. *Developmental Psychology, 22,* 562–579.

van Kleeck, A. (1990). Emergent literacy: Learning about print before learning to read. *Topics in Language Disorders, March,* 25–45.

Watson, M. W. (1990). Aspects of self development as reflected in children's role playing. In D. Cicchetti & M. Beeghly (Eds.), *The self in transition* (pp. 265–280). Chicago: University of Chicago Press.

Waxman, S. R., & Senghas, A. (1992). Relations among word meanings in early lexical development. *Developmental Psychology, 28,* 862–873.

Weir, R. H. (1962). *Language in the crib.* The Hague: Mouton.

Wellman, H. M. (1990). *The child's theory of mind.* Cambridge, MA: Bradford.

Wellman, H. M., & Bartsch, K. (1988). Young children's reasoning about beliefs. *Cognition, 30,* 239–277.

Wellman, H. M., & Estes, D. (1986). Early understanding of mental entities: A reexamination of chilhood realism. *Child Development, 57,* 910–923.

Wellman, H. M., & Gelman, S. A. (1992). Cognitive development: Foundational theories of core domains. *Annual Review of Psychology, 43,* 337–375.

Wellman, H. M., & Woolley, J. D. (1990). From simple desires to ordinary beliefs: The early development of everyday psychology. *Cognition, 35,* 245–275.

Whitehurst, G. J., Falco, F. L., Lonigan, C. J., Fischel, J. E., DeBaryshe, B. D., Valdez-Menchaca, M. C., & Caulfield, M. (1988). Accelerating language development through picture book reading. *Developmental Psychology, 24,* 552–559.

Wilcox, S. A. (1991). Children's understanding of modal expressions: Understanding the relative certainty of beliefs. (Doctoral dissertation, University of Michigan, 1990). *Dissertation Abstracts International, 52,* 3B.

Wimmer, H., & Perner, J. (1983). Beliefs about beliefs: Representation and constraining function of wrong beliefs in young children's understanding of deception. *Cognition, 13,* 103–128.

Woolley, J. D., & Wellman, H. M. (1990). Young children's understanding of realities, nonrealities, and appearances. *Child Development, 61,* 946–961.

Yaniv, I., & Shatz, M. (1988). Children's understanding of perceptibility. In J. W. Astington, P. L. Harris, & D. R. Olson (Eds.), *Developing theories of mind* (pp. 93–108). New York: Cambridge University Press.

Yaniv, I., & Shatz, M. (1990). Heuristics of reasoning and analogy in children's visual perspective taking. *Child Development, 61,* 1491–1501.

# INDEX